D1593016

The Burden of Dependency

The Burden
of Dependency

Colonial Themes in
Southern Economic Thought

JOSEPH J. PERSKY

The Johns Hopkins University Press
Baltimore and London

This book has been brought to publication with the generous assistance of the Karl and Edith Pribram Endowment.

The Johns Hopkins University Press
701 West 40th Street
Baltimore, Maryland 21211-2190
The Johns Hopkins Press Ltd., London

Library of Congress Cataloging-in-Publication Data

Persky, Joseph.
    The burden of dependency : colonial themes in southern economic thought / Joseph J. Persky.
      p. cm.
    Includes bibliographical references and index.
    ISBN 0-8018-4422-3 (alk. paper)
    1. Southern States—Economic conditions.   2. Deendency.   I. Title.
HC107.A13P48 1992
330'.0975—dc20   92-10844

For my parents,
my wife, Victoria,
and my children

Contents

Preface and Acknowledgments

In 1844, Nathaniel Ware observed that his *Notes on Political Economy* had been written "partly to give expression to thoughts that occurred to the author, and partly to occupy and amuse his leisure moments." I could hardly offer a better defense of this essay, which, like Ware's, trespasses on disciplines and centuries of which the author had, at the outset, limited knowledge.

In college and graduate school I began to work on the economics of the South, prompted by the civil rights movement and a rather poorly articulated notion that a more prosperous South might be able to transcend the worst features of its historic legacy. Outside a few large urban areas, the South, even then, looked like an underdeveloped country. The radical populism of the 1960s held that the "System" had exploited the South, black and white. I did a piece called "The South as a Colony." I thought I was in some sort of vanguard.

Over the years, in a rather haphazard fashion, I came to realize that my ideas paralleled one of the oldest intellectual traditions of the region. From the seventeenth century to the middle of the twentieth, southerners had pondered their economic dependency. I became fascinated with both the repetition and the variety in this history. Its intellectual roots, shared with the dependency theories of the Third World, stretched back to the mercantilism of the early nation-states. The southern critiques of dependency bound together the region's intellectual history, providing a continuity between antebellum and postbellum thought grounded in material conditions.

Throughout this essay a reader will have to wrestle with the ambiguities surrounding any definition of the South. Is Baltimore a southern city? Or is Kentucky a southern state? These problems of geography confront all those who study the South. A more difficult issue plagues any discussion of "southern thought." Who can speak for the South? Even worse, when a sentence begins "southerners were likely to believe . . . ," to exactly *whose* thought does the author refer? Obviously, these questions defy precise answers. Differences between rich and poor, men and women, city dwellers and farmers all compromise any attempt at generalization; but in the case of the South, there has long been a division even more fundamental than these. Southern whites and blacks have lived in close geographic proximity but at the greatest imaginable social distance. For most of southern history, African-Americans were excluded from participating in the region's formal intellectual life. This observation prompts a warning: unless otherwise indicated, in this work *southerners* refers to white southerners. A separate section considers black thought on the southern economy. This historiographic segregation reflects the region's own peculiar history.

Writing on southern political economy has been for the most part a lonely exercise. The topic is of little interest to economists and is only a bit more interesting to historians of economic thought. Nevertheless a synthetic essay like this one must depend on the scholarship of others. While I deal directly with the written ideas of the South, I draw heavily on secondary sources for historical context. The bibliographic notes at the end of this work recount this indebtedness.

I must acknowledge the support provided me by the librarians at the University of Illinois at Chicago. They have shown a generous graciousness in shuttling older books back and forth from the campus at Champaign-Urbana and in arranging other interlibrary loans. I am also grateful to the university for granting me two quarters of sabbatical leave to pursue my research on southern economic thought. My colleagues William Grampp, George Rosen, and William White have given friendly attention to this project.

Two sections of this work, in somewhat altered forms, have appeared previously in print. "The Political Economy of George Fitzhugh," in chapter 3, bears a striking resemblance to "Unequal Exchange and Dependency Theory in George Fitzhugh," which was published in *The History of Political Economy* by Duke University Press. Similarly, "Black Thought and the Colonial Analogy" in chapter 5 contains only slight modifications from "Black Economic Thought and the Southern Economy," found in *The Review of Black Political Economy*. I am grateful to the editors and reviewers of both journals for substantive and constructive criticism.

I owe a considerable debt to Robert J. Brugger, who has supported this project and has, without intrusiveness, helped me to sharpen and focus my thinking. He approached his work as editor by opening a wide-ranging and constructive dialogue. To the final editing of the manuscript Anne M. Whitmore brought enthusiasm and a high level of professionalism. Undoubtedly, errors yet remain. In part these must reflect my intellectual abandon in traversing such a wide expanse of history. Yet, in advancing a broad thesis a bit of recklessness will, I hope, prove a virtue. If not, I can only offer the apology of Mr. Ware: "Whatever defects may be found in the work, the author hopes to get credit for good intentions."

My family has lived with this project for a number of years. Without their warm support, I would have deserted it long ago. This essay carries a dedication to parents, wife, and children. Each of them deserves a book of his or her own, but the egregiously long time it took me to put together this slim volume makes a full set of individually dedicated future works highly unlikely.

The Burden of Dependency

Chapter One

Introductions

Geography has dictated many of the political and economic conflicts that punctuate the history of the United States. Often these conflicts have set North against South. Almost always they have pitted the interests of cities—commerce, industry, "progress"—against agrarians. From their side of the ramparts, many southerners have accused the urban North of exploiting the South's economy as a colonial dependency. This charge dates almost from the beginning of southern history. Some years ago, C. Vann Woodward suggested that the various burdens of southern history, including the region's poverty, gave the South's experience a universal character. Perhaps, then, it should come as no surprise that many southerners, like early British mercantilists, German nationalists, and Latin American *dependistas,* have attributed the persistence of their region's underdevelopment to a debilitating economic dependency.

Dependency and Southern Economic Thought

The colonial analogy so popular in the South stands at odds with much of modern economics, which persistently minimizes the significance of geography. Despite their reputation for dismal pessimism, most economists optimistically believe that economic development tends to diffuse from the center outward, gradually homogenizing the world economy and erasing accidents of place. This faith, most closely associated with neoclassical economics, also infects Marxian scholars eager to pronounce the arrival of an international proletariat. Academic orthodoxy, left and right, has shunned the notion of dependency.

Nevertheless, southern colonial analogies drew from and contributed to a broad intellectual tradition. Observers in many societies caught in the paradoxes of economic underdevelopment have listed the dangers of dependency. The theme originated in the mercantilist fear of powerful competitors, it infected the work of Adam Smith, and it appears full-blown in the writings of nineteenth-century nationalists from the United

States and Germany. At the beginning of this century notions of dependency laced the economic thought of Eastern Europe and Russia.

More recently a frustration with stifled and dependent development has become a commonplace across the Third World. In Latin America the "dependency school" of economic thought has strongly challenged the orthodoxy of free trade and free markets. From a similar perspective Arghiri Emmanuel and Samir Amin have advanced a theory of "unequal exchange" between metropolis and periphery in the modern capitalist world. All of these Third World critics question the basic assumption of an inevitable tendency toward economic homogenization on a world scale. They argue that since the mercantilist era Western European expansion has produced an ever-greater geographic specialization and differentiation, as it has brought far-flung places into considerable interdependence. From their vantage point, this process of spatial differentiation continues today.

Persistent conditions breed persistence in intellectual outlook. Southerners championed their own versions of dependency theory well into the twentieth century. In the late seventeenth and early eighteenth centuries southerners who had the time to think about economic theory protested the effects of the British mercantilist system on their region's development and puzzled over how best to build an independent southern economy. Later, the rise of northern commerce complicated these dilemmas as southerners tried to define their relation to this new power. In the nineteenth century the development of cotton textiles linked the South to the very engine of the Industrial Revolution, requiring a reappraisal of the nature of southern dependency. Finally, consolidation of the American industrial base in the post–Civil War period brought forth new perspectives from the periphery. Like the southern economy itself, southern economic thought reacted to changes that originated elsewhere. This recurring need to redefine the nature of southern dependency can be offered in itself as a minor proof of the region's dependent position.

The southern colonial analogy contributed ideas to movements as diverse as antebellum secessionism, populism, and the New Deal. In all of its guises it maintained a critical attitude toward the course of U.S. economic development, and this attitude gave its various critiques a surprisingly radical tone. With an emphasis on self-determination, the colonial analogy often drew on liberal hostility to authoritarian centralism. At the same time, its attachment to local society and culture was profoundly conservative in outlook. The coupling of colonial arguments first with numerous defenses of slavery and subsequently with apologies for racism gave some versions of the critique a reactionary, even fascist, taint.

A colonial critique necessarily begins with a geographic conception of economics, the usefulness and continuing relevance of which this work accepts. Like the stratification of society into classes, the economic stratification of regions requires explanation. Among the many factors that might influence geographic variations in economic development, every colonial critique identified economic exploitation as the most significant. While agreeing on this basic point, they differed, sometimes dramatically, in their description and analysis of the mechanisms of exploitation.

Two broad camps can be identified in southern attacks on dependency. First and most classically, many southerners argued that all systems of legislated commercial and economic regulations favored urban interests and exploited the agrarian economy. From a rather different perspective, others in the South maintained that southerners' own unbridled pursuit of short-run self-interest left the region open to exploitation from outside. The first of these explanations called for liberal and even libertarian policies that would allow a greater freedom of individual action; the second warned that an unregulated, undisciplined society left itself easy prey to those with greater consciousness of purpose. The first led naturally to a focus on freeing the regional economy from the drag of taxation and outside interference, while the second implied a need for regional cooperation and planning to offset the economic advantages of already-developed centers in Britain and the North.

These alternative explanations of the South's dependency established a tension in southern economic thought. First one and then the other of them dominated the colonial arguments southerners advanced. An early version of the colonial critique put forth an essentially laissez-faire view of economics; another version concentrated on developing an appropriate mercantilist program for the South. Yet these approaches shared the colonial analogy and on occasion the same spokesmen. The same person, say a John C. Calhoun, would argue first one variant and then the other. Whichever line they took, southerners rarely doubted the dependent character of their economy.

The South's economic thought evinced other tensions as well. Only a bit less important than the conflict between laissez-faire and mercantilist interpretations of dependency was a basic ambivalence about urbanization. While southerners generally spoke as agrarians, they were unsure of regional urban growth. Should the South raise up large, commercial cities of its own? Comparisons to the more prosperous North suggested that the South was artificially underurbanized. Against this notion stood the traditional conviction that cities lived parasitically off the countryside. Typically an emphasis on building a southern urban base was part and parcel of a mercantilist program, but not always. Again, the same individual might advance the most contradictory propositions about the value of cities. Thomas Jefferson endorsed Virginia's hopes to become the commercial outlet for the interior and yet firmly believed that the share of farmers in a country's population measured its virtue.

In a similar way, the issue of industrial diversification caused considerable trouble for southern economic writers. Even those southerners convinced of the dependent nature of their economy could doubt the desirability of diversifying that economy. While mercantilists generally argued for diversification, many in the laissez-faire camp maintained that a specialized economy, if unencumbered by tariffs and other interferences, could perform perfectly well. On occasion, some southerners even called for a return to a self-sufficient and individualistic economy— a call that drew on deep popular suspicions of commercial activity. The appeal of a more primitive division of labor fluctuated inversely with the economy, falling in the boom and rising during hard times. Of course, such arguments played on the romantic nostalgia for frontier conditions that southerners shared with their northern cousins.

Thus, contradictory ideas about free markets, urbanization, and diversification appear throughout this peculiar literature, to which southern statesmen and politicians, professors and amateur social scientists, populist farmers and agrarian poets all contributed. With only an occasional dash of formal economics, popular political economy freely explored the dependency of the region. These wranglings seldom conformed to modern demands of discipline and rigor, yet they often produced originality and insight.

In tracing the popular debates over southern dependency, one naturally looks for patterns. I originally suspected that the mercantilist urbanization-diversification position embodied the platform of a frustrated urban bourgeoisie, while the agrarian free trade—specialization view represented the intellectual defense of ensconced slaveowners and landlords. At certain places and certain times this characterization held true, but the exceptions are too rich to prove the rule. At crucial points in American history the leadership of the South's landed aristocracy dreamed of a well-regulated regional economy and significant new commercial centers. Many of those southerners who fought in the revolutionary struggle and then agitated for the Constitution followed just such a vision. On the other hand, urban southerners, enmeshed in an agrarian society, were often seduced by the rural hostility to commerce. The Nashville Agrarians by and large lived in cities and marketed their work in distinctly urban settings. Rather than championing programs of urban development, they fashioned an eloquent and penetrating attack on the very commercialism that sustained them.

Debates over dependency produced more than a side show to the region's class conflicts and marked more than the regional preoccupation with race. In the twentieth century, hostility to the struggles of blacks for economic and civil rights has often tainted the traditional agrarian position, while cautious support for the goals of blacks has characterized the advocates of a new southern urbanism. But this simple correspondence will not bear close scrutiny. There are exceptions on both sides. When we look back to the nineteenth century and earlier, the correspondence breaks down entirely.

Some twentieth-century writings might suggest that the agrarian versions of the colonial critique derive from the romantic tradition in the South while the more urban-oriented versions represent a refreshing realism in the region. There is some truth in the charge, but again, no easy generalization holds. Some of the most romantic southerners wrote poetically of the new metropolises that would rise to challenge the northern Babylons. Southern agrarians had no monopoly on romanticism.

The intellectual history of the South involves more than quarrels over class interests, anguish over slavery, and tensions between romantics and realists. For three centuries southerners have analyzed their economic dependency. The literature of dependency supplies insight into the mind of the past. Perhaps more importantly, it challenges us to ascertain what might still be novel and valuable in the southern critiques of colonialism, and it brings into sharper focus the universal character of the region's experience. As Woodward first suggested, the South's history, while often divergent from the dominant American themes of "opulence and success and innocence," has reflected burdens common to much of the world. Southern thinking on the burdens of dependency particularly deserves attention, since similar ideas continue to generate controversies in conflicts now played out on a global stage by far more populous Norths and Souths. Exploring this intellectual tradition in our own South provides a much needed link between American history and the experience of dependency shared by so many peoples.

The Meanings of Dependency

Although it has been denied a place in modern textbooks of economic orthodoxy, the concept of dependency has a rich history. Three major schools stand out: the English mercantilism of the seventeenth and early eighteenth centuries; the political economy of the "American System," including the closely related work of the German nationalist, Frederick List; and the dependistas of modern Latin America. Each of these intellectual traditions emphasized that a trade relationship in no way implies equality of the trading parties. Each school provided fuel for an upsurge of nationalism and led to the advocacy of aggressive programs of protection, diversification, and government intervention. And yet most southerners advocated free trade, not protection. They usually cited Adam Smith, not the mercantilists. In their hands Smith's attack on mercantilism became an argument not only for individual freedom but also for regional independence. Thus, in seeking an understanding of dependency we must also explore Smith's classical economics.

From the perspective of the twentieth century Adam Smith's thought seems the very antithesis of dependency theory. With his strong espousal of free markets and his hostility to government interference in the economy, Smith aggressively attacked the mercantilist doctrines that carried considerable influence in his day. His famous metaphor comparing the market system to an invisible hand working to achieve efficiency has become an epigram for the laissez-faire position. That southerners concerned with their region's dependency would attempt to build upon Smith's foundations might first seem surprising. If we shift our vantage point back two hundred years, however, Smith's economics are revealed in a quite different light.

In 1776, when *The Wealth of Nations* appeared, Smith's liberal attack on monopoly and privilege spoke to the aspiring middle class. For Smith and his readers monopoly bore an even more powerful stigma than it does today. Describing a mixture of economic exploitation and political manipulation, monopolies carried a connotation similar to that of trusts at the beginning of this century. Smith's stand against monopolies, especially state monopolies, had great appeal to those in the Americas who saw themselves as the victims of monopolistic malefactors. Not only did Smith attack monopoly, but more importantly he attacked the logic of British efforts to regulate colonial trade. Writing at the start of the American Revolution, Smith took strong exception to British colonial policy, categorizing it as "a project fit only for a nation of shopkeepers."

Worse yet, it could not even turn a profit. In effect, Britain had attempted to establish a monopoly over colonial trade. "[That] monopoly is the principal badge of their [the colonies'] dependency, and it is the sole fruit which has hitherto been gathered from that dependency." According to Smith the cost of administering and defending the colonies had become a subsidy for the support of monopoly. British policy claimed to encourage manufactures, but, Smith said, "its real effect has been to raise the rate of mercantile profit" while reducing home production. Merchants might benefit, but the distant and time consuming trade could not absorb as much product as more competitive trades closer to home. In Smith's view American dependency actually had cost both America and Great Britain.[1]

These writings against a politically maintained economic dependency obviously appealed to Americans eager to establish an independent economy. Southerners as well as New Englanders took heart in Smith's attack on colonial policy. With Smith, they asserted that free trade promised an escape from dependency.

In a somewhat different vein, Smith also argued for the primacy of agricultural over commercial development. This focus had considerable appeal for a southern audience concerned with building a strong agriculturally based economy. Smith maintained that the "natural progress of opulence" began with agriculture, then moved to manufactures, and only in the last phase turned to commerce. Smith based this argument on necessity, security, and human nature: The need for food, the most essential good, must be satisfied before the desire for items of comfort or luxury; hence, food commands large profits in the early phases of development. As for security, capital invested in agriculture could be kept under close scrutiny and protected from the numerous risks of commerce; the capital of the landlord is "as well secured as the nature of human affairs can admit of." Finally, human nature encourages agricultural investment. According to Smith, by nature men would ever retain a "predilection for this primitive employment," because of the beauty, tranquility, and independence of country life.

Smith bemoaned the fact that in most of Europe economic development had followed an "unnatural and retrograde order" from commerce and industry back to agriculture. This inversion of the natural sequence resulted from the feudal system, which had reduced incentives in agriculture and created a class of profligate large landholders. Energy had early been directed to commerce, and only when those efforts proved successful had investments been made in agriculture. Smith thought that inversion of the natural order of development produced serious problems. Commerce takes an inherently unstable course. Even worse, "a merchant, it has been said very properly, is not necessarily the citizen of any particular country."

With delight, the revolutionary generation of American agrarians read that their country, unlike Europe, was following the natural path to wealth. According to Smith, not just the availability of land, but also its division into relatively small efficient holdings accounted for the rapid growth of the North American economy. This agricultural base would naturally promote the growth of other industries over time. Rural surpluses would generate local demand and manufactures. Trade between town and country would anchor the national economy. All this would come to pass if only markets were left free.[2]

Smith's hostility to the mercantilist system grew out of his conviction that it attempted to force resources into an unnatural pattern of development. Throughout *The Wealth of Nations,* Smith points to the natural barriers of distance and time that work to discourage long distance trade and investment. The natural desire for security directs investment toward the domestic economy and especially toward agriculture. Left to the wisdom of these natural forces, the laissez-faire economy will develop in the most rapid and efficient manner possible.[3]

One can read Smith as an economist profoundly concerned with the problems of dependency. He attacked most forms of monopolistic exploitation. In this spirit he opposed efforts by developed countries to monopolize the trade of their colonies and less developed nations. Dubious of the value of international commerce, he encouraged developing countries to rely on internal development led by agriculture. In the absence of government intervention, he maintained, natural barriers would provide considerable incentive to local reinvestment. These barriers, not the mercantilist policies developed by "shopkeepers," provided a path to economic strength and independence. Attempting to add to these natural barriers was likely to produce more bad than good.

Adam Smith argued for a liberal path to economic development. Having identified the failures and excesses of mercantilist policy, Smith quickly asserted that there had never been any need for such policies in the first place. In doing this he drew a caricature of mercantilism that hardly did justice to the subtlety of thought underpinning it. Emphasizing the early concern mercantilists showed for the international flow of bullion, he ignored the more sophisticated arguments associated with the best of mercantilist theory. He also lost sight of the political realities that had so influenced that school. Although often critical, historians of mercantilism have painted a much richer picture—one that makes plausible the persistent appeal of mercantilism as a strategy of economic independence.

Starting with Gustav Schmoller's famous discussion of the economic policies of Frederick the Great, mercantilists have received at least partial rehabilitation. For Schmoller mercantilism emerged from the problem of state building. Only statesmanship could fashion a cohesive national economy. The state builder had to overcome local insularities, while protecting an emerging economy from hostile international competition.[4]

Although twentieth-century historians have balked at the breadth of Schmoller's thesis, clearly the role of statesmanship in a competitive setting dominates many mercantilist writings.[5] This idea reached its highest elaboration in the works of Sir James Steuart, the somewhat unfortunate foil for Adam Smith's pithy brilliance. For Steuart, "the trading nations of Europe represent a fleet of ships, every one striving who shall get first to a certain port. The statesman of each is the master."[6]

Writing in the second half of the eighteenth century, Steuart demonstrated a confidence that Britain could best the competition. His countrymen, writing a hundred years earlier, worried greatly about the vulnerability of their domestic economy. They continually warned that if the government did not follow an aggressive mercantile policy other states soon would subject England to dependency. "Whatsoever trade they beate us out of and engrosse into their owne hands, will bleede us with a bit and blow, making us pay for it what they please, which will not only impoverish us, but ruine our Navigation, and subject us to become a prey at pleasure," wrote Henry Robinson.[7]

The mercantilists feared the dependent position of a supplier of raw materials and consumer of finished products. Uniformly they railed against the exportation of unfinished goods. An anonymous tract, *Britannia Languens; or, A Discourse of Trade*, dramatically expressed these concerns. After noting that manufactures "will make a return of five, ten, or twenty times more Treasure to the Nation than the raw Materials," the author went on to a pointed warning:

> Besides, it is most dangerous to Export the Materials of Manufacture, since it may transfer the Manufacture it self into some Neighbour Nation, and with it the incident Riches and Populacy: by which means a Neighbour-Nation may become five, ten, or twenty times richer and stronger than that Nation which doth Export its Materials, and those

innocent Materials may in a short time return in the shape of armed
Men and Ships, to the Terror and Confusion of an unwise and lazy
People.[8]

The author admitted the wisdom of working up materials provided by
other nations and thus gaining activity for one's own. This policy not
only put people to work and reduced the need to import finished goods,
but it might also provide a new export. *Britannia Languens* also encouraged
the nation to eschew foreign luxuries in favor of domestic products even
when the latter were somewhat cruder.

Many of the mercantilist policies make considerably more sense when
viewed as advice in the art of state building and not as abstract exercises
in the study of equilibriums. The encouragement of colonial expansion
to achieve access to raw materials, the insistence on developing one's
own merchant marine, and the willingness to use state subsidies to build
fledgling industries all grew out of national rivalries and royal ambitions
rather than scholarly study.

For mercantilists a broad program encouraging finished exports and
import substitution could help the domestic economy in the international
struggle among the commercial states of Europe. Each country must try
to develop its commerce and its industry before it found itself reduced
to a dependent supplier of raw materials. Failure in this competition
promised to leave a country impoverished and, worse yet, vulnerable to
direct military action.

As Smith maintained more than two hundred years ago, not a few
mercantilists sought only their own private advancement. Eli Heckscher
has suggested that mercantilists put so great an emphasis on national
power, that they often lost sight of national affluence as an important
goal of policy.[9] Nevertheless, the mercantilists advanced an intelligible
analysis of the dangers of a resource-based, export-oriented economy.
While their understanding of the balance of trade was crude, their
underlying theory of economic development cannot be easily dismissed.
These ideas naturally attracted attention from Americans eager to build
a new nation in the wilderness.

Historians of economic thought now consider early American political economy as something of an archaic curiosity. The success of the
neoclassical school, as codified by Alfred Marshall at the end of the last
century, has obliterated all but the most important classical works from
serious academic consideration. Economists particularly avoid that band
of nineteenth century thinkers who attempted to integrate political econ-

omy with a broader social science. (The fact that Marshall himself drew on this tradition causes minor embarrassment.) Henry Carey, the Philadelphia economist and publicist, viewed economics, political science, and what we now call sociology as whole cloth. Little wonder that Carey wins only passing mention in the history of economic thought.[10]

By the early nineteenth century Adam Smith's intellectual attack on mercantilism had succeeded completely. To finish the job, David Ricardo had expounded his theory of comparative advantage, which provided a rather bloodless but highly rigorous demonstration of the mutual advantages of trade. These lessons of classical economics are still taught in American universities today, yet many in the young United States rejected the free trade argument and instead endorsed protectionist policies as a means to break the country's dependence on Great Britain. Henry Carey agreed. He set out to provide a rationale for protectionism that could stand up to Smith's arguments.

Carey's system starts from a distinction between a healthy concentration of economic activity and an oppressive centralization of the same. According to Carey, close association with others in towns raises labor productivity. Carey outlined a natural progression of economic development: An increasing density of population allows an expanded division of labor in nearby towns and hence increasing returns to scale. The growth of urban areas further encourages agriculture and facilitates the increasing productivity of that industry as well. Far from the grim Malthusian doctrine, Carey's was an optimistic vision in which population growth promoted heightened productivity. And with producer and consumer in close proximity, spatial concentration saved the wasteful "tax" of transport charges.[11]

Against the abundance produced by concentration, Carey described the sterility of what he called centralization. By forcing all the surplus of the periphery into a single metropolitan center, a centralized economy discourages the development of the former and squanders the wealth of both. Ostentatious consumption by the metropolis and the machinery of the state form an unnecessary burden on the population at large. Without a healthy local economy, underinvestment, low productivity, and an overweening dependence on export characterize the agricultural sector.

The sorry state of the Irish economy provided the obvious proof of Carey's theory. English rule had prevented Ireland from developing an autonomous concentration of economic activity. The poverty of Ireland resulted from "the pertinacious determination of England that Ireland shall send her wool to England, accompanied by food for the man that

is to twist and weave it: the whole then to be carried back in the form
of cloth, which the poor wretch who raised the food cannot buy, because
he has not even potatoes for his family."[12]

In Ireland, as elsewhere, centralization created great wealth for only
a few. In doing so it had preempted the spontaneous products of concentration. Indeed, the policies of centralization must necessarily oppose
the natural tendencies of concentration and undermine the contributions
of small independent farmers and capitalists. Everywhere centralization
worked to limit the opportunities opened to these classes. The British
Empire stood as a direct threat to the individual small producer and to
local concentration. The Irish could not protect themselves, nor could
the residents of India, but Americans could.

The answer was a protective tariff system, not to raise revenue, but
to encourage the spread of development in which producers and consumers were close at hand. Once in place, such local production would
yield a far better living standard than might be obtained by trading with
Britain. Indeed, Britain's centralized system forced an unequal exchange
on the periphery. Carey reckoned, for example, that with good machinery
the labor necessary to work up Indian cotton was less than that to grow
it; but because of the oppression of colonial peoples, because
of the unnecessary cost of transportation and the other indirect taxes of
the British system, the Indian farmer was forced to give up six times
the labor he should have in exchange for English goods. The Irishman
traded two to four times what he should, and similarly the Tennessee
planter or Ohio farmer. All three of these dependent nations thus had
their economies distorted to fit the needs of Great Britain. Only by
protecting themselves from Britain's rapaciousness could they develop
in a robust fashion.

Carey's theory of dependency and economic development presented
an exciting and dynamic alternative to the dry analytics of Ricardian
comparative advantage. His attack on British centralization raised serious
doubts about the unprecedented expansion of England's manufacturing
economy. Not surprisingly, the growth of British industry and commerce
had stimulated similar feelings on the Continent—most notably dis-
played in the work of Frederick List. List had spent several years in
America and had studied the writings of American protectionists including Carey. In constructing his "national system" of political economy
List argued strongly against the distortions produced in the international
economy by the "dominant power," Great Britain. "In the actual state
of the world, free trade would bring forth, instead of a community of

nations, the universal subjection of nations to the supremacy of the greater powers in manufactures, commerce and navigation."[13]

List, like Schmoller at the end of the century, gave high marks to the mercantilists, whose theories and policies he saw as the product of pragmatic experience. And, like Schmoller, List put a particularly nationalistic interpretation on the problems of dependency. While small nations could not be expected to maintain alone either their political or their economic independence, a nation of reasonable size must necessarily follow just such a course.

List was far more cautious in his recommendation of protection than Carey was ultimately to become. List continually emphasized that protection should be only a temporary measure to allow the development of new or infant industries in a balanced fashion as part of the "industrial education" of a nation. On the other hand, diversification into manufactures could provide a steady market for national agriculture. Agriculture oriented to foreign markets might achieve sporadic successes, but it left a nation's trade vulnerable to interruption by war or new sources of supply. Long-run development required a balanced economy.

Orthodox economics has dismissed both Carey and List as mere protectionist pamphleteers, and both surely did support protective measures; but in neither case did their protectionism reflect a misunderstanding of the message of comparative advantage as propounded by David Ricardo. Quite the contrary, they maintained that the Ricardian theory was simply too static. The mere fact that free trade might provide short-run advantages did not prove that it promised long-run development.

Oddly, both of these early economists advocated a balanced economy very similar to that advanced by Adam Smith, whom Carey on several occasions cited as an authority for his views. If they sponsored protectionist policies, which Smith would have found excessive, they did so in support of goals that he would readily have endorsed. In assembling their arguments they developed a dramatic conception of dependency. Great Britain's spectacular success prompted envy and fear. Both Carey and List argued with considerable scholarship and much emotion. In their day both commanded the attention of politicians and statesmen, and both had an influence on southern writers.

Unfortunately for academic economics, neither Carey nor List was able to formalize an analytical scheme capable of competing with the impressive edifice of Ricardo's classical economics. With the perfection of the neoclassical machinery constructed by Marshall and others, the work of these nineteenth-century nationalists was dropped from the canon of economic theory. Nevertheless, their themes did not disappear totally. First they were taken up by Marx and assimilated into his own brand of classical economics. Then, in the twentieth century, they again emerged as the justification of one or another form of nationalism. These two developmental streams have merged in the work of the dependency theorists of Latin America. In the debate over their theories, the analysis of dependency has reached its most serious expression. To put nineteenth-century notions of dependency in perspective, we do well to consider their intellectual descendants as well.

Most of the Latin American economists who have contributed to dependency theory trained in traditional economics. Many took graduate degrees at prestigious American universities. Their first-hand exposure to the poverty of underdeveloped economies made them receptive to nonorthodox approaches, including Marxism. Stimulated by the emergence in the 1950s of economic development theory as a policy-oriented discipline, the founders of the dependency school mounted a considerable challenge to the traditional faith in laissez-faire policies. Nevertheless, these dependistas, like most of their forerunners, have been plagued by an overabundance of insight and a lack of rigor.[14]

For the dependency theorists, development and underdevelopment are two sides of the same coin. As Andre Gunder Frank put it, "before there was development there was no underdevelopment." Developed and underdeveloped nations share a "common historical process"[15] The dependent economy does not simply lack this or that; dependency implies a relation, and most dependistas see that relation as highly exploitative. More than simply lagging behind on the path to development, the dependent economy finds itself locked into a relation with developed economies that undermines it potential.

Typically the dependent economy enters the world market as a provider of raw materials, trades for the most part with only a few developed economies, and quickly becomes a market for the simple manufactured goods of the metropolis. The dependent economy has a "concentration of reliances." The greater this concentration, "the greater the vulnerability" of a nation, since it would have greater difficulty "adjusting to a break in relations."[16]

Much of this has a familiar ring to us. It clearly reflects the thinking of List and other continental critics of the Pax Britannica. The dependistas, however, explore these notions in a far richer manner. They insist that dependency reaches past simple trade relations, that it insinuates itself into every response the dependent nation makes to changing world circumstances. Hence, programs of import substitution and protection can provide no simple remedies for dependency.[17] Even the domestic bourgeoisie becomes so entwined in the dependent relations of the colonial economy that it cannot chart a course of independent development. When it attempts to do so it becomes helplessly befuddled in compromising activities as it constantly turns to the developed world for capital, technology, and political support. In Frank's words, a "lumpenbourgeoisie" produces "lumpendevelopment." Even for its mode of thought, its culture, and its ideology, the *compradore* class of the periphery must draw on the center.

The dependency school has produced a broad sociopolitical critique of both the external relations of the underdeveloped country and the domestic social structures these relations engender. The dependistas strongly linked the notion of dependency to a self-critical jeremiad against the social psychology that dependency itself has produced. At times this critique of the psychology of dependency has taken precedence over the description of the external relations. In this respect the dependistas have searched for an analytical mode much broader and more difficult than that of traditional economics.

References to Adam Smith, James Steuart, and Frederick List punctuate the works of southerners attempting to explore their own dependency. Strong similarities exist between southern economic thinking and the various theories of dependency developed elsewhere. Southerners, too, had their theory of unequal exchange, and they also had their jeremiads. The universality of the southern colonial critiques becomes clearer when viewed in terms of the intellectual history of dependency theory. Nonetheless, the southern experience had its own peculiarities, and those peculiarities also influenced southern economic thought. To understand the meaning of colonial analogies in southern writings, we start with the region's own colonial experience.

The Colonial South

Latin American economists have formulated the modern theory of dependency as an explanation of the common experience of many Third World nations. These nations emerged from colonial status into extended economic disappointment.[18] The southern section of the United States also had a long colonial apprenticeship. The history of southern economic thought reaches back to these earliest beginnings.

While struggling with the practical problems of governance during the colonial period, southerners developed nothing so formal as a system of political economy. Early southern economic writings, like the mercantilist pamphlets of Great Britain, dealt with the immediate issues of policy. The first southerners to dabble in political economy bore the mercantilist stamp.

To understand the concerns of these "provincial" mercantilists, we must keep in mind the role assigned to colonial appendages in the imperial scheme.[19] Mercantilists first seriously dealt with the economic significance of the new colonies of America in the context of a self-conscious policy of diversification. Given their belief that England was underemployed, not overpopulated, the mercantilists approached the colonial initiative with extreme caution. From their vantage point, the eagerness of some individuals to emigrate to the colonies hardly proved the social usefulness of those colonies. Mercantilists maintained a fundamental mistrust of what Adam Smith would later celebrate as the invisible hand. For Samuel Fortrey, a merchant economist of the seventeenth century, it was an obvious dictum that "private advantages are often impediments of publick profit." Thus, Fortrey emphasized the importance of a controlled colonial policy that would complement the diversification program at home:

> I conceive, no foreign Plantation should be undertaken, or prosecuted, but in such countries that may increase the wealth and trade of this nation, either in furnishing us, with what we are otherwise forced to purchase from strangers, or else by increasing such commodities, as are vendible abroad; . . . but otherwise it is always carefully to be avoided, especially where the charge is greater than the profit, for we want not already a country sufficient to double our people, were they rightly employed; and a Prince is more powerful that hath his strength and force united, then he that is weakly scattered in many places.[20]

Mercantilists criticized especially the colonization of New England, which they saw as adding little to the British economic base. Josiah Child, the famous director of the East India Company, made a sharp distinction between New England and the other colonies in America. Child argued: "All our American Plantations except that of New England produce commodities of different natures from those of this Kingdom, as Sugar, Tobacco, Cocoa, Wool, Ginger, sundry sorts of dying Woods, etc. Whereas New England produces generally the same we have here." New England's ideal location for the building of ships and breeding of seamen most worried Child. Child felt that "there is nothing more prejudicial, and in prospect more dangerous to a Mother Kingdom, then the increase of shipping in theire Colonies, Plantations or Provinces." Finally, he claimed, one Englishman working in the West Indies with "ten or eight Blacks" made work for "four men in England," while ten immigrants to New England "doth not employ one man in England."[21] England benefited from the colonies other than New England to the extent that they provided employment in England itself. In turn, employment determined population, and concentrated population determined the prosperity of the kingdom.

Mercantilists like Fortrey and Child actually presented a fairly sophisticated argument against unplanned expansion. In their view, the problems facing England did not originate in poor soil and overpopulation but rather reflected a lack of proper organization and direction of labor. Spreading population willy-nilly over the globe could hardly be expected to address these needs, no matter how fertile the soil elsewhere. On the other hand, the provision of crucial commodities and the forced labor of other peoples could make a contribution to full employment and rapid expansion at home.

As long as the mercantilist remained safe at home in England, little could disturb the comforting consistency of his thought. He stood for a diversified, dense, and well-regulated economy and could maintain that the usefulness of colonies lay only in their ability to complement the economy of the mother country. However, once a mercantilist ventured across the Atlantic, mingled with the colonists, and became concerned with the quality of the colonial economy itself, naturally enough his basic commitment to a well-regulated division of labor might come to the fore. Viewed from the colonial side, a highly specialized colonial economy appeared almost profligate. If the poor ordering of the English economy led to a substantial loss of output and productivity, imagine the potential losses in the economy of the New World, where labor marched off into the forest in search of the quickest short-run profit. Reflecting on such questions led directly to a mercantilist-based critique of colonialism.

The logic of a well-balanced community seemed so powerful to seventeenth-century colonial mercantilists that even the loyalists among them questioned policies that encouraged a disorganized and highly specialized economy. Perhaps the best example of this phenomenon was William Berkeley, the royalist governor of Virginia.[22] The well-educated Berkeley came from a prominent court family. He strongly supported the Crown in England's Civil War. Here was no colonial rebel. Berkeley fully accepted the notion that Virginia's products should complement the home economy. But beyond that given, the colonial economy should diversify as much as possible, he felt. Berkeley saw Virginia's economy as greatly overspecialized in tobacco and argued, "Such staple commodities as Iron, Silk, Flax, Hemp and Pot-ashes, may be easily raised in Virginia, and high imputation will lye upon us, why we have not all this time endeavorred to evidence the truth and certainty of it, to our own and the public advantage."[23]

For Berkeley, the unfortunate concentration on tobacco derived not from any natural advantage in this area but rather from the government's encouragement of its cultivation and lack of support for other endeavors. A chaotic oversupply had resulted in low prices for what King James described as the vile weed. According to Berkeley the planters understood their situation and wanted to rectify it. The lack of skilled labor presented the major obstacle to diversification. The planters were like "those Architects, who can design excellent Buildings, but have no skill to square their Timber, or lay their Bricks, and for want of money to procure men for these labours, their models remaine only in their imaginations or papers."[24]

In identifying community with well-ordered villages and town concentrations, Berkeley reflected the dominant thought of English mercantilism. Mercantilists had a powerful faith in the productivity of proximity. English colonial policy had always assumed that new lands should be settled in a compact and controlled fashion.[25] Berkeley aggressively pursued efforts to legislate town development in Virginia. Whatever their original intent, such proposals came close to advocating the development of urban industries and a further diversification of the colonial economy. No wonder the royal government balked at fully implementing such plans.[26]

If, in the area of town formation, Berkeley pressed hard on mercantilist orthodoxy, when it came to trade and commerce he clearly broke with it. "Confining the Planters to Trade only with the English" might be justified if it benefited the "Crown or our Mother-Nation," but Berkeley doubted that such a case could be made. He therefore petitioned the home government to allow ships from the colonies to trade with any country, contending that this would save the timber resources of England and allow trade to be carried out more cheaply. Clearly, from the vantage point of the colony, an otherwise solid mercantilist might call into question the very linchpin of mercantilist policy.

Berkeley was no early harbinger of laissez faire and free trade. Quite the contrary; he advocated governmental intervention in matters of town development and industrial diversification. Berkeley was only applying mercantilist thinking to Virginia, herself. Undoubtedly he felt that the regulated development of that colony would be useful to the mother country, but his concern to build a viable economy (and society) in the mercantilist image overshadowed his commitment to the narrower theory of mercantilist colonialism.

It is against this background that we must read Berkeley's denunciation of the Navigation Acts. According to Berkeley the restrictions on colonial trade benefited only a small group of English merchants. Berkeley portrays himself and his colonial constituency as part of the King's dominion, in conflict not with a nation but with a class or interest group. Berkeley wrote, "We cannot but resent that forty thousand people should be impoverished to enrich little more then forty Merchants, who being the only buyers of our Tobacco, give us what they please for it, and after it is here, sell it how they please; and indeed have forty thousand servants in us at cheaper rates, then any other men have Slaves, for they find them Meat, Drink and Clothes, we furnish ourselves and their Sea-men with Meat and Drink, and all our sweat and labour, as they order us, will hardly procure us course clothes."[27]

Berkeley's argument falls considerably short of a full-blown anti-colonial critique. At the analytical level it is rather simple. His plea for greater commercial freedom has an opportunistic ring, and he fails to directly address the mercantilist argument for concentration in the home country. Nevertheless, Berkeley represents a major departure for economic thought in Virginia and the South. He did not so much reject mercantilism as "go native." His plans all involve using standard mercantilist techniques to build up the Virginian economy. They amount to a mercantilism centered on Virginia rather than England. Berkeley's Virginian mercantilism addressed pressing policy questions of the day. However, it also stands as the source of a major theme in southern economic thought.

The general mercantilist outlook carried over into the next generation of leaders in Virginia. Born in the colony, these men quite naturally saw Virginia's economy as their central concern. The most notable home-grown southern mercantilist of the early eighteenth century was Robert Beverley, author of *The History and Present State of Virginia*. Beverley had high respect for the diversification policies of Berkeley and praised Edmund Andros, a later governor, for his encouragement of manufacturing. He himself consistently supported efforts to designate ports for trade as a means of encouraging urban growth. Beverley offered an analytic defense of "cohabitation":

It is thought too much for the same Man, to make the Wheat, and grind it, bolt it and bake it himself. And it is too great a charge for every Planter, who is willing to sow Barley, to build a Malt-House, and Brew House too, or else to have no benefit of his Barley; nor will it answer if he would be at the Charge. These things can never be expected from a single Family: But if they had cohabitations, it might be thought worth attempting. Neither as they are now settled, can they find any certain Market for theyr other Grain, which if they had Towns, would be quite otherwise.[28]

Beverley's political economy built on standard mercantilist themes, but his emphasis on developing an extensive division of labor within the colony contradicted mercantilist colonial policy.

Beverley paid lip service to the imperial view of the colonies' place. He dedicated his book to Robert Harley, Speaker of the House of Commons, and emphasized his commitment to those measures that were "due to a loyal People whose Lives are devoted to the Benefit of their Mother-Country."[29] Even so, Beverley repeatedly criticized those agents of the Crown who attempted to limit the collective initiatives of the colonial populace. He saw as particularly blameworthy any opposition to the program of town formation and diversification. In his specific defense of these same programs he offered no rationalization as to how they would benefit England. Instead, he continually emphasized their importance to Virginia. Beverley was exasperated with the foolishness and lethargy of the colonists who seemed eager to cultivate only tobacco. Their short-term pursuit of profit had made them dependent in an unnecessary fashion and had reduced their productivity. Nowhere in his argument does Beverley even attempt to demonstrate the value to the empire of a more diversified Virginian economy. Beverley, like Berkeley, Fortrey, and Child, feared the wasteful dissipation of effort over the new lands. This was a fundamental mercantilist principle. However, he increasingly saw the loss in terms of the Virginia and not the imperial economy.

Between Berkeley and Beverley mercantilist ideas had been firmly planted among the dominant landholders of Virginia. But the hope to use mercantilist policies to establish a well-ordered society in the colony inevitably ran counter to British concerns to maximize the production of the tobacco staple. Hence, the call for diversification and urbanization became linked to potentially radical criticisms of imperial policy. While these arguments were still rather rudimentary, they would have a lasting appeal in the South.

William Berkeley and Robert Beverley advocated a Virginia-centered mercantilism, but not all Virginians saw their problems in a mercantilist context or saw the answer as one of expanding the role of government in the economy. Virginia's mercantilists felt that the majority of planters underestimated the evil of a specialized economy. They thought that the planters were much too eager to waste resources in maximizing their profits from tobacco. Beverley's book emphasized the shortcomings of the planters' practices as much as those of the colonial administration.[30]

Early mercantilist writings in Virginia foreshadowed the recurring southern introspection about the region's colonial mentality. Men like Beverley, aspiring to a more complete economy, found considerable fault with their neighbors. Although disparaging of colonial restriction, the mercantilists were the last to suggest a laissez-faire abandon. Many of the common tobacco farmers, however, sought freedom from officious home-grown mercantilists as well as from British interference. Basically they chafed at any attempt to limit their ability to grow and sell tobacco as they pleased. While they fully opposed the Navigation Acts, they had no interest in replacing them with a Virginia-based mercantilism. They did not want to have to carry their tobacco to Virginia towns when it could more easily be loaded directly at their own riverside wharfs. They did not want high taxes to subsidize commercial or industrial ventures of dubious value to themselves. And they wanted the freedom to press into the interior for fresh and cheap land. At least in part, the failure of early attempts to alter the southern economy can be traced to the unwillingness of these planters to devote their political energies to a coherent program of mercantilist reform.[31]

Significant irony surrounded this libertarian theme in early southern economic thought. As the southern mercantilists often pointed out, it was precisely the unregulated pursuit of tobacco profits that contributed most to colonial dependency. These mercantilists nonetheless led popular opposition to imperial schemes of trade regulation. To some extent, this collaboration blurred the distinction between two very different perspectives on the colonial predicament, one espousing freedom that would lead to economic independence, the other counseling regulation that would foster diversity. But the underlying contradiction remained and would continue throughout southern history. This tension fostered the development of rich and varied critiques of colonial dependency and an economics full of politics and geography.

The tension in southern economic thought between mercantilist and libertarian conceptions of dependency has its roots in these first efforts to formulate economic policy for the region. But to what extent did southerners share this tension with settlers further north? There can be little doubt that mercantilist notions also influenced colonists in the North. And surely hostility to the Navigation Acts infected the North as well as the South.[32]

Until the twentieth century, southern economic and social thought maintained a sensitivity to issues of dependency that the North originally shared but had much earlier repudiated. Even late in the seventeenth century a difference between southern and northern thought had appeared. This intellectual difference reflected the material differences already emerging in the two regional economies.

The South, with its concentration on staple products, especially tobacco, had already enmeshed itself in a monetized, highly specialized agriculture. This fact lay behind both the southern mercantilist's emphasis on diversification and the southern planter's individualistic commercialism. Reflecting this internal conflict, southern thought, particularly that of southern mercantilists, included far more self-criticism than did that of the North. The mercantilists berated not only Great Britain but also their fellow southerners. In this they showed a sensitivity to the dangers of colonial co-optation that was unique in the writings of the day.

The early commercialization of southern agriculture played a fundamental role in the differentiation of northern and southern economic thought. This commercialization expanded during the eighteenth century. Slavery in Virginia and the other southern colonies rapidly spread into the system of commercial agriculture. In turn slavery validated that agricultural system.[33]

The very resistance of the North to slavery can be interpreted as another manifestation of the early regional difference in agricultural specialization. More than one researcher has argued that northern farmers perceived their society and economy in a fundamentally different manner than did southern colonists.[34] They did not undertake a business; they lived as farmers. Farming obviously had its commercial side, but at the same time it carried a broad range of social meanings. Northerners thought about farming in terms of European models. For all the differences between England and New England, the New England farmers probably perceived themselves as scarcely distinguishable from the English farmer. Southern planters could hardly deny the colonial nature of their own role. Slavery had an obvious instrumental meaning in the southern context. The North, starting with a far less focused commercialism, rejected slavery and thus created a less colonial, less profit-oriented society.

Ironically, the North, more isolated from world trade, created a less commercial agriculture that ultimately provided a base for a successful diversified capitalism. The South followed a course dictated by the spirit of commercial calculation that defined the region as a highly specialized colonial appendage to the emerging capitalism of Europe. In places like Cuba, Jamaica, and Barbados, the dialectical confusions of this irony of modern slavery caused little concern. The calculating, commercial white settlement on those islands always remained small and elite. Indeed, those settlers strove for absentee status, a return to the center of the empire. Not so in the southern colonies, where many ambitious white settlers continually attempted to imitate the exploits of their more successful countrymen by working on their farms. The number of planters grew, but owners of slave plantations were left with a sense of incompleteness and remoteness. The very opportunism of slavery invited repression and denial of its acquisitive motive. The commercial slave economy appeared too different from the British manorial model to be of value in itself. Already in Beverley (and more in his contemporary William Byrd) we can hear, in the attack on southern dependency, a strong element of self-defense or rationalization. This apology for slavery became even more pronounced in the writings of the revolutionary generation.

In this rather convoluted fashion, in the midst of the most commercial of all forms of agriculture, a hostility to commerce itself developed. This hostility strongly colored all varieties of the early southern colonial critiques, distinguishing them from the economic thought of the northern colonies.

Chapter Two

Agrarianism and the Paper System

Anticolonial revolutionaries in our century have found justification for radicalism in theories of economic exploitation. Southerners, especially leading Virginians, played critical roles in the American Revolution. Unlike more recent colonial rebels, however, southerners produced precious little in the way of serious economic argument, before or during the revolutionary war. While concerns over dependency contributed to revolutionary enthusiasm in the South, the pressing need for unity muted potentially divisive economic debates.

Southerners differed among themselves on the best cure for a colonial economy. Not a few southerners suspected the economic motives of their northern allies. The struggle to form a new system of government brought these issues to the surface but left them unresolved. Southern arguments against a strong Congress drew on a libertarian interpretation of the region's dependency. The southern "nationalists," including Washington and Madison, supported strengthening the central government and flirted with mercantilist thinking but proposed no clear plan of economic development for either the South or the new nation as a whole. Over the years, the nationalists showed considerable ambivalence toward the South's dependency and uncertainty about how best to overcome it. In the midst of this confusion Jefferson began to shape the agrarian ideology that ultimately played a central role in southern thought. The equivocal economic thinking of the revolutionary period provides a useful foil to the agrarian synthesis.

Revolutionary Thoughts

Throughout the eighteenth century southerners had continued to worry about their economic dependence on producing a few staples. Tobacco prices had fluctuated considerably over the years since the introduction of the crop.[1] Planters had ridden out more than one wave of boom and bust. Within a colonial context they puzzled over their own ability to expand the area of cultivation devoted to tobacco and their inability to contract it. This simple issue haunted southern agriculture through its entire history. However beneficial to planters as a group, any effort to regulate tobacco always angered a significant number of producers. Even governmental establishment of standards and official warehousing in the early eighteenth century alienated many marginal producers.[2]

The Crown could propose little in the short run to deal with the cycles of expansion and indebtedness. At the same time, many planters continued to be critical of profits accruing to British merchants in the tobacco trade. As Governor Berkeley had noticed early on, regulations such as the Navigation Acts seemed strongly to favor this group. For the first half of the eighteenth century this conflict remained below the surface. However, the deterioration of tobacco markets in the 1760s and the resulting debt incurred by planters greatly intensified fears of economic dependency.[3] In this context any efforts to reform colonial economic policy had to address the anxieties of the colonists themselves.

Successful prosecution of the French and Indian War had left Great Britain with a much-enhanced North American empire and an opportunity to rationalize its colonial operations. The revised British colonial policy showed little sensitivity to the aspirations of southern planters. Predictably it provoked an angry response. The British focused almost exclusively on raising revenues and restricting expenditures in the colonies. This approach made some sense in the troublesome northern colonies, as long as the Crown stood ready to enforce it. Yet, in the southern colonies, whose economic aspirations Britain presumably shared more deeply, this policy hastened the alienation of already suspicious planters.

The Quebec Act of 1763, for example, forbade settlement west of the Alleghenies. This statute attempted to contain British military expenditures along the frontier. A rapid and chaotic settlement of the trans-Allegheny region could only bring additional expense and little profit to the home government. This British policy came into conflict with one of the fondest hopes of the mercantilists in the southern provinces. For years advocates of urban development in Virginia had looked on westward expansion as a force that could guarantee the commercial importance of the colony's stunted towns. Toward this end (and with some considerable hope of private profit), more than one prominent Virginian of the revolutionary generation had speculated in western lands—among them George Washington and George Mason, heavy investors in the Ohio Company.[4]

Restricting settlement in the West made sense from the point of view of enlightened mercantilist policy. The Quebec Act would have complemented efforts to diversify the remaining economy, encourage urban development, limit the ravages of price fluctuations, and protect agriculture from financial crisis. Such a program might have directly addressed those aspirations of the colonial mercantilsts that hinged on a better regulated economy, yet the Quebec Act came with no such broader program.

Similarly, Lord Townshend's efforts to tax British imports to the colonies only exacerbated the Virginia planters' deep-seated hostility toward British merchants. The planters mounted an ambitious boycott. Even though the nonimportation agreement failed miserably, it reflected a growing distrust of the central government's economic policies. Lord Townshend had sought to raise revenues; instead he raised colonial consciousness. The historian T. H. Breen concludes that the boycott helped "to crystallize largely inchoate ideas about the moral dangers of dependence."[5]

Southern colonists protested, but they could not agree on a clear economic strategy. The traditional mercantilist emphasis on order and planning did not blend well with an increasingly shrill political debate focusing on rights and liberties. Debating mercantilist notions could only divide the colonists. Many southern leaders of the revolutionary generation maintained their confidence in well-conceived public intervention of the mercantilist type. In the years before the Revolution, however, the designing of such a program could easily be postponed. As hostility mounted, the Revolutionary rhetoric drew increasingly on the libertarian version of the colonial critique and less and less on that of the mercantilists. Political attacks targeted the oppressive regulations of the British government; better and more elaborate planning held little appeal as a rallying cry.

Thomas Jefferson's "Summary View of the Rights of British America" (1774) provides a good example of how revolutionary rhetoric favored libertarian political economy. Jefferson did allow the existence of a public interest, but he endorsed no system of economic regulations. Jefferson asserted that individual efforts had developed the American colonies and, therefore, Britain had to allow a greater individual freedom to the Americans. In Jefferson's words, "America was conquered, and her settlements made and firmly established at the expense of individuals, and not of the British public. Their own blood was spilt in acquiring land for their settlement, their own fortunes expended in making that settlement effectual. For themselves they fought, for themselves they conquered, and for themselves alone they have right to hold."[6] Jefferson then launched into a tirade against British trade regulations and British merchants. Americans had a right to greater economic freedom. Britain must not "think to exclude us from going to other markets, to dispose of those commodities which they cannot use, nor to supply those wants which they cannot supply."[7]

Jefferson himself, after the Revolution, advanced several plans in the spirit of the early mercantilism of Virginia, but during the revolutionary struggle he emphasized individual economic rights. Indeed, resistance to the various regulatory policies of the British government created an alliance of disparate classes and interests. The restriction of western settlement brought together small farmers and those large planters who had investments in western land schemes. Whatever doubts about frontier democracy the great planters may have had, they became champions of the rights of British subjects. Had such men advocated a new mercantilist order, they must have seriously threatened the grand alliance.

The heady pronouncement of liberties and the excitement of revolution also obscured important differences between northern and southern colonies. Even before the Revolution the North had begun to develop a diversified economy with growing commercial centers. The northern economy appeared a younger (and perhaps more energetic) version of the European states. The South had a much less certain identity. Not simply a slave colony in the West Indian mode, but surely not an urban-dominated commercial economy, it was betwixt and between. The South brought together an incongruous combination of elements from the mercantilist age. Given this odd mix, American independence raised fundamental questions about how best to decolonize the southern economy. In struggling over these questions, southerners naturally drew and expanded upon the two critiques developed during the colonial period.

The libertarian perspective had always focused on British regulatory mechanisms and their role in channeling a portion of the colonial surplus to the metropolitan centers. As enunciated during the Revolution, the libertarian argument called for the unfettered pursuit of individual gain—for free trade and open frontiers. Yet, despite its explicitly commercial character, or perhaps as a defensive reaction to that character, the libertarian critique often came coupled to a precapitalist agrarian ideal embodying a broad hostility toward all commercial activity. The libertarians wished to benefit from commerce, not be ruled by it. Such ideas intensified the opposition to mercantilist policies and centralized government. Southerners who subscribed to the more libertarian version of the colonial critique especially feared that a central government would attempt the imposition of a "commercial system." In these arguments southerners easily slipped into a broad attack on commerce as such.

The fear of a new centralization showed most clearly in the writings of Richard Henry Lee. Lee came from one of the oldest and best-established Virginia families, which might have made him an advocate of order and government controls. Lee's own economic situation being highly strained, however, he identified with the interests of the wide range of common planters.[8] Lee saw the major economic achievement of the Revolution as the destruction of the British commercial system. Freed of that system, what could be simpler than to declare an open commerce and institute a laissez-faire commercial policy? Lee saw little reason for entering a strong union with the North to promote a new, American commercial system. That would simply be trading one master for another. In a 1785 letter to Madison, Lee made clear his hostility to any national commercial system:

> Giving Congress a power to Legislate over the Trade of the Union would be dangerous in the extreme to the five Southern or Staple States, whose want of Ships and Seamen would expose their freightage and their produce to a most pernicious and destructive Monopoly. With such a power eight states in the Union would be stimulated by extensive interest to shut close the door of Monopoly, that by the exclusion of all rivals whether for the purchasing of our produce or freighting it, both these might be at the Mercy of our East and North. The Spirit of Commerce throughout the world is a spirit of Avarice and could not fail to act as above stated.[9]

Richard Henry Lee distrusted all commercial powers, including the northern states. Political independence, however, could protect agriculture from the worst excesses of commercial regulation. For Lee, as for many southerners of the eighteenth century, "commerce" raised images not of peaceful merchants and trade but of stockjobbers, influence peddlers, and Whiggish aristocrats.[10] While denouncing commerce, Lee advocated unbridled free trade. His inconsistency in this reflected a fundamental contradiction in the South's vision of a commercial-agrarian economy.

In the postrevolutionary period, this argument reappeared in the thinking of many southerners—perhaps most notably in the heat of the

Constitutional Convention, where George Mason fought against federal commercial regulation. Mason worried that giving the congressional majority power to pass navigation acts "would enable a few rich merchants in Philadelphia, New York and Boston, to monopolize the staples of the Southern States, and reduce their value perhaps fifty per cent."[11] Like Lee, Mason saw no reason to expect the central government to play a constructive role in the decolonization of the southern economy.

Early southern arguments against nationalizing control over trade stood in sharp contrast to traditional mercantilist thought in the South. Nationalists, northern and southern, argued that effective regulation could come only from a strong central authority. Without such coordinated intervention, political independence could not bring economic independence. The dependency of the colonial period might well reassert itself in some form of neocolonialism.

In Great Britain powerful men had already laid just such plans. Lord Sheffield cheerily argued that the new states would likely remain economic appendages of the mother country. He laid a strong claim to the dubious honor of inventing neocolonialism.[12] Sheffield provided a strategy for continued British influence in his *Observations on the Commerce of the American States* (1783). No modern representative of the dependency school has offered a clearer statement of the multiple ties that continue to bind a newly independent colony to its colonial economic patterns. Sheffield's basic premise was, "No American articles are so necessary to us, as our manufactures are to the Americans."[13] Britain continued to hold great advantages over other European carriers and manufacturers: "Few trading Americans speak any foreign language; they are acquainted with our laws as well as with our language. They will put confidence in British merchants, which they will not in those of other nations, with those people they are unacquainted as well as with their laws and language."[14] But Sheffield did not rely only on the ties of culture. British merchants also enjoyed important advantages in their ability to provide credit: "Experience will operate every day in favour of the British merchant. He alone is able and willing to grant the liberal credit which must be extorted from his competitors by the rashness of their early ventures; they will soon discover that America has neither money nor sufficient produce to send in return, and cannot have for some time."[15] Cheerfully Sheffield observed that the independence of the colonies freed Great Britain from the cost of maintaining American government. Moreover, Great Britain no longer had any reason to allow the bothersome competition of American ships in the West Indian trade.

Clearly, Sheffield wrote in the mercantilist logic of the eighteenth century. As the "provincial mercantilists" had understood, that logic naturally suggested a set of mercantalist counterarguments. In the post-revolutionary period an independent South, with few towns and virtually no merchant marine, would hardly provide a strong base on which to build a commercial power, hence the appeal of a North-South alliance in a federal system. But southerners schooled in the mercantilist tradition also appreciated the dangers that an overreliance on the North carried with it. At a practical level most southerners with mercantilist leanings solved this dilemma by supporting a stronger national government based on state representation. Yet the Constitution, in solving the immediate political problem, did little to clarify theoretical issues surrounding southern economic development.

While Lee epitomized the libertarian attack on colonial policy and mercantilism more generally, Washington and Madison, Virginia's foremost nationalists, proved more pragmatic—critics might say opportunistic—in their political economy. There can be little doubt that the nationalists descended from the older generation of mercantilists. That influence showed most clearly in the thinking and works that George Washington recorded between the Revolution and his election to the presidency. During this period Washington strongly advocated mercantilist schemes of internal improvements, with the purpose of winning the riches of the western territories for Virginia.

Washington's notions of the West derived not from idle speculation, but from land speculation. Washington had direct and significant experience with the frontier. His family had played a major role in the opening of western Virginia, both by personal settlement and by corporate development. Something of a failure as a planter, with expenses far greater than his crops could maintain, Washington had attempted during the prerevolutionary period to reconstitute his wealth through land speculation and development. Washington, like many Virginian planters, looked to the western lands to subsidize his position. During the period immediately after the Revolution he devoted much of his attention to shaping a new policy toward the West. With a bit of the theatrical, he descended on the Virginia assembly in 1784 and won its approval of improvements for the James and Potomac rivers, with an eye to a western canal connection. For all of his American nationalism, he argued that Virginia had to act quickly or risk competition from New York and Pennsylvania.[16] To that end Washington eagerly advocated state subsidies for a southern commerce based on western farming.

Commerce has an infectious quality; not all southerners could stay immune. James Madison also had the infection for a while. Madison argued strongly for Virginia to limit international shipping to Norfolk, or perhaps Norfolk and Alexandria, a plan directly descended from the seventeenth-century mercantilists. By such legislation, he hoped to raise up a city in Virginia to rival Baltimore for the profit of southern commerce. His proposal aimed at destroying the monopsonistic position of the British merchants who had brought their business directly onto the navigable rivers of Virginia. Madison enthusiastically led the fight for Washington's proposed internal improvements and linked these to a broader system of economic development for the Commonwealth. Madison believed that the state must do for the common good what individuals could not achieve.[17]

Washington and Madison endorsed the development of a more diverse economy in Virginia. They, almost as much as Lee, looked on the North as a potential threat to Virginia's economy. They drew heavily on the early tradition of mercantilism in Virginia. It may seem odd, then, that they became two of the staunchest champions of the nationalist principles underlying the Constitution. How can these positions be reconciled? The simplest answer, appearing often in Constitutional commentaries, builds on the confidence of the southern nationalists that their region would dominate the federal government.[18] They anticipated not so much the spread of slavery, which in the late eighteenth century seemed in decline, as the agricultural penetration of the Ohio valley and the old Southwest. They saw little reason to fear that such areas would tie themselves closely to the Northeast. For southern mercantilists, a stronger federal government sensitive to southern interests might work to build up the region's economy as part of a broader plan of national development.

This seems reasonable enough, but there may have been another dimension to southern nationalist thought. As in the jeremiads of Beverley years before, mercantilist aspirations for a more diverse economy could lead to a sense of impotence—no one knew how to achieve the vision. Taking measure of their countrymen, so eager to escape the yoke of all regulation, Washington, Madison, and their followers might well have despaired. The mercantilists had always criticized their own class of large landholders and (even more harshly) the common planters. Perhaps they feared the kind of government their neighbors might institute. Perhaps by contrast northerners appeared more energetic and creative.

Even the nationalists had considerable misgivings about the new constitution. Sectional conflicts in the Constitutional Convention more than once threatened to destroy it.[19] Virginian nationalists feared giving up too much. Still, they succeeded in carrying their reluctant constituents into the new union. They continued to hope that such a union would hasten southern economic development. Only the prestige of Washington and a bit of dubious politicking won Virginia's ratification. Events may have carried the nationalists further than they had anticipated.

Two generations later, apologists for the Republican party would see the Constitution as the product of a "slaveowner conspiracy," a view with some credibility.[20] Yet the story was clearly more complex. In union Virginian nationalists hoped to find a way to develop their state and the South, to decolonize them; but their approach involved a difficult balancing act. These men, mercantilist by inclination, had to take into account their neighbors' enthusiasm for a more independent and laissez-faire approach. The southern nationalists' ambivalence may have limited their ability to formulate a clear plan of economic development. Without such a plan, they ran the risk of merely asserting a natural harmony of interests among the sections. Such thinking always played well in the North. Some northerners eventually argued that economic differences between sections made for a mutually advantageous regional division of labor and thus provided an important and natural bond tying the nation together. That view of course turned the southern nationalist hopes on their head. Rather than promoting southern regional development and diversification, the sectional cohesion of such a position projected the never-ending specialization of the southern staple economy—dependence everlasting.

Under the circumstances, many southerners doubted the promises (and premises) of the nationalist project. Although politically successful, southern mercantilist nationalists produced little in the way of regional development. Their strategy left the fragile commercial economy of the South in direct competition with the North. The new federal government, like British rule before it, threatened to become a burden to the producer and an agent of the exploiter. This threat provided fertile ground for a new southern agrarianism.

Agrarianism and the Neocolonial Predicament

In all of southern history, Thomas Jefferson stands out as the most important and most impressive intellectual force. While Jefferson's influence spread across the nation (indeed, the world), his philosophy of agrarian republicanism had a profound and persistent impact on southern thought. Jefferson's preoccupation with dependency played a central role in that philosophy.

Jefferson's primary concern was social, not economic. He took as his own the classical philosophical problem of how to so order the state that it would encourage both private and public virtue. Jefferson's interest in political economy grew out of his suspicion that economic conditions strongly influenced character. In this he subscribed to an economic determinism common in his day (and not altogether naive). For Jefferson, economic independence fostered virtue while economic dependency sorely eroded it. Jefferson puzzled over the relation between individual and national dependency. Indeed, this question occupied the bulk of his economic writings. Since his agrarianism focused on the protection of personal and public virtue through individual independence, Jefferson's use of the colonial theme often had a libertarian rather than a mercantilist ring; we have already seen a good example of this in his "Summary View of the Rights of British America." But Jefferson never endorsed a uniformly passive approach to government. Government, he believed, had a responsibility to shape an economy capable of sustaining virtuous individuals.

Like Adam Smith, Jefferson thought that most people, if given the choice, preferred agriculture to all other pursuits. Farming built both self-reliance and virtue. The vast area of the United States could allow the great bulk of its population to take up an agrarian life. A wise government, Jefferson reasoned, should support a prosperous agrarian economy, thus nurturing a virtuous citizenry. Despite his preference for limited government, he advocated economic policies to actively aid agriculture. Jefferson most feared those economic developments that might force self-reliant farmers into dependency. Clearly he saw British commerce as the greatest danger in this regard, but he also suspected that the commercial Northeast, with its continuing ties to the British, also posed a considerable threat. National policy had to guard against these dangers, not exacerbate them.

This did not mean a complete renunciation of commerce. He hoped that government could shape commerce to serve the interests of an independent and highly diversified agriculture. To maintain a reasonable standard of living, the rural economies of the South and West required commerce as their handmaiden. Jefferson struggled to formalize economic policies to support his agrarian republic.

The farmer's superiority to other citizens derived from his independence. In a famous passage from his *Notes on the State of Virginia* (1784), Jefferson wrote:

> Those who labour in the earth are the chosen people of God, if ever he had a chosen people, whose breasts he has made his peculiar deposit for substantial and genuine virtue. It is the focus in which he keeps alive that sacred fire, which otherwise might escape from the face of the earth. Corruption of morals in the mass of cultivators is a phenomenon of which no age nor nation has furnished an example. It is the mark set on those who, not looking up to heaven, to their own soil and industry, as does the husbandman, for their subsistence, depend for it on the casualties and caprice of customers. Dependence begets subservience and venality, suffocates the germ of virtue, and prepares fit tools for the designs of ambition. This, the natural progress and consequence of the arts, has sometimes perhaps been retarded by accidental circumstances: but generally speaking, the proportion which the aggregate of other classes of citizens bears in any state to that of its husbandmen, is the proportion of its unsound to its healthy parts, and is a good-enough barometer whereby to measure its degree of corruption.[21]

The problem of how to foster "virtue" haunted the republican consciousness.[22] Other southern writers, most notably Richard Henry Lee, had already developed the theme. Like Lee, Jefferson wanted to build a political economy that would nurture virtue and in turn be supported by it. "Virtue," for these eighteenth-century citizens, meant a generous concern for public matters and a stoic disposition.[23] Virtue required independence. For both men a dependent individual always risked corruption of character. Their concern showed the influence of classical educations, but it also must have reflected their experiences with the slave economy of the South. Both Lee and Jefferson openly criticized slavery. In the South slavery gave dependency a meaning that was far more immediate than it carried in other regions or back in Britain.

Much of the revolutionary rhetoric of the southern patriots had interpreted British policy as an attempt to enslave the colonies. This analogy must strike us today as rather ludicrous, and yet slavery may teach a love of independence to the slaveowner as well as the slave.[24] Surely Jefferson had something like this in mind when, in a now famous letter, he described southerners as "zealous for their own liberties, but trampling on those of others."[25] Nor does it seem accidental that in his *Notes on Virginia* Jefferson's paean to the independence of agriculture came immediately after his denunciation of slavery in Virginia. Slavery eroded virtue. Allowing half the "citizens thus to trample on the rights of the other, transforms those into despots and these into enemies, destroys the morals of the one part, and the amor patriae of the other."[26] Relatively few southerners followed Jefferson and Lee into open criticism of slavery. Nevertheless, southern sensitivity to the onus of dependency often reflected a common appreciation of the abject dependency of the plantation slave.

Consideration of the slave's dependency made it clear that agricultural work alone did not guarantee independence. Even among white landholders poverty might place the virtues nursed by the rural life in considerable jeopardy. The goal had to be both liberty and prosperity. John Taylor of Caroline, the most aggressive of the southern agrarians, made this point forcefully. As Taylor put it, "an order of men earning a bare subsistence, in low circumstances and whose inferior rank is wretched in the extreme, cannot possibly constitute a moral force, adequate to either . . . liberty or prosperity."[27]

While many agrarians bemoaned the decadence of unbridled luxury and urged a rustic simplicity, the agrarian philosophy never endorsed poverty. Agriculture encouraged virtue because it rewarded virtue. Only a prosperous agriculture guaranteed virtue. For all of Jefferson's genuine sympathy for the poorer class of farmers, he, like Taylor, saw the landed gentry as the epitome of the good and virtuous life. Ultimately, agrarians differentiated themselves from urban "stockjobbers" by their more wholesome appreciation of wealth and not through any wholesale renunciation.

The Jeffersonian image of agrarian independence still holds a powerful charm. Jefferson drew it with broad romantic strokes. Only with some difficulty and a bit of embarrassment do we keep in mind the historical role of this creed. Whatever his misgivings about slavery, Jefferson strengthened the common ground between planter and small farmer. By placing the agricultural interest at the center of his philosophy Jefferson provided an ideology and a politics comfortable to both frontier farmer and southern plantation owner.

American agrarianism sought to attain rural prosperity through commercial expansion. Like many statesmen of the revolutionary generation, Jefferson thought that the abundance of land in the United States permitted an international division of labor in which the United States might specialize in agriculture. Thus, in a letter to Jean Baptiste Say, a French economist, Jefferson argued that Malthus's theory of overpopulation held little threat for America, with its plentiful supply of land. "Here the immense extent of uncultivated and fertile lands enables every one who will labor, to marry young, and to raise a family of any size. Our food, then, may increase geometrically with our laborers, and our births, however multiplied become effective."[28]

In advocating a commercialized agriculture, Jefferson immediately confronted the question of how to keep such a commerce independent. He judged that the colonial policies of Great Britain had weighed heavily on American prosperity. In the postrevolutionary period an even graver threat emerged from the neocolonial policies of Britain. Land for farmers was of little use if traditional markets were closed.[29] For Jefferson and many of his fellow Virginians, free commerce had become a central plank of the agrarian program. Jefferson, as secretary of state, directly addressed this problem in his 1793 report to the House of Representatives on commercial policy.[30]

In his report Jefferson first reviewed "the extent of the privileges and restrictions of the commercial intercourse of the United States with foreign nations" and noted the particularly opportunistic policy of Great Britain. "Instead of embarrassing commerce under piles of regulating laws, duties and prohibitions," he wrote, paying deference to Adam Smith, "could it be relieved from all its shackles in all parts of the world, could every country be employed in producing that which nature has best fitted it to produce, and each be free to exchange with others mutual surpluses for mutual wants, the greatest mass possible would then be produced of those things which contribute to human life and human happiness; the numbers of mankind would be increased, and their condition bettered."[31]

This introduction hints strongly at the agrarian program for the United States and even its optimistic implications for the Malthusian dilemma of Europe. Unfortunately, Great Britain's policies threatened American agriculture. How best might the country meet this challenge? Jefferson considered three cases. If any nation showed a willingness to extend open commerce to America, the United States should reciprocate, "since it is one by one only that it [free trade] can be extended to all." From those countries that approached trade strategically, the United States might win considerable concessions, because the size of potential American purchases from abroad made the United States an attractive customer. Yet some nations would still enforce considerable restrictions. Toward them, Jefferson advised taking a retaliatory stance. "Free commerce and navigation are not to be given in exchange for restrictions and vexations; nor are they likely to produce a relaxation of them."[32]

Both southerners and northerners broadly endorsed Jefferson's cautious free-trade position. To commercial centers along the Atlantic such a policy seemed simply pragmatic, but for Jefferson an open commerce represented a critical prerequisite to agrarian independence and virtue. Could this approach to free trade secure these agrarian goals? Jefferson's case provided no guarantees. His commercial policy depended on European nations' recognizing their long-run self-interest in the American initiative. Even if successful in the short run, his strategy required an ever-expanding dependence on world markets. Could such a dependence prove costly itself?

Jefferson's criticism of urban artisans had rested in large measure on their need to curry favor in the selling of their wares. Such activities undermined their independence and hence their virtue. By contrast farmers participated in an open market, the anonymity of which presumably left the farmer's virtue safe. The logic of the market protected the individual farmer. Jefferson hoped that such a relationship could be replayed at the level of nations. If the new republic could be made one among many trading countries, then it too could achieve independence in the market place. Such national independence would provide a fitting basis for individual liberty. But, as the experience of the postrevolutionary period made painfully clear, the European powers had no intention of acceding to this new world order. If, as a result, the national economy fell into a demeaning neocolonial dependency, then surely the prosperity necessary to support individual virtue would be lost. National dependency could not build a virtuous citizenry.

A too-simple resolution suggested itself. If farmers could accept an ascetic self-sufficiency, then those farmers individually and the national economy collectively would achieve independence. Jefferson toyed with the notion of self-sufficient farms as an ultimate protection of political and economic independence. The obvious limitations of such a policy, however, compromised greatly the promise of agrarian solutions to decolonization.[33] Whatever the abstract classicism of self-sufficient agriculture, Jefferson as a man of affairs realized the lack of such a program's appeal.

Failing to institute free trade and rejecting self-sufficiency left one obvious alternative: diversifying the economy via manufacturing. Jefferson acknowledged from the start that his approach to free trade might force the development of manufactures. In particular, retaliatory tariffs against the British would provide a stimulus to such activities. Jefferson hoped that the result would take the form of artisanry and household manufacture, as opposed to concentrated factory production, but such hopes failed to appreciate the power of the ongoing Industrial Revolution.

Madison may have seen these problems more clearly than Jefferson did; his advocacy of a balanced economy of agriculture, commerce, and manufactures was perhaps the best that could be done under the circumstances.[34] Earlier Madison had shown sympathy for the mercantilist programs of Virginia's aristocracy. His support of the Constitution showed a sense of realpolitik that many of his agrarian colleagues lacked. Madison attempted, more explicitly than did most southerners, to integrate the various themes of the colonial critiques.

After the War of 1812, Jefferson too accepted the necessity for a manufacturing sector. To some extent his new position reflected the growing importance of manufacturing in the Atlantic economy. Jefferson offered an explanation that focused on the threat of dependency. Toward the end of the war, he concluded, "To be independent for the comforts of life we must fabricate them ourselves. We must now place the manufacturer by the side of the agriculturalist. . . . He, therefore, who is now against domestic manufacture must be for reducing us either to dependence on that foreign nation [Great Britain] or to be clothed in skins and to live like wild beasts in dens and caverns. I am not one of these; experience has taught me that manufactures are now as necessary to our independence as to our comfort."[35]

This is the circuit that Jefferson rode. While Jefferson's agrarian philosophy built on a classical definition of virtue, it also reflected the colonial condition of the Virginian economy. Jefferson had hoped to maintain the independence of the frontier by developing a prosperous commercial agriculture. His agrarian solution promised an inverse colonialism, in which the former colony would live passively, almost parasitically, off the developed nations. In this way a new nation might avoid the social and moral problems of concentrated urban manufactures while maintaining a reasonably high standard of comfort.

Jefferson's image of a prosperous commercial agriculture powerfully appealed to white southerners of his time. Although largely insensitive to the hypocrisy of slaveholding in a republic, they shared Jefferson's hostility toward urban classes. The agrarian program also demanded little in the way of structural change and endorsed the customs of rural life. This reassuring philosophy continued to capture the imagination of southerners for generations.

Ultimately, Jefferson himself recognized the serious shortcomings of his program. Rejecting self-sufficient farming, he reluctantly accepted the need for a manufacturing sector. But such a program raised the very specter that Jefferson had hoped to avoid in the first place: a more diverse economy probably would lead to a more corrupt economy. Jefferson never plausibly explained how American manufacturing operatives would avoid the dependency he so despised. Unwilling to accept a frontier existence but imbued with frontier values, Jefferson moved from one contradiction to another. Why should manufactures at home be any less exploitative or demoralizing than manufactures abroad?

Jefferson had hoped to keep the entire nation agrarian. Even if this could not be achieved, many southerners were convinced of the need to maintain at least an agrarian region. It was this goal as much as the subsequent debates over slavery that caused southerners in the nineteenth century increasingly to turn inward.

The Political Economy of John Taylor of Caroline

Jefferson and Madison toyed with the idea of a new agrarian commonwealth supported by domestic manufactures. In sharp contrast to that experimental mood, John Taylor of Caroline stood squarely for agrarian principles, opposing all flirtations with mercantilist industrialism. Ultimately Taylor's thought and not Jefferson's came to epitomize southern agrarianism. Taylor's ideas, not Madison's, dominated the region's antebellum economic thought.

Taylor drew a sharp line between productive classes and capitalists (his own choice of epithets). He deeply feared that the independence and liberty of the former were at risk. The federal government itself had become an instrument of oppression. The manipulation of federal powers threatened the productive classes of the South particularly. Taylor described southern dependency in far richer detail than had any seventeenth- or eighteenth-century writer. A product of the revolutionary experience, Taylor formulated an economic theory that had political and economic liberty at its center. For Taylor, only the corruption of government could impose economic dependence on southern agriculture. Despite his continuing commitment to the Constitution, Taylor played a crucial role in transforming Jeffersonian agrarianism into a regional ideology. From Taylor's rendering of agrarianism southerners formalized the libertarian version of the colonial critiques.

James Taylor, John's father, died when John was only six years old. John's mother, Ann, sent him to live with his uncle Edmond Pendleton, a successful lawyer and active participant in Virginia politics.[36] Although his uncle treated Taylor as a son, this early experience may have sensitized Taylor to the sting of dependency. Pendleton had used the income from his legal practice to restore his family's plantation holdings. He brought John Taylor up in the style of the Virginia gentry. After Taylor had spent two years at William and Mary College, he joined Pendleton's successful law practice in Caroline County. Admitted to the bar in 1774, he quickly became involved in the revolutionary politics sweeping Virginia at the time. He fought in the Revolution, although his war record lacked distinction. Returning to Caroline he actively participated in the state legislature, engaged with his uncle in a bit of land speculation, and prospered in his law practice. He married Lucy Penn, the daughter of an affluent planter. With the dowry she brought and his own earnings he established himself as a planter, retiring from legal work in 1789.

John Taylor's political life had an erratic quality. His early experiences in the Virginia assembly involved him in the Revolution's tumult. Even early in his career Taylor demonstrated a sensitivity to regional issues. In 1781 he was the major author of a "remonstrance" denouncing northerners for failing to support the revolutionary struggle once it had shifted to the South.[37] Despite these forays into regionalism, other more mundane matters dominated the young Taylor's attention. While a legislator, he aggressively lobbied for bills in which he had a personal interest. This blatant use of official position to bolster his land speculation, while quite common at the time, hardly appears consistent with his denunciations of influence peddling, a central theme of his writings.

Taylor's most notable legislative accomplishment occurred in 1798. As a member of the Virginia House of Delegates Taylor introduced the Virginia Resolutions, written by James Madison. Like Jefferson's Kentucky Resolutions, this protest of the alien and sedition laws claimed for the states the right to review the constitutionality of congressional legislation. Taylor apparently wished to push the point a good deal further than Jefferson did, but the vice president, anticipating his victory over the Federalists in the upcoming presidential election, checked his disciple.[38] On three occasions Taylor was appointed senator from Virginia. In each case he served only briefly. Taylor advanced the agrarian cause more through his writings than in direct political action. In this role, however, he became the major prophet of republican agrarianism.

Taylor loved agriculture. He had worked hard as a lawyer but always aspired to the status of a country gentleman. Convinced of the nobility of the challenges and rewards of agriculture, Taylor saw in farming "inexhaustible sources of human pleasure." In *Arator* (1813), a collection of his journalistic pieces on the practice and politics of agriculture, Taylor waxed eloquent on the "Pleasures of Agriculture." He particularly emphasized the active intellectual quality of agriculture: "The novelty, frequency and exactness of accommodations between our ideas and operations, constitutes the most exquisite source of mental pleasure." Thus, it was the multiplicity of possibilities that made agriculture attractive. Listing the varying factors that influenced farming, Taylor noted that "their combinations are inexhaustible, the novelty of results is endless, discrimination and adaptation are never idle, and an unsatiated interest receives gratification in quick succession."[39] Agriculture then gives exercise "both to the body and to the mind, it secures health and vigour to both."

Like all the agrarians, Taylor saw agriculture as "the mother of wealth." Taylor argued that agriculture offered the most productive activity for labor. He even went so far as to endorse the physiocrats' notion that commerce and manufacturing only changed the form of value, that only agriculture created value.[40] Like Adam Smith, Taylor held that the natural progression of economic development began with agriculture and only later moved on to commerce and manufacturing. America obviously stood at the beginning of this course and needed to remain an agricultural nation for a considerable time.

In the best Jeffersonian tradition, Taylor asserted that agriculture not only mothered wealth but also guarded liberty. He did not base this argument on the inherent virtues of the farmer. Indeed, for these purposes he lumped together all "labourers, mechanical or agricultural." He then went on to make a materialistic argument that in many ways anticipated Karl Marx's identification of the interests of the proletariat and humanity. Since agriculture and the mechanical arts must include the vast majority of the population, and since they created the vast majority of wealth in the society, these productive classes could not possibly live off the efforts of others. The minority could never support the majority. "Consider, however splendidly a minority may live upon the labours of a majority, that a majority cannot subsist upon those of a minority, and you will see that it is impossible for experience in future to teach a different lesson."[41] Hence, agriculture had nothing to gain from governmental bounties or redistributions; such intrigues could only favor a minority. Farmers and the other laboring classes could only hope for government to protect them and the fruits of their own efforts. "Those who compose these majorities, if they are wise, never fail to see that their interest points to a republican form of government, for the very purpose of preventing the passage of laws for quartering or pasturing on them minor interests."[42]

While the productive classes had a clear interest in defending pure republicanism, they might prove less than "wise," allowing themselves to be "duped" by one special interest or another. "Whenever bounties are pretended to be bestowed on labour, by privileges to feudal barons to defend it, to bishops to save it, or to capitalists or bankers to enrich it, an aristocratical order is unavoidably erected to pilfer and enslave it."[43] Taylor saw a crucial link between agriculture and political liberty. A wise agriculture would strive to maintain an open republican form of government that protected all citizens in their labor. By contrast Taylor detected everywhere minorities ready to ruin agriculture and destroy liberty.

From a modern vantage point, the very argument Taylor uses against feudal barons would seem easily extended to his fellow slaveowners, living off the surplus created by their slaves. The owner of scores of slaves, Taylor demonstrated considerable ambivalence over the region's peculiar institution. In one of the few passages in which he questioned Jefferson, Taylor denied that slavery eroded the virtue of the southern masters. In a somewhat defensive tone, he argued that slavery forced slaveowners to contrast constantly their behavior and standards with those of the slaves. Yet, like many of the revolutionary generation, Taylor felt that slavery was "a misfortune to agriculture, incapable of removal, and only within the reach of palliation."[44] While Taylor desperately wanted to think of black slaves as talented domestic animals, he recognized their humanity and the tensions it created in southern society. Free blacks constantly put dangerous ideas in their path and set a bad example, slaves eager for their freedom ran away, and those slaves who had developed a "vicious disposition" took up the "habit of indiscriminate theft, so ruinous and disheartening to industry."[45] In the short run Taylor advocated strong laws to transport out of state free blacks, runaway slaves, and slaves found stealing. Over a longer period of time, he hoped that the gradual colonization of blacks in Africa would provide a promising solution to the South's problems. These ideas seem totally inconsistent with Taylor's philosophical libertarianism. The deep psychology of the slaveowner eludes us.

If slavery posed impossible dilemmas for the South, it simultaneously served to ameliorate potential conflicts between poor and rich farmers in the region. Rich planters directly exploited slaves, not tenants or white laborers; poorer farmers aspired to slave ownership. All the mysteries of racism bound poor and rich whites together. More immediately, yeoman and plantation owner shared a range of interests. While engaged in market competition, they prospered or failed together. The sun shone the same on both; market prices fluctuated the same for both; the tariff bore down the same on both. In an increasingly democratic age, Taylor and many of the South's planters came to see themselves as only the most prosperous and talented of the class of farmers.

Taylor never disparaged a healthy interest in accumulating property. A "love of property" was essential to establishing a viable economy. Yet, excessive greed could easily transform ambition into a socially destructive force. "In either extreme, like many other passions necessary to our happiness, it becomes pernicious."[46] In the open competition of America's free farmers, this passion played a useful role, but in Europe "separate interests, goaded on by an avarice, awakened by unjust laws, and rendered unconscious of guilt, by the sanction of the statute book, have filled the old world with crimes, and perverted the primitive end of society to secure property, by making it the instrument for its invasion."[47] The most eager of these special interests were the moneyed capitalists and their political allies.

Unlike Madison, Taylor never seriously considered mixing agricultural, commercial, and industrial employments. He was far more completely convinced of the efficiency of the market than the crypto-mercantilist Madison. Taylor had fully imbibed the message of Adam Smith. According to Taylor, "the products of agriculture and manufacturing, unshackled by law, would seek each for themselves, the best markets through commercial channels."[48] Certain of the productivity of agriculture, Taylor had little doubt that the great mass of Americans could and should remain farmers for the foreseeable future. Market forces, left to themselves, enforced this simple truth. Because of the richness of American natural resources, farmers with a little industry could enjoy a high standard of living. Never an advocate of American autarchy, Taylor saw Europe as the natural market for the agricultural surpluses of the United States.

While Taylor thought it proper for the government to encourage agricultural reform, he opposed governmental interference in the economy. "Opposed" is far too mild a word, for Taylor knew that government could not truly aid the economy, and he deeply feared that Congress could destroy it. In Taylor's mind, when governments insisted on tinkering with the economy, they generally pursued illegitimate ends. Public intervention never represented mere misguided enthusiasm; throughout history government activity had provided the means for the minority to rob and exploit the majority. In the modern age, he felt, government had become the primary agency of a false aristocracy, centered in the Northeast, which threatened to reduce southern and western agriculture to a state of dependency.

Taylor allowed that in the distant past an aristocracy of "virtue, talents and wealth" had perhaps existed. Such an aristocracy "ought to govern." But the monopoly of virtue that had justified the aristocracy of Rome had been undermined by technological and economic developments. The printing press had spread knowledge and virtue. Commerce and open markets in land had produced a wide distribution of wealth.[49] This broad dissemination of virtue, knowledge, and wealth implied a democratic government of limited powers. Presumably, this understanding had motivated the framers of the Constitution. The cause of aristocracy did not disappear, however, just because its historic justification had been eroded. In Great Britain aristocracy artificially maintained itself through "the system of paper and patronage" established by governmental fiat. The mass of people had inherited the right to govern, but a paper aristocracy using "modern taxes and frauds to collect money" manipulated the government exclusively for its own interest. This fundamental danger of modern political economy did not stop at Britain's shores but extended to the United States as well. The northern capitalists of the paper system threatened the very heart of the republic.

American citizens had little excuse for tolerating the aristocratic misuse of government. Unlike the ancients, encumbered by religion, superstition, and awe of the nobility, Americans had consciously rejected a hierarchical system.[50] Taylor asked why the people were so blind. He concluded that the paper aristocracy had turned to its own purpose "plausible phrases," phrases such as "publick faith, national credit and private property." They slyly confounded the public good with an artificially bloated system of funding, banks, and patronage, with devastating results.[51] Capitalists, largely from the North, had launched a massive campaign of disinformation to confuse the public.[52] These moneyed capitalists necessarily corrupted the government in order to live off the industrious population. Taylor knew that even in a system of elected government the moneyed interest could bribe the legislature. With such subterfuge the capitalists had won commercial regulation, the funding of the national debt, and the creation of the banking system.

Taylor's attack on tariffs ventured into deep issues concerning the relation of geography and economic dependency. Playing devil's advocate, he argued that "if the policy [protective duties] be wise and good between the United States and England, it must also be wise and good between the nations composing our union. If it be injurious to the United States, to admit the importation and use of foreign manufactures, subject to competition, it must be more injurious to the southern states, to suffer the use of northern manufactures, enhanced by a monopoly."[53] Clearly Taylor meant this as an argument in favor of free trade, but his formulation of the issue almost invites an argument for a compact and diversified southern region.

Taylor insisted that protection failed to serve even the interest of northern manufacturing as a whole. Rather, like the national debt and banking, the drive for protection represented a cleverly disguised effort of the capitalists to tax the productive community. In the end, Taylor argued, "monied capital . . . will seize upon and appropriate to itself, the whole profit of the bounty extorted from the people by protecting duties."[54] Paying only minimal subsistence wages, this moneyed capital in protected activities "drives industry without money out of the market, and forces it into its service." Taylor drew a sharp distinction between moneyed capital and manufacturers. Taylor, the agrarian, saw the enemy not as productive labor employed in other industries but as exploitative moneyed capital committed to no industry. At least in this respect Taylor, like Jefferson himself, saw agrarianism as a national, not a sectional, ideology. Northern workers, Taylor declared, should join southern agrarians in checking the schemes of northern capitalists.

In attacking the paper economy, Taylor continually emphasized the sterility of the federal debt. Here Taylor anticipated a major agrarian concern, the profits of financial speculators from cycles of inflation and deflation. The American paper system had allowed speculators to earn large gains from buying depreciated notes and then demanding full payment. The populace suffered twice: first from the devaluation, which robbed them of their savings, and then from the taxation necessary to pay the face value of the notes. Taylor struggled to understand these burdens of the national debt. He denied that such borrowing in any way allowed the country to "anticipate the riches of posterity." The government most often went into debt during wartime. Simple logic demanded that the living suffer every hardship and cost of war. In no way could they share that cost with future generations. Yet, the speculators of the paper system could fasten onto the "unborn" a burden equal to that already paid by the living.[55]

Taylor's argument made sense. It anticipated that of the Progressive historian Charles A. Beard. Taylor made a serious analysis of the speculative profits earned on the national debt. At times, though, his misgivings about that debt seemed to spring from a simpler hostility, his aversion to compound interest and all paper profits. Taylor estimated that if, over fourteen years of war, the nation devoted its entire surplus to that effort and funded it by debt, then the resulting obligation would require that the nation use its annual surplus in perpetuity simply to pay the interest on the accumulated debt.[56] These effects of compound interest would sap the productive energies of the nation. Taylor never made clear how he thought the revolutionary war should have been financed.

Once established, predictably, the funding system tempted the legislature and government to corruption. Egged on by the paper faction, the Congress pushed measures that otherwise they never would have considered. The people had difficulty determining who had been corrupted. The profligacy of the government exacerbated the burden of the debt. Those who profited by funding, eager to "deceive, plunder and enslave" the nation, "artfully" likened the practice to "the case of a man who buys an estate on credit, or who gives bonds to himself."[57] This lie obscured the transfer of wealth that the funding system had brought about. In one of his most telling passages, Taylor argued that nations "are not one homogeneous mass of matter, but capable of a thorough divisibility into individuals, and into a multitude of separate interests (such as payers and receivers, masters and slaves, impostors and dupes . . .)." Taylor anticipated a political economy sensitive to the class and sectional differences in the population, but he brought little subtlety to the distributional issues at hand. In his view, the funded debt had forced the mass of landholders to mortgage their lands without receiving anything in return. The interest on that debt had simply become a feudal tribute.

For Taylor the emergence of modern banking in the United States ushered in the "third age" (after the ancients and the feudal lords) of aristocracy. Banking insidiously grafted itself onto the body politic. Taylor's diatribe against banking echoed down through the years. Its most spectacular manifestation came in Andrew Jackson's famous attack on the bank of the United States.[58] Beyond that battle, and perhaps with even more effect, it crystallized agrarian hostility to the paper system and gave reason to southern mistrust of northern finance capital.

The banking system amounted to modern feudalism. It left the entire productive population bound to a new aristocracy. "Had banking been called 'a paper feudal system,' and had the barons proposed to take it by that denomination as a reimbursement for their abolished tenures . . . it would have been clearly seen by the people that the money to be collected by 'a paper feudal system' for their lords, was the representative of the services rendered under the landed feudal system."[59] Money simply provided a more convenient form in which to pay labor services.

Taylor believed that "gold and silver, the universal medium" had been "legislated out of sight." As a result the nation had no alternative but bank money. "This is banking. By the help of law it creates a necessity for its own currency." Forced to turn to the banks, the people found that those institutions had an effective monopoly that allowed them to charge outrageous rates for the circulating medium. Moreover, he claimed, "if fluctuations in currency, produced and managed by chartered monopolies, can affect price or value, it follows, that through his income, his money, and his property, an individual is reached by the tax of this currency, although he never borrowed or used it."[60]

The right to establish this power to tax, that is, to charter banks, became the most dangerous corrupter of representative democracy. It seduced the people's representatives into speculative banking activities with the hope of profiting from their prerogatives. A stockjobbing legislator no longer represented the vast majority of citizens but only a small minority—bankers. Taylor denied that the nation or any "industry" could benefit by such shenanigans. Such "political alchemy" was more fraudulent than "the chymical," since "one proposes to make gold out of something; the other out of nothing."[61] The banks might appear as a "few rich individuals" benefiting a poor country, but in reality these banks taxed the entire nation for the benefit of a few. The only legitimate function of money was to facilitate exchange. Bank paper could only imitate specie in this respect. The profits of the banking system represented a tax paid for the circulating medium, a tax that could be avoided with specie. The currency created by banks was in no way a stimulus to industry. Confident of the workings of free markets, Taylor denied any need to encourage investment through bank credit. Any gain to the borrowers simply derived from losses to those who held existing notes deflated by the expansion of the money supply. To add to the nation's plight, British investors drew off much of the tax collected by banks. These investors enjoyed profits that they never could have extracted from the American colonies before the Revolution. Taylor, like Sheffield, understood neocolonialism.

Taylor provided the Jeffersonians with the most serious defense of the political economy of agrarianism. It is clear that Taylor conceived his arguments as the base for a broad alliance of producers. While he undoubtedly saw the southern landed gentry as the natural leadership of this alliance, he envisioned a national, not a sectional program. Nevertheless Taylor's economics became hard-core southern orthodoxy and provided a major stimulus to the further elaboration of the libertarian versions of the colonial analogy.

The critical impetus to this transformation came from the growing conviction that the capitalists had successfully hoodwinked the people of the North. Capitalist influence in that region endangered the delicate machinery of the federal Constitution. Taylor "believed that capitalists threatened northerners as well as southerners . . . [but] Northern states, in their excitement against the South, allowed themselves to be enslaved by a capitalist minority."[62] Capitalists wielded demagogic arguments about slavery to their own political purposes. As Taylor put it, "the spectacle of slavery was therefore a cunning device to draw their attention from home."[63]

Taylor put no faith in the logic of a balance of power, as between North and South. He consistently held that the legislature should reflect the broad interests of the agrarians and their allies. He opposed regional parties as just another manifestation of capitalist trickery. Northern capitalists aimed to seize the machinery of government for the further expansion of the paper system. This would benefit the northern producers no more than the southern producers.

Taylor argued that if the people of the United States allowed themselves to be swept up in senseless bickering over slavery, disunion must follow. This disunion would reflect not a fundamental difference of interests but rather a quasi-religious conflict over morality. In the meantime all the profit accrued to the capitalists, busy at work while the people engaged in the senseless struggle. Taylor pointed to the fight over the Missouri Compromise as a prime example of the waste of energy the emerging sectional conflict fostered.[64]

Toward the end of his life, despite his nationalist sentiments, Taylor acknowledged the reality of regional economic interests. In a letter written in December of 1820, he considered the consequences of laws for "making one portion of the Union tributary to another." Such legislation could not be imposed on the South. While "the Southern States might long submit to their (natural) commercial disadvantages, so beneficial to the Northern, they will not long bear an aggravation of them by geographical legislation."[65]

Similarly, in his last attack on tariff legislation, in 1824, he concluded that the northern states extracted $28 million per year from the
southern states. This tribute had greatly limited the ability of the South
to itself build a merchant fleet.[66] Here Taylor came close to fully identifying the northern states with the evils of the paper system.

Taylor did not live to complete this transformation from nationalist
to sectionalist. His work remained a tribute to republican ideas and an
attack on the class of paper capitalists. Still, later southern sectionalists
were able with only modest revisions to revamp Taylor's theories into a
full-blown regionalist critique. Thus, while radical Jacksonians attempted to complete the attack on money capital, the southern agrarians
increasingly perceived exploitation in terms of geographic dependency.
In doing so, they had to identify the emerging industrial society of the
North with the evils they had earlier ascribed only to the minority faction
of the paper system.

Defining a Southern Interest

At the close of the War of 1812, the postrevolutionary generation of
southern leaders hardly seemed ready to retreat into idiosyncratic regional
agrarianism. Indeed, the most energetic southerners, under the leadership of John C. Calhoun, attempted to construct a new economic
nationalism. They hoped to use agrarian political dominance to tame the
aristocratic paper system. The young southerners looked forward to building
a diversified economy. Their plan included both manufactures and commerce, to free the nation as a whole and the South in particular from
British neocolonialism.

By 1816 the notion of diversifying the regional economy of the South
already had a history. For years before the Revolution both southerners
and northerners had threatened the establishment of American manufactures if the Crown denied this or that commercial favor.[67] During
the Revolution and in the early years of the republic, craftsmen and
artisans in the South, like those in the North, firmly supported the
creation of a national protected market. The artisans of Charleston had
entered the Revolution with the slogan "Encouragement to American
Manufacturers."[68] From the start of the nineteenth century there had
been several modest efforts to establish textile mills in Virginia and the
Carolinas.[69]

Despite this history, conversion of important southerners to the
gospel of economic activism seemed to portend a major turn. Ironically

enough, these new converts took over more or less completely the program of their former nemesis, Alexander Hamilton. It had been Hamilton, in his famous *Report on Manufactures,* who had argued the need to develop a diversified national economy. Hamilton had pushed for manufactures on the grounds that commerce with European markets would likely prove unpredictable. While Europe, and especially Britain, stood ready to export, foreigners had shown a willingness to import only irregularly. Hamilton concluded that agricultural interests that depended on European markets would find their produce considerably undervalued. By contrast, he had argued that if the United States went ahead and developed a manufacturing base, this would provide an important domestic market to absorb the agricultural surplus.[70]

How strange that these ideas should subsequently be voiced by southerners in support of the tariff of 1816. Stranger still that they should be most forcefully argued by just those men who would eventually represent an intransigently free-trade ideology. Hamilton had built his argument on the contention that the North and the South shared a harmony of interests. He had expected that manufactures would concentrate in the northern states. However, he explicitly denied that this should be of concern: "Ideas of a contrariety of interests between the Northern and Southern regions of the Union are, in the main, as unfounded as they are mischievous. This diversity of circumstances, on which such contrariety is usually predicated, authorizes a directly contrary conclusion. Mutual wants constitute one of the strongest links of political connection; and the extent of these bears a natural proportion to the diversity in the means of mutual supply."[71] Because northern manufacturers would demand southern agricultural products, and southerners would demand northern manufactures, a powerful harmony of interests promised benefits to both regions.

Hamilton advanced a national policy of protection, a play that always risked a charge of regional favoritism. John Taylor led the charge: if the North needed protection against Britain, did not the South need protection against the North? In defending his policies, Hamilton had anticipated such objections: Free trade was impractical for the world as a whole. A stable international division of labor, although desirable, was unobtainable; but a country the size of the United States could build a mutually beneficial interregional division of labor within its borders, protected from erratic international markets. America could not remain purely agricultural, but the South could.

The Hamiltonian vision titillated the younger generation of southerners. At the close of the War of 1812, John C. Calhoun, then in the House of Representatives, became one of the firmest champions of the new departure. Emphasizing the current dependence of both agriculture and commerce on foreign markets, Calhoun argued, "When our manufactures are grown to a certain perfection, as they soon will under the fostering care of Government, we will no longer experience these evils. The farmer will find a ready market for his surplus produce; and what is almost of equal consequence, a certain and cheap supply of all his wants." And if international commerce leaves the nation dependent, manufacturing will "bind together more closely our widely-spread republic. It will greatly increase our mutual dependence and intercourse." Ultimately the "liberty and union of this country were inseparably united."[72]

Calhoun was less concerned than Jefferson over the effects of manufacturing employment on the virtue of the citizenry. Acknowledging that manufacturing "produced a greater dependence on the part of the employed than in commerce, navigation or agriculture," he argued that this observation should not be decisive. The personal dependence of the individual worker was more than offset by the greater independence created at the national level. Where Jefferson contrasted manufacturing and agriculture, Calhoun sensed a parallel between factory and slave plantation: both institutions encouraged a dependency in the labor force, and perhaps not everyone could or should be independent. This comparison appeared repeatedly in Calhoun's later thought.

The southern Republicans, triumphant in 1816, firmly controlled an agrarian government. They no longer needed to identify themselves as anti-Federalist. With confidence that agrarian interests naturally dominated in the new nation, the mercantilist leanings of a Madison could be tolerated, even encouraged. With considerable élan, the more adventurous southerners pored over Hamiltonian policies.[73] Calhoun assembled an imaginative program building on the southern nationalism of Washington and Madison. First came support of protection. Calhoun then attempted to link internal improvements to a rechartered Bank of the United States. Calhoun in his "bonus bill" had developed a scheme for controlling a sophisticated financial structure in the interest of the agrarians. His proposal to link the returns on the shares held by the government in the national bank to the construction of roads and canals made a purposeful statement on socially useful public works. At the same time the bill struck a balance among the investments in each region. This balance would have allowed the southern cities—Baltimore, Washington, Richmond, Charleston, and Savannah (explicitly mentioned by

Calhoun)—to compete more evenly with New York and Philadelphia. Calhoun also looked forward to improving transport between the West and New Orleans. Taken as a whole, Calhoun's proposal offered a comprehensive plan of internal improvements driven in large part by the engine of finance harnessed to agrarian interest.[74]

Between 1816 and 1824 the younger generation of southerners turned from their imaginative agrarian nationalism to an increasingly provincial regionalism. The usual explanation for the South's retreat from nationalism emphasizes the intensification of animosity over the slavery issue. The bitter conflict over the Missouri Compromise left deep scars in the South, and surely slavery became a preoccupation of the antebellum United States. But slavery alone was not an obvious reason for southerners to put in jeopardy their agrarian alliance with the West. At the heart of the new sectionalism was the growing conviction that the South's economic dependency on the northern states had become far more dangerous than the threat from Britain.

An intelligent proponent of agrarian nationalism like Calhoun balked at the sheer energy shown by northern capitalists in putting together their own American system. Far from a careful, complementary relationship between agriculture and industry, Calhoun saw emerging an ungodly collection of peculiar interests without shape or form. This new system grew independent of any southern agrarian purposes. Northerners continued to run ahead, with little concern for how their activities impinged on the South. In 1816 southerners hoped that they could control the new nationalism. Calhoun and the others had endorsed a rough-and-ready mercantilism. The young Calhoun, as much as any figure of his generation, personified the amalgam of frontier democracy, southern agrarianism, and northern federalism. Through the 1820s Calhoun seemed increasingly afraid of the economic and political strength of emerging northern capitalists. The arguments of the Old Republicans appeared stronger and stronger. Calhoun's move from mercantilism to laissez faire (significantly matched by the move of Daniel Webster in the opposite direction) summarized the most sophisticated southern thinking on the subject. In the context of the new economic realities, Calhoun and his like could no longer imagine how to control the process of industrialization. Calhoun, the natural ally of John Quincy Adams from the North and Henry Clay from the West, could not put together the machinery the situation required.

In 1816 the most acute southern leaders, including John C. Calhoun, had recognized the needs of the West and small farming interests. They had tried to put forth a cogent program. However, by 1824, with Adams in the White House and Clay pushing his American system through the Congress, southerners were in a headlong retreat from their own initiative. Increasingly, Calhoun and the southern planters he represented did not see the nationalist position as a plan of leadership to guarantee independence but rather as the basis for a new and limiting dependency. While aware that manufacturing and urban areas could provide additional markets to agriculture, the bulk of southerners increasingly feared that such a policy, once instituted, could not be kept under agrarian control. Already the American system had produced a barrage of lobbying and interest groups.

In this scramble for governmental favors, southerners saw the realization of Taylor's prophecies. They listened with renewed respect to the Old Republican John Randolph of Roanoke, an ally of Taylor in earlier years, when he attacked the tariff bill of 1824: "I declare that this bill is an attempt to reduce the country south of Mason and Dixon's line, and east of the Allegheny Mountains, to a state worse than colonial bondage; a state to which the domination of Great Britain was, in my judgment, far preferable."[75] Randolph, never one to hold back, concluded that if the South could not stop this grab for power through the federal government, then the region must secede, just as the colonies had seceded from Great Britain. The North, he declared, now corrupted by its capitalist leadership, had become the central problem. Northern capitalists now threatened to fasten the South in a new more vicious dependency based on all the mechanisms Taylor had decried.

Great Britain and its neocolonial policies had previously been the danger, but now the South must look to Britain and Europe for allies. Randolph called on the southern agrarians to reaffirm their traditional faith in free trade. As the cotton culture of the South continued to expand, as Britain became ever more eager for the region's fiber, southern economic thinking tried mightily to justify this conclusion. The most compelling arguments hinged on the oppressive dependency associated with any surrender to the northern capitalist program.

The 1820s and 1830s witnessed the classical era of southern economic thought. In this period three serious southern economists, Jacob Cardozo, Thomas Dew, and Thomas Cooper, advocated free trade and laissez faire. Despite the erudition of this new generation of southern economists, their formal contributions to the region's economic ideology remained nominal. Staunchly committed to Adam Smith, they elaborated classical economics with only modest originality.

Of the three, Jacob Cardozo probably had the strongest analytical faculty. Cardozo, who came from a Sephardic Jewish family, participated actively in the intellectual life of Charleston. He became editor of a major paper and helped to found *The Southern Review*. In the antebellum period his grasp of classical political economy made him one of the best economists in the nation.[76] Cardozo took an optimistic view toward technology and denied the dismal conclusions of Malthus and Ricardo. With respect to the tariff, however, Cardozo stuck to classical orthodoxy. He emphasized the absolute advantage of America in following an agricultural development policy and the reciprocity of the trade with England.[77]

Similarly, Thomas Dew, professor of history, metaphysics, and political law at William and Mary College, took the classical position that the burden of tariffs necessarily fell on consumers.[78] Dew maintained, however, that manufacturers in protected industries would not permanently gain, because the returns to capital tended to equalize between industries. The net effect would only be to slow down the otherwise efficient emigration of labor and capital to the West.

Thomas Cooper, from the University of South Carolina in Columbia, argued that a tariff amounted to a "tax on the whole mass of consumers." Essentially, tariffs raised prices and "the whole fortune of every consumer is affected by every fluctuation of price in the articles of consumption; the cheaper they are, the richer he is, and vice versa." And since "the whole nation is included in the class of consumers," the nation suffers when prices rise.[79]

Classical economists of the South were particularly fond of emphasizing that everyone, North and South, consumed. These same men did suggest one special burden of their region under a tariff. They often argued that, either for economic reasons or as a result of conscious policy, the demand for American exports, especially cotton, would fall as a result of tariff legislation. Cooper held that a reduction of imports must necessarily reduce exports and force the producers of exports into other, presumably less profitable, domestic pursuits. Thus, he argued, "every prohibition to buy, is in effect a prohibition to sell." Clearly this would most directly affect southern exporters.

Ironically, among these early southern economists, only Cooper, who moved to the region after the age of sixty, fully embraced the colonial argument. The Virginian, Dew, an ideologue of slavery, tended toward philosophical abstractions. Cardozo strongly supported measures to diversify the southern economy, but his conservative nature mixed poorly with the colonial rhetoric. Cooper, however, reveled in rhetorical excess.

Thomas Cooper came to the South after a dramatic and frustrating life. He began as a British radical in Manchester, an advocate of free speech and an early supporter of the French Revolution. Emigrating to America at the same time as his close friend Joseph Priestly, Cooper settled in Pennsylvania, shunning the South because of its slave system. Imprisoned under the alien and sedition laws before the election of 1800, Cooper entered into a lifelong correspondence with Thomas Jefferson.

Cooper had a harsh and argumentative personality. Although a democrat, he had little patience with "the people" and, once appointed to the Pennsylvania judiciary in 1804, began to shift toward order. He lost his position under Republican pressure and resorted to academia, winning an appointment in chemistry from the University of Pennsylvania. Jefferson sponsored him for an appointment to the new University of Virginia but could not overcome the hostility of the state's clergy to Cooper's materialist philosophy. Instead, almost by default, Cooper landed in South Carolina.[80]

Cooper's life followed an eccentric course, from eighteenth-century radical British thought to nineteenth-century southern sectionalism, that paralleled the South's own path. Cooper, like many in his adopted region, recanted his early radicalism but still sensed that central authority threatened the political and economic independence of individuals. Even more dramatically than his neighbors, he channeled old rhetoric into the new cause.

In his famous "value of the Union" speech, Cooper broached the central question: "We shall 'ere long be compelled to calculate the value of our union; and to enquire of what use to us is this most unequal alliance? By which the south has always been the loser and the north always the gainer? Is it worth our while to continue this union of states, where the north demand to be our masters and we are required to be their tributaries? Who with the most insulting mockery call the yoke they put upon our necks the American system! The question, however, is fast approaching to the alternative, of submission or separation."[81]

Despite these stirring words, Cooper added little of analytical significance to the argument southern statesmen already had made. Accepting the framework of classical laissez-faire economics, Cooper saw little need to innovate. Adam Smith had just about said it all. Indeed, in this period southern politicians, not southern academicians, made the most original contributions to political economy.

Like John C. Calhoun, George McDuffie, of South Carolina, had supported the tariff of 1816. By 1824, McDuffie had followed Calhoun into the mainstream of southern free-trade thought. He made a considerable tribute at that time to Adam Smith, who he felt had "done more to enlighten the world on the science of political economy than any man of modern times."[82] Like the classical economists, McDuffie had become particularly concerned with the effect of tariffs on exports. He asserted that "if we make everything we consume at home, we will, of course, import nothing; and if we import nothing it is a self-evident proposition that we can export nothing."[83] He developed this idea along the basic line that Britain would retaliate against U.S. tariff policy by encouraging cotton production in South America. This argument covered familiar ground.

By 1828 McDuffie's position was beginning to evolve into something new. These ideas reached their clearest statement in his speech in the House of Representatives in 1830. McDuffie now advanced an original and explicitly colonial argument. In his speech, he considered a planter who used all of the revenues he earned abroad to import foreign manufactures for resale in the United States.[84] A planter who sold a hundred bales of cotton might purchase a hundred bolts of cloth for resale in the United States. When the planter brought that hundred bolts back to the United States, he had to pay a tariff of say 40 percent. Thus, the proceeds of forty bolts must go to cover the tariff. It is just as if the government had taxed away forty bales to start with.

McDuffie knew that planters did not generally engage in the import business, and he went to considerable lengths to establish that this was not relevant to the final burden of the tariff. As the economist Earl Rolph explains, McDuffie's conclusion held as long as "foreign exchange rates are allowed to adjust freely in a balanced trade setting."[85] Thus, McDuffie made the plausible, and rather sophisticated, argument that the tariff had the same effect as a direct tax of 40 percent on planters' exports. Unlike the standard wisdom, McDuffie assumed that "the planter is subjected to precisely the same burden, as a planter, that he would pay if he had no factor or commercial agent, but exported his own produce himself and imported what he obtained for it abroad."[86] Not surprisingly McDuffie's views soon became known as the "Forty-Bale Doctrine."

McDuffie's theory presumed the colonial nature of the South's economy. Many southerners, including McDuffie, had formerly argued that tariffs would reduce foreign trade. But this would imply that southerners had at least reasonable alternatives to growing cotton. McDuffie's Forty-Bale Doctrine focused sharply on the inability of the southern economy to adjust. Slaves were profitable only if they could be used to produce for the market. Increased production for direct consumption by slaves was of no value to slaveowners. Domestic markets could not absorb all that slaves could produce. The slaveowner extracted a surplus from slave labor, but to realize that surplus planters had to sell a large portion of their product on international markets. This lack of alternatives left them highly vulnerable.

McDuffie's argument attempted to demonstrate that the tariff amounted to a blatant transfer of a large portion of the southern-generated surplus to the federal government. For McDuffie this amounted to a colonial tribute of the worst kind. Although many southerners sympathized with his conclusions, most could hardly have appreciated the subtlety of the argument. Classical theory treated tariffs as taxes on consumers. This easily understood proposition appealed to the majority of southerners. In its standard form it implicitly assumed that producers of export goods could fairly easily transfer resources to domestic uses. McDuffie's case rested on the contrary assumption that southern planters must continue to produce for export even after tariffs subsidized domestic production. McDuffie presented a serious economic argument.

For McDuffie the South's specialization naturally followed from its climate and geography. Unlike the southern mercantilists of the seventeenth and eighteenth centuries, he saw no attractive options for redirecting the region's economic activities. In the prosperity of the cotton boom of the early 1830s, he hardly considered a major restructuring of the region's economy. Arguing that the South lacked economic alternatives, he insisted on the need for a political remedy.

McDuffie's arguments pushed toward a sophisticated appreciation of southern vulnerability. Whether or not southerners understood or accepted McDuffie's views on who paid the tariff, virtually all of them could appreciate the climax of every attack on tariffs. The tariff, even if raised proportionately among the regions of the country, would obviously be oppressive if the bulk of the revenues generated went to enrich only one region. The North reduced the South to a tributary status not only by exploitative taxation but also by unfair patterns of federal expenditures. This familiar theme had the considerable advantage of avoiding the complex economic analysis that characterized McDuffie's tariff argument.

According to McDuffie, Calhoun, and most other southern politicians, the federal government built its internal improvements disproportionately in northern areas.[87] This represented a transfer from all other regions to the North. The North could have its internal improvements without a reduction in its own consumption. In particular the North might continue to import, even though it did not export, because the distribution of federal revenues subsidized that region.

This emphasis on the political nature of southern dependency led many southerners to search for essentially political solutions to the region's dilemmas. In this spirit, Calhoun constructed his theory of concurrent majorities. Behind that theory lay his conviction that "universal experience in all ages and countries . . . teaches that power can only be restrained by power, and not by reason and justice; and that all restrictions on authority, unsustained by an equal antagonist power, must forever prove wholly inefficient in practice."[88]

In a similar vein, McDuffie claimed to derive the theory of nullification from the sovereignty of the states, which he explicitly contrasted with colonial dependency. "Thank God! No one has yet been found bold enough to maintain that South Carolina is short of that high and sacred prerogative [sovereignty], and reduced, politically, to the condition of a corporation or a colony," he declared; "yet many reason upon the subject precisely as if this were the case."[89] The problem derived from the unwarranted governmental interference in southern affairs. Left to its own devices, the southern economy would do quite well. McDuffie presented a quintessential libertarian version of the colonial critique.

The nullification crisis in South Carolina provided a welcome platform for economic debate. Now, southerners have always been attracted to a bit of flowery overstatement, but surely the speeches and writings of this period defined the high-water mark in southern rhetoric. And yet, we would be wrong to dismiss this rhetoric out of hand. Their words carry both an intuition and a conviction that formal economics sometimes can only glimpse. Thus, in the *Exposition* Calhoun wrote, "We are the serfs of the system, out of whose labor is raised, not only the money paid into the Treasury, but the funds out of which are drawn the rich rewards of the manufacturer and his associates in interest."[90]

Comparisons to the revolutionary experience provided another meaningful rhetorical tool. After all, the burdens of the tariff far exceeded anything that Britain had attempted to impose on the colonies. McDuffie argued that the comparison to the revolutionary period was particularly apt, since the South, like the American colonists, could gain little from proportional representation. "There is no form of despotism so utterly intolerable as an interested majority, acting upon the peculiar and adverse interests of the minority." Like the British, the South's oppressors were geographically removed from those they victimized; hence: "They act without control, moral or political, and are utterly destitute of the sympathy which would be felt by the most absolute aristocracy, when residing among their subjects. We are, in fact, the subjects of the very worst species of aristocracy in the world, an upstart, mercenary aristocracy of absentee landlords, who know very little about our sufferings, and care still less."[91] McDuffie here once again comes close to the heart of the matter: what is the appropriate geographic scale of the polity?

McDuffie and the nullifiers defended free trade, and he heartily endorsed an international division of labor. However, as the older agricultural areas of the Southeast failed to prosper, some southerners again asked whether a highly specialized economy could be anything but dependent. Their arguments for diversification reintroduced into southern economic thought the mercantilist quest for a balanced economy.

Chapter Three

Unequal Exchange

The tariff debates of the 1820s and early 1830s made clear to many southerners the increasingly important role of cotton in the American export trade. In the chaotic conditions surrounding the War of 1812 southerners had despaired of building regional cities on a base of international commerce. With the enhanced importance of the cotton trade, however, such a conclusion now seemed premature. Exporting cotton promised a good deal more stability than the short-lived re-export business of the Napoleonic period. All in all, southerners expressed a renewed interest in commerce. Especially in the Southeast, politicians and journalists looked to establish a new urban commercialism, similar to that envisioned by the mercantilists of colonial Virginia and later by Washington and Madison. Public and private plans to stimulate the development of transport and finance abounded. These ideas gained considerable momentum because of the low returns of southeastern agriculture, increasingly in competition with that of the Southwest. The renewed call for an expanded commerce addressed the longstanding southern sense of dependency and vulnerability. Any service—commercial, financial, or transport—bought from the North came much too dearly.

Voluntary Tribute

The two decades from 1820 to 1840 had brought only modest urban growth to the Southeast. If the artificial commercial prosperity of the early nineteenth century had strongly favored the coastal cities of the Northeast, the end of the War of 1812 left some uncertainty as to the ultimate fate of the southern Atlantic ports. For those eager to build a southern commerce, the spectacular growth of Baltimore might have signified incipient southern strength or threatening northern hegemony. By 1840 there was no doubt; in the interim no great southern commercial city had arisen south of Baltimore and east of New Orleans. Charleston, Savannah, and Norfolk had not participated in the general economic expansion of the Atlantic seaboard. The significant decline in the price of cotton in the late 1820s had left the Southeast in considerable difficulty, while the cotton boom of the 1830s had drawn off a large share of its potential population growth, leaving the region demoralized. Virginia could not grow cotton, and increasingly South Carolina could not grow it cheaply enough. The Southeast faced economic stagnation.[1]

Thoughtful people along the south Atlantic shore looked to the Northeast and saw those states enjoying strong population growth despite considerable western migration. They saw a bustling commercial base spawning an emerging manufacturing sector and urban areas along the coast profiting from the growth of interior settlements. In contrast, the southwestern cotton boom of the 1830s provided little stimulation to southern coastal cities. While the economy of the Northwest seemed to complement that of the Northeast, southern subregions were locked in a competitive struggle that could hardly bode well for the older areas. Observing the sustained rise of the northern commercial cities, southerners from Virginia and South Carolina tried to explain this basic difference. The tariff theories of the nullifiers accounted for only a portion of the thought surrounding these matters. Those theories emphasized the coercion lying behind the tax tribute that the South paid to the North. Increasingly, in the 1830s, southerners began to identify other mechanisms of exploitation. As tariff levels fell in response to southern political successes, the southeastern economy hardly improved. Its continuing sluggishness prompted a broader analysis of the South's colonial position.

If the tariff amounted to forced tribute, some southerners now identified a long list of mechanisms whereby the North extracted "voluntary tribute" from the South. These pervasive mechanisms caused more damage than the direct intervention of the federal government. The resulting dependency, precisely because of its voluntary nature, posed a serious threat to the prospects of the South, especially the Southeast. And, like it or not, this line of analysis pointed away from a laissez-faire view back toward mercantilist policies.

In the 1830s the lawyer-planter leadership in South Carolina continued to dominate discussion. Men like McDuffie, Robert Hayne, and James Hamilton provided the most penetrating analysis. They presented some of their most cohesive work at the various commercial conventions that became popular in Georgia and South Carolina in the late 1830s.[2] Merchants and lawyers—southern men of affairs—made up most of the delegates, rather than any incipient or frustrated urban bourgeoisie.

The conventions in no way represented a challenge to the planter class. Rather, they fitted quite nicely into the old Virginia mercantilist tradition. They aimed at building an independent commerce based on the agricultural exploitation of the interior.

George McDuffie expanded his colonial view of the southern economy to include the sources of voluntary tribute. In a report prepared for the first commercial convention, held in Augusta, Georgia, in 1837, McDuffie reworked and broadened his approach. After presenting the basic tariff argument, McDuffie went on to consider other major mechanisms of transferring wealth to the North. Among these he chiefly denounced the domination of southern foreign trade by northern merchants. The rise of the northeastern ports had distorted southern commerce. Despite the fact that the South exported staples directly to England and other countries, relatively little in the way of direct imports landed in southern ports. McDuffie pointed out that regional imports from abroad amounted to about one-seventh of exports. The South purchased some $72 million worth of indirect imports, mostly through merchants in New York City. McDuffie claimed the northern merchants cleared 15 percent profit on these transactions, and he estimated that the "annual loss of the exporting states by the indirect course of their foreign trade" was over $10 million. From McDuffie's vantage point these developments paralleled the inroads made by the tariff: "We are opposed to an absorbing centralism in commerce as well as in government."[3]

McDuffie's comments addressed the widely held dismay at the relative decline of southern ports. Denunciations of New York and its imperial ambitions commonly appeared in southern newspapers of the day. For example, a "Friend of the Old Dominion" wrote in the *Norfolk Beacon* that the town "was better off as a colony. The present system takes away our foreign trade, and I have little hope for the preservation of our liberties, when one city is to swallow up all the commerce of the country."[4]

In looking for an explanation of the success of the northern ports, New York City in particular, McDuffie found no evidence of real competitive advantages. The tariff had done considerable damage, but the financial power of the North played the most important role in forging the commercial dependency of the South. The pattern of long-term credits being extended by northern commercial houses to southern merchants and through them to southern planters had fettered local commerce. To right the situation, he said, "a radical change must be made in [the planters'] system of economy. The habit of laying out their incomes before they get them, and requiring a credit in all their dealing for the year, till the close of it, or until they sell their crops, even if it be longer, is the root of the evil of our whole system of credit."[5]

Reform obviously required that the planters no longer buy on credit. They should spend last year's income, not next year's. McDuffie estimated that such a change would reduce by half the capital required to carry out direct trade with Europe. Moreover, this capital could easily be raised from the planters themselves. Here McDuffie built on his basic insight concerning the costs of the inflexibility produced by overspecialization. The reason planters needed financing to import their goods and produce their crop—the reason they had nothing to invest in commercial houses—lay in their overweening tendency to spend on land and slaves for the staple crop. While this approach generated short-run profits, it undermined the planters' long-run interests in an orderly expansion of the cotton trade. To avoid the pitfall of overproduction, the planters would need to redirect their investments. What better technique for accomplishing this than to diversify into commercial ventures?

In this spirit McDuffie summed up his argument:

> Widely dispersed over an immense territory, without the means of consultation or concert among themselves, [the planters] cannot prevent the habitual occurrence of excessive crops, unless they adopt a system which will of itself have a constant tendency to prevent it. The basis of that system should be the investment of at least a fair proportion of their set annual income in some other profitable pursuit, instead of investing it in land and negroes; and we believe there is no such pursuit that promises a more abundant reward to industry and enterprise than the direct importation of foreign merchandise through our southern seaports.[6]

McDuffie requested that planters invest half their net income in such enterprises.

The issue of credit haunted all of the commercial conventions. For example, Robert Hayne looked for planters to invest 10 percent of their crop outside agriculture. He also encouraged southern banks to discount the long paper of small merchants. Finally, he advocated using foreign sources of capital to carry out the trade. Somewhat surprisingly, Hayne did not suggest that foreign capital might pose dangers to southern commerce.[7]

Both McDuffie and Hayne appreciated the connection between the availability of regional credit and the growth of regional commerce. Both proposed concerted southern action to stimulate southern commerce. Some have argued that the positions taken by these men in the commercial conventions ran counter to their defense of free trade in Congress; and surely, when these southerners waxed eloquent on free trade as the economic equivalent of political liberty, they must have had a few qualms about their own hopes to redirect commercial development.

Such inconsistencies originated in the overlapping versions of the colonial critique held by many southerners. These critiques drew freely on both mercantilist and libertarian ideas. After the War of 1812 many southerners, including McDuffie, had committed themselves to an expansive program of a broad agrarian alliance to defeat the British commercial system. As the northern star rose, they saw a new, more proximate danger. Adam Smith and free trade made sense to them when they were fending off the aggressive commercial policies of the North. Nevertheless, a McDuffie could remain eager to build a regional consciousness among southern planters and farmers. In the context of the commercial conventions, these men felt free to denounce the dependency produced by market transactions and to advocate concerted regional efforts to build the southern economy.

The problems of trade and credit already had a long history in the United States. Washington, at the time of the Revolution, predicted that the collapse of the established credit system would be beneficial if it forced planters out of staple production into more diversified farming. War had disrupted financing during the Revolution, and the new business cycles caused much the same result in the early nineteenth century. Several speakers at the commercial conventions in 1837 and 1838 suggested that the confusion in northern financial markets at the time created a good opportunity to establish a greater independence in the South. The notion of credit as something that ensnares appeared in virtually all versions of the colonial critique. Warnings to avoid northern credit drew on the basic anticommercial theme common in the region. They often degenerated into moralistic admonitions—neither a borrower nor a lender be. At times, however, this stance produced serious attempts to find pragmatic alternatives to established channels of credit. The idea of running the plantations of the South without short-term credits was quixotic. Antebellum planters found such financing a profitable expedient. In good years high cotton prices justified their leveraging their capital. Bad years might wipe out the small fry, but a farm of average size could generally absorb the loss. Appeals to virtue, bolstered only by the promise of remote gains of economic independence, fall on deaf ears in any epoch. While southern planters remained highly sensitive to their region's dependency, they also remained wedded to their individual sources of credit.

A similar problem bedeviled various attempts to solicit pledges to buy only those imports that entered the country through southern cities. The most common pledge required retailers to buy from merchants engaged in direct trade, "provided those merchants would sell as cheaply as the northern merchants." A few southerners tried to demonstrate that goods purchased through direct importation would actually be cheaper than those obtained from northern ports.[8] Yet most men of affairs doubted that southern merchants could compete with northern ones. The North's accumulated advantage in importing—its large markets, specialized financial services and abundant transportation facilities—would require a concerted attack. Various pledges to "buy southern" had no great effect. Matthew F. Maury, the talented southern oceanographer, compared these pledges to the "oath which old Neptune administers to sailors when crossing the Line, — 'Never to kiss the maid when they can kiss the mistress, unless they like the maid best . . . never to eat hard bread when they can get soft, unless they prefer the hard.' " According to Maury the direct-trade conventions had resolved that "southern merchants should never buy in the North, when they could purchase at the South, unless they could buy cheaper in the North."[9]

Whatever their misgivings, the proponents of direct trade advanced a wide range of concrete plans including schemes for developing transportation services and for establishing companies with facilities on both sides of the Atlantic. These southerners hoped that European financial markets would supply the capital for their ventures.[10] Few direct-trade projects ever came to fruition; dozens of importing ventures launched with much fanfare disappeared into oblivion. The simple profit calculus of commerce favored the northern ports. Whatever the causes of the initial discrepancy, by the late 1830s importing through New York remained significantly more profitable than working through southern ports. The sheer size of the New York market guaranteed ready buyers at reasonably stable prices. The smaller southern cities, with their circumscribed hinterlands, promised only uncertainty.

As an obvious complement to the quest for direct trade, southern cities sought to use the region's political influence to improve transport links to the interior. Every southern seaport viewed the dramatic example of the Erie Canal as a model. Fifty years after Washington's proposal to strengthen the competitive position of Virginia's ports through canal construction, many of those concerned with southern dependency continued to espouse much the same argument. With internal improvements, and especially a tie to the Ohio River–Mississippi River basin, the seacoast might be able to achieve sufficient demand to justify a greater direct trade.

McDuffie and Calhoun had both advocated southern internal improvements early in their careers. In the 1820s when the strict constructionists like William Crawford of Georgia and Philip Barbour of Virginia declared federal help for internal improvements unconstitutional, older southern "nationalists" paid little attention, finding Clay's arguments on this matter more convincing. Before he gave up on the notion of a political alliance with the West, McDuffie attempted to make clear that that region stood to gain much more from internal improvements than from tariffs. Again in the 1830s, as he considered the problem of commercial development, it was natural to emphasize the importance of transportation to the interior. A railroad to the Mississippi Valley would play a crucial role in breaking the "shackles of our commercial dependence" and making the southern cities meeting places of Europe and the West.[11]

The new emphasis on railroads grew out of the surprising success of the Baltimore and Ohio Railroad. For years Virginians had been seeking a commercial link to the Ohio River. The Virginia assembly had squabbled with the federal government over support for the Chesapeake and Ohio Canal, with its terminus in the Washington vicinity, and the James and Kanawha Canal, favoring Richmond and Norfolk. The Virginians could never agree on the constitutionality of federal assistance, let alone concentrate their political forces to advance one or another of these possible routes to the interior. The Baltimore and Ohio Railroad rendered the entire matter academic.[12] Eyeing these developments, Charleston, which possessed no natural waterway to the interior, began to promote a rail link to Cincinnati.

In the early nineteenth century the schemes for internal improvements offered by the South's political and commercial leadership lacked a clear vision. Generally eager to imitate the successes of others rather than to experiment, southerners began their projects late. Consequently, their routes only helped to fill in a system with an already well-established northern focus. Where the Erie Canal and the Baltimore and Ohio Railroad brought the profits due pathbreakers, southern projects hardly lived up to expectations. Virginia's efforts, racked by internal squabbling and petty jealousies, proved the most disappointing.

From the late 1830s on, southerners advocating internal improvements emphasized the need to catch up with the North. Neither the capital nor the political muscle for such an effort materialized. The planters and their bankers remained wary of large-scale projects. Southern politicians had only limited success in winning federal dollars for their region. The resulting pattern of scattered improvements left the South poorly served in comparison to the North.

The call for credit reform, direct trade, and internal improvements grew out of a colonial analysis of the southern economy. This analysis increasingly emphasized the ways in which voluntary market transactions led to dependency: the South produced wealth, but, through a multitude of indirect channels, the North siphoned off that wealth. Like Jefferson and other early agrarians, McDuffie and many of the other participants in the commercial conventions advocated an expanded commerce as a means of freeing the region's agriculture from this persistent extortion. Some advocates went further, asking whether agriculture itself had contributed to the problem.

Much of the tariff debate of the 1820s had been over the issue of whether to protect manufacturing, meaning northern enterprises. In 1816 Calhoun had been generous toward manufacturing. By the 1820s even "mercantilist" southerners had developed a deep mistrust of these new pursuits. They worried that the industrial revolution in the North had spun out of control, that a new class of manufacturers had been able to take a leading position in the government, and that the promises made by northern politicians had won over the South's traditional ally, the agrarian West. Southern agrarians responded to these developments by attacking the new manufacturing as an artificial product of sectional favoritism in the central government. A return to free trade would immediately check this rapid expansion and restore the country as a whole to its agrarian destiny.

Some of the strongest tariff opponents, however, carried their analysis in a different direction. The wealth produced by northern manufacturing in the 1830s and 1840s convinced them that a modern regional economy required an industrial sector. At a theoretical level they began to develop a sophisticated view of exchange as between nations and sectors. Proponents of southern manufactures, such as James H. Hammond, governor of South Carolina, mounted a broad defense of a diversified economy. These men, although familiar with Adam Smith's argument for specialization and trade (several had even used it in attacking the tariff), increasingly borrowed from the economic logic of the American System in advocating a diversified South. In this they drew freely on the ideas of David Raymond and the Careys, economic writers who had supported the development of northern manufacturing. In addition, the advocates of southern industrialization quaintly argued that the diversified talents of the southern people demanded a diversified economy.[13] More concretely, they drew attention to the geographic limits of staple production. These limits involved both supply and demand.

Hammond pointed to South Carolina's own experience. No region could easily maintain a monopoly in provisioning staples. In the 1840s, declines in cotton prices made it painfully clear that the tremendous increase in production on new southwestern lands had undermined South Carolina's position. What had happened to the Southeast would happen to the Southwest when cotton inevitably expanded to other parts of the world. Hammond made the point quite neatly: "In the present state of the world, when science and industry, backed by accumulated capital, are testing the capacity of every clime and soil on the globe, and the free and cheap communications which is now growing up between all the ends of the earth, enables wealth and enterprise to concentrate rapidly on every favored spot, no such monopoly can be enjoyed if sufficiently valuable to attract the cupidity of man."[14]

Notice that Hammond in this proposition points out the roles of "science" and "accumulated" capital. He drew a particularly acute picture of the transient character of the staples boom that is common in the early economic history of many dependent regions and countries. Good soil, good harbors, and good seed yielded profit for only so long. A fully developed capitalist order rendered inevitable an attack on every staples monopoly.

Against this background, advocates of a more independent southern economy advanced a second theme, that of an inherent difference in the productivity of agricultural labor and industrial labor. William Gregg, the most famous of contemporary southern cotton mill owners, argued, "If we will but look at the vast difference in productiveness between the mechanic or factory operative and agricultural laborer we will be led at once to the conclusion that every country should have the workshops at home which supply her with all the actual necessaries of life."[15] Gregg explained that this difference in productivity emerged from the higher input of capital per worker in manufacturing. In addition, manufacturing workers acquired more skill and education than farm laborers did. Nineteenth-century observers of such phenomena regularly attributed them to the positive effects of high population density. One of the most popular approaches to political economy in early American writings drew on the old mercantilist principle that the density of population had an important influence on productivity. This idea was common in the North as well as the South, and it played a central role in the work of Henry Carey of Pennsylvania, perhaps the most creative American economist of the nineteenth century.[16]

In the South, throughout the eighteenth century, there had been a strong mercantilist concern to develop a more concentrated pattern of settlement, including the development of urban ports. Early in the nineteenth century Thomas Cooper had argued that cities played a crucial role in the process of economic development: the pressure of population on subsistence, far from being a negative, provided "the source of all human improvement."[17] Drawing on this tradition, George Tucker, the Virginian who first catalogued the statistics of interregional differentiation, ascribed the difference in northern and southern living standards to "the different densities of population, different degrees of fertility and different distances from market."[18]

Faced with an apparently growing gap between the economic development of South and North, some southerners began to argue that the relation of an industrial power to an agricultural one necessarily bred exploitation. Transactions between such partners inevitably took the form of unequal exchanges. At the same time, the increasing importance of urbanization in commerce and manufacturing underscored for southerners their dependence on the cities of the North and Great Britain. Southern reliance on a few staple crops had led to dependency. From this perspective, the Smithian laissez-faire doctrines that dominated southern economic thought greatly constrained the colonial analogy. McDuffie, Hayne, and even Calhoun moved back and forth between libertarian and mercantilist versions of the critique, and their analysis suffered from that inconsistency. To develop the notion of "voluntary tribute" in a powerful manner, southerners had to break with the classical principles of political economy. The academic economists of the region could hardly contemplate such a step. In the end, it was not one of the South's prominent professors but rather an eccentric pamphleteer who fashioned the South's longstanding uneasiness over diversification and urbanization into a full-blown theory of dependency and unequal exchange.

The Political Economy of George Fitzhugh

The classical economists of the South—Cooper, Cardozo, and Dew— uniformly rejected protectionist arguments. Their traditional views left little room for aggressive policies to promote regional diversification and urbanization. As a result a few southerners began to reconsider their economics. Among these heretics, George Fitzhugh, of Virginia, stands out. Later known primarily for his reactionary defense of slavery, Fitzhugh also mounted a telling attack on classical economic thought. More clearly than any northern opponent of free trade, Fitzhugh developed the idea that long-run dependency grew out of the very advantages that recommended free trade in the short run. This argument rationalized the program of men such as J. B. DeBow, editor of *DeBow's Review* and crusader for southern industrialization.

Oddly, Fitzhugh's critique of free trade drew heavily on versions of the labor theory of value propounded by socialists and abolitionists. At the same time, it reflected the reactionary thinking of Thomas Carlyle's defense of feudal institutions. The eccentric Fitzhugh stirred this curious pot to produce the most interesting political economy ever to emerge from the South. For him the South's problems originated not in northern tariffs or financial manipulations but in the necessarily exploitative relationship of industry to agriculture. Fitzhugh argued that voluntary and mutually beneficial exchanges between such societies inevitably led to grossly uneven development. His formalization of this argument largely anticipated twentieth-century theories of dependency and unequal exchange.

Despite his prominent ancestry, George Fitzhugh, born in 1806, was a marginal member of the Virginia gentry.[19] His parents, Lucy Stuart and George Fitzhugh, an army surgeon, had owned a plantation but in 1825 had been forced to sell it at auction. Fitzhugh acquired only the skimpiest formal education at a primitive grammar school. He avidly read the British literary reviews popular at the time and once admitted to a friend that his "pseudo-learning" was "all gathered from Reviews. I never read a Socialist author treating his subject philosophically in my life. Newspapers, novels, Reviews, are the sources of my information."[20] His writings lacked erudition, but they overflowed with an instinctive critical insight.

As a rather unsuccessful lawyer, Fitzhugh depended heavily on the property of his wife, Mary Brockenbrough, whose estate lay near Port Royal in Caroline County, earlier the home of one of the Old Republican essayists, John Taylor. There, Fitzhugh concentrated on his writing, which met with a measure of journalistic acceptance. He published frequently in the Richmond papers and placed longer pieces in *DeBow's Review*. Although he stayed on good enough terms with Democrats (and obtained a rather menial clerkship during the Buchanan administration),

Fitzhugh played no significant role in Virginia politics. Both friends and adversaries generally viewed him as something of an intellectual eccentric. In the 1850s Fitzhugh published two important works that summarized his economics and sociology: *Sociology for the South* (1854) and *Cannibals All!* (1857). These rather thin volumes presented Fitzhugh's clearest statements of his mix of socialism and reaction.

Fitzhugh consciously took as his starting point the philosophy of Thomas Carlyle. Carlyle had become the champion of a reactionary romanticism with considerable appeal to the Tory England of his day. He also had shown what many southerners interpreted as sympathy for their own slave system. In an explicitly racist essay, "The Negro Question," Carlyle had scathingly criticized the charitable societies that had effectively lobbied for the abolition of slavery in the British West Indies. According to Carlyle, the strong and intelligent had a responsibility to guarantee the industry of the improvident. The West Indian blacks had "an indisputable and perpetual right to be compelled, by the real proprietors of said land, to do competent work."[21]

All of this appealed strongly to southerners who were searching for a broad rationalization of slavery. The reactionary logic of Carlyle offered a clean break with the Jeffersonian liberalism that had dominated southern thought.[22] Carlyle's work pointed toward a positive defense of slavery, but a systematic neofeudal argument for slavery required a major shift in the world view of southern intellectuals. Fitzhugh in particular recognized that Carlyle's thoughts on slavery were part of a frontal assault on both the political philosophy and the political economy of liberalism. Condescending toward his "philanthropic friends" with their misplaced faith in the equality of mankind, Carlyle disdained liberal political economy. Carlyle's Tory radicalism challenged not only John Stuart Mill's criticism of slavery but also Mill's defense of laissez-faire markets.[23]

Here was an attack worth mounting. But Carlyle's denunciation of supply-and-demand and the cash nexus left unclear what principles, if not the market, should govern exchange. Fitzhugh eagerly searched for a more rigorous, less literary base for his attack on orthodox political economy. He did not merely parrot Carlyle's broad denunciation of the market system; he used it as an introduction and motivation for a far more analytical critique of the dismal science.

Strangely enough, his inspiration here came from the far left of the political spectrum. The Ricardian version of the labor theory of value lent itself to all types of radicalism. At root, that theory identified a surplus, the difference between value and cost of production, which accrued to the capitalist. It seemed obvious to Ricardian socialists such as William Thompson that labor deserved "to possess all that it produces." The separation of labor and capital left the "Competitive System" a sham, engendering "enormous inequalities of wealth, the parents of almost all the crimes and vices that desolate society."[24] Like Robert Owen, Thompson saw the natural answer in worker cooperatives. He maintained a profound faith in the malleability of human beings. All humans had much the same capabilities, but unequal remuneration forced the great mass of the laboring classes into ignorance, while hypocritically claiming to reward intelligence and merit.[25] Thompson denounced the high wages of "mental labor." Such labor carried an exorbitant price only because of an artificial scarcity created by unequal access to education.

Although Thompson had nothing but scorn for the slave South, he saw little to praise in the free North. There, as in Great Britain, one found "the same eternally-succeeding distresses, arising from the impossibility of suiting regularly the supply of commodities to the demand" and "nearly the same degradation, attached to manual labor."[26] Thompson and his fellow Ricardian socialists provided a damning argument against the excesses of capitalism. Fitzhugh, of course, had no truck with Thompson's egalitarianism. But what was false for individuals might be true of societies. Fitzhugh's sociological imagination suggested that the radical arguments might prove a powerful cudgel to wield against the liberal economics of free trade.

Fitzhugh drew most heavily on the thought of Stephen Pearl Andrews, a disciple of Josiah Warren, who in turn had been strongly influenced by Owen and Thompson.[27] In Andrews's words (extensively quoted by Fitzhugh in *Cannibals All!*), "Suppose it costs me ten minutes' labor to concoct a pill which will save your life when nothing else will. . . . It is clear that your life is worth to you more than your fortune. Am I, then, entitled to demand of you for the nostrum the whole of your property, more or less?" Andrews goes on to describe the "value principle" as the "commercial embodiment of the essential element of conquest and war—war transferred from the battlefield to the counter." In words that Fitzhugh could well understand, Andrews pronounced that, "in bodily conflict, the physically strong conquer and subject the physically weak. In the conflict of trade, the intellectually astute and powerful conquer and subject those who are intellectually feeble, or whose intellectual development is not of the precise kind to fit them for the conflict of wits in the matter of trade."[28]

In a passage that Fitzhugh also quoted, Andrews expounded: "If, in any transaction, I get from you some portion of your earnings without an equivalent, I begin to make you my slave. . . . If I obtain the whole of your services without an equivalent—except the means of keeping you in working condition for my own sake, I make you completely my slave." And finally we are informed that upon "scientific analysis . . . the slaveholder will be found . . . to hold the same relation to the trader which the freebooter holds to the blackleg. It is a question of taste which to admire most, the daredevil boldness of the one, or the oily and intriguing propensities and performances of the other."[29]

Little wonder that Fitzhugh eagerly rebroadcasted this message. Fitzhugh drew on Andrews's rich socialist critique of the immorality of the market system; he enjoyed nothing better than turning these radical guns on northern merchants and capitalists. Like Carlyle, he used the socialist attack of capitalism to bolster a glorified notion of paternalism. Fitzhugh acknowledged in particular his debt to "the socialists," who "stumbled on the true issue, but do not seem yet fully aware of the nature of their discovery." They appreciated that "liberty" must be controlled, "competition arrested, the strong restrained from, instead of encouraged to, oppress the weak—in order to restore society to a healthy state."[30]

Fitzhugh took more than a vague indictment from the socialists. From Andrews, Fitzhugh acquired Thompson's conviction that labor must be exchanged "at cost," hour for hour. For Andrews and his colleagues this proposition grew out of their egalitarian volunteerism. In Fitzhugh's hands it became something quite different. Fitzhugh obviously rejected the broad egalitarianism of the socialists. Indeed, he advanced an ideology based on a paternalism of the more able toward the less able. At first glance it seems ludicrous that this Junker should draw on an economic theory constructed to realize egalitarian individuality. Nevertheless, Fitzhugh saw a certain logic within the socialist position.

What might be false for individuals might be very true for a community, region, or nation. From his sociological perspective, Fitzhugh argued that two sizable samples of people should not differ all that much. Any large group of people must include a broad range of potential abilities. While local custom and culture would realize some of these abilities, many aptitudes would remain only potentialities. At root, however, a large region like the South could engage in virtually any type of production. On average, the South's labor was the equivalent of that in the

North and Britain.[31] Fairness in exchange required that the goods produced in the South trade on a par with those produced elsewhere. An hour's worth of southern labor should exchange for an hour's worth of northern labor. Fitzhugh believed that in principle this rule should hold but that in practice the market could not achieve such fair exchanges.[32] He then set about explaining why southern labor did not trade at par against the labor of the North. In doing so, he developed a theory of regional dependency.

Fitzhugh's critique of free trade makes one of the most challenging and original economic arguments to come out of the South.[33] The southern free-trade tradition had always held that if tariffs and other barriers to an open commerce could be overcome, international markets would appropriately reward the region's labor. Cardozo, Dew, and Cooper all had taken this position. John Taylor of Caroline had held to it, and the Jeffersonian agrarian program made it a central tenet. In stark contrast Fitzhugh denied that markets could be relied on to achieve equitable exchange: despite the appearance of fairness and even the reality of short-run mutual advantage, interregional and international trade must necessarily exploit the South.

What characteristics of the South guaranteed its exploitation? Fitzhugh singled out just that agrarian base the Jeffersonians had so praised. Agricultural labor inevitably remained unskilled and uneducated labor. Like other types of "hand-work," its price would always be determined by the cost of subsistence. Like Thompson's and Andrews's common laborers, agricultural labor, because of its abundant supply, could never command a reward greater than its cost. However, the products and hence the labor of an industrial region had just the opposite character. In carrying out their "head-work," merchants and manufacturers could command high premiums, premiums that reflected not costs of production but scarcity in the market. Paraphrasing the socialists, Fitzhugh asserted that "peoples and individuals must live by hand-work or head-work, and those who live by head-work are always in fact, the masters of those who live by hand-work. They take the products of their labor without paying an equivalent in equal labor. The hand-work men and nations are slaves in fact, because they do not get paid for more than one-fourth of their labor." And for sure, such exploitation victimized his own region: "The South has, heretofore, worked three hours for Europe and the North, and one for herself. It is one of the beautiful results of free trade."[34]

Fitzhugh never denied that trade implied mutual advantage. Indeed, the gain from trade seduced the agricultural region or country into a dependent position. The more primitive partner traded with the more developed precisely because in the short run it acquired goods cheaply. But the very process of exchange between an agricultural partner and a nonagricultural one reduced the capacity of the former to participate in the ongoing advance of technology and skill. The process left the agrarian economy dependent. While the North grew more and more like industrial Britain, the South grew more and more like a colonial appendage, like India or Ireland.

Fitzhugh believed that a region like the South eventually could produce most of the products it needed or wanted. The various skills of a community did not result from any innate abilities in its people, but were generated from education, experience, and the human environment. In this spirit, he entitled his first book *Sociology for the South.* From a much more consistent perspective, Fitzhugh shared with Thomas Cooper the conviction that cities, or at least towns, played a crucial role in both invention and productivity. For Fitzhugh, too, environment largely determined these developments.

Fitzhugh saw wealth in natural resources as something of a curse. Economic development most often emerged in less-favored areas. "Necessity compels people in poor regions, to cultivate commerce and the mechanic arts, and for that purpose to build ships and cities. They soon acquire skill in manufactures, and all the advantages necessary to produce them with cheapness and facility." By contrast, richness in natural resources reduced the need for initiative and encouraged a passive reliance on trade. Unless a region is cut off from the rest of the world, as "China was and Japan yet is," trade "will supply everything they need, except the products of the soil."[35] The result was dependency:

> As they [an agricultural people] are unskilled in mechanic arts, have few towns, little accumulated capital, and a sparse population, they produce, with great labor and expense, all manufactured articles. To them it is cheaper, at present, to exchange their crops for manufactures than to make them. They begin the exchange, and each day the necessity increases for continuing it, for each day they learn to rely more and more on others to produce articles, some of which they formerly manufactured,—and their ignorance of all, save agriculture, is thus daily increasing.[36]

One cannot imagine a more cogent statement of dependency theory. These are propositions that could easily win the endorsements of the modern dependistas of Latin America as well as the advocates of unequal exchange. And perhaps this is not so surprising. After all, Fitzhugh employed the same Ricardian labor theory of value that inspired Marx and many twentieth-century radicals, and similar premises lead to similar conclusions. Like the first dependency theorists, Fitzhugh argued for a conscious program of import substitution. While other southerners had taken the same position, Fitzhugh based his recommendations on a theory of labor cost and skill acquisition:

> It is cheaper for a man, little skilled in mechanics, to buy his plough and wagon by the exchange of agricultural products, than awkwardly, clumsily and tediously to manufacture them of bad quality with his own hands. Yet, if this same man will become a skillful mechanic, he will be able to procure four times as much agricultural products for his labor, as he can now secure with his own hands. His labor, too, will be of a lighter, less exposed, more social character, and far more improving to his mind. What is true of the individual, is true as to a nation, the people who buy their manufactures abroad, labor four times as hard, and as long, to produce them, as if they made them at home.[37]

Of course, the "infant industry" argument had become commonplace in the early nineteenth century, and the protectionist economists of the American System, Daniel Raymond and the Careys, had emphasized the importance of density and self-reliance as spurs to productivity, but none of them had drawn so clearly the inevitable dependency following on unequal exchange. Fitzhugh's more sociological view of the economy lent him a sharper sense of the evolution of productivities. In a passage that almost belied Fitzhugh's racism, he argued that the very progress of civilization among "savages" was destroyed by free trade, because it undermined the "necessity that alone can beget" civilization. In contrast to the standard protectionist fare, Fitzhugh offered a dynamic analysis of how richness of resources could undermine development.[38]

Fitzhugh believed in the need for diversification, because he saw manufacturing as a vibrant sector likely to spawn continuous techno-logical improvements. This productivity growth would allow a manufac-turing region to exploit agricultural areas even as the prices of manu-factures fell. Again, high density furnished "the opportunity for association and division of labor, and the division of charges and expenses." Agri-culture could never enjoy a similar growth of productivity. The low population density in an agricultural country also made the cost of obtaining education prohibitive. Finally, the very failure of an agricultural society encouraged the emigration of her population; the rich left for pleasure and the poor left for employment. Ultimately this drain demoralized the community as a whole.

Fitzhugh's analysis of the dependent position of agrarian society was by far the most acute of the antebellum period. Rather than emphasizing tariffs and politics, he struck at the core of the free-trade argument and attempted to demonstrate not just imperfection but a systematic failure. Moreover, he honestly confronted the similarities between the North and Britain. Playing off one against the other or choosing the lesser of two evils promised no gain, he claimed. In the natural course of things, either one would exploit the South. The root of the problem was that free trade undermined regional independence. Breaking only the political connection to an industrial center was an insufficient solution to the colonial predicament. For Fitzhugh, real solutions necessarily involved a dynamic and intelligent turning inward.

The work of George Fitzhugh represents the epitome of the mercantilist stream in southern economic thought. Emphasizing the colonial position of the region, Fitzhugh argued the necessity of diversification, even at the cost of a reduced commerce. Like J. B. DeBow and other advocates of industrialization, he saw the basic problems of the South as originating in the region's exaggerated dependence on staple crops, but Fitzhugh had at least the beginnings of an analytical apparatus with which to explain the nature of that dependency. Working backwards from a theory of unequal exchange, he constructed a dynamic view of colonial dependency, which in turn provided a logically compelling argument for the diversification of the region's economy.

The reputation that Fitzhugh has in American historiography rests largely on his apology for the South's "peculiar institution," slavery. Unlike most defenders of slavery, he voiced a paternalism that he would have extended over white employees as well as black slaves. The reactionary character of his work has attracted some attention from historians. Louis Hartz extensively analyzed Fitzhugh's work because of its sharp break with Jeffersonian liberalism and concluded that Fitzhugh's Carlylian position was hopelessly contradictory. Hartz rightly pointed out that in America, where feudal institutions had never taken root, a call for a paternalistic feudalism was not conservative or reactionary but, rather, extremely radical. As a result Fitzhugh, who continually asserted his connection to time-honored values, in fact had to advocate a sharp break with American traditions. Perhaps this implicit radicalism explains

Fitzhugh's extensive involvement with the philosophical anarchists and socialists of his day. Perhaps he saw in them kindred souls, also eager for a radical restructuring of their society. In any event this fundamental inconsistency in Fitzhugh's political thought convinced Hartz, while ever respectful of Fitzhugh's originality, to reject his intellectual arguments as fraudulent.[39]

By contrast, Eugene Genovese sees in Fitzhugh the quintessence of the slave society and in his work nothing less than an ideology for slave society. Genovese argues that the work of Fitzhugh and the southern sociologists George Frederick Holmes and Henry Hughes commanded increasing respect in the antebellum South as it approached secession. For Genovese, the inconsistencies in Fitzhugh's arguments pale in comparison to the historical importance of his attack on capitalism and his defense of paternalism.

Hartz and Genovese both make clear their respect for Fitzhugh's intellectual insight, if not his scholarship. The dispute between them centers on whether his philosophy represented a viable ideology for the slave South. This is an interesting question, but its relevance ended when the Civil War destroyed the antebellum South. By contrast, Fitzhugh's anticipation of dependency theory, although the product of his region's early history, has a continuing relevance to the broad problems of economic development.

This in no way implies that Fitzhugh's work can be sanitized by emphasizing his theories of dependency and unequal exchange. Like all southerners of the 1850s, Fitzhugh was caught up in the central conflict of that decade; he consciously organized his work around his defense of slavery. In many ways, however, his reactionary prescription for the shortcomings of world capitalism can be separated from his analysis of dependency. While we rightly place intellectual work in its immediate context, we cheat ourselves if we ignore the universal in yesterday's theories. The underlying continuity in southern economic history from the seventeenth century to the twentieth was dependency, not slavery. The relevance of southern economic thought to political economy today stems more from its treatment of dependency than from its treatment of slavery.

Slavery as a Burden

An emphasis on regional dependency in no way implies that southern intellectual history can or should ignore slavery. Slavery affected southern dependency. It affected all features of southern life before the Civil War. As we have already seen, southerners often made use of the metaphor of slavery to represent their dependent economic condition. The rhetorical excesses of the nullification controversy reduced this long-standing habit almost to the status of cliché. More significantly, at least a few southerners saw slavery not just as an occasional metaphor for their economic dependency but as its direct cause.

Even in the seventeenth century some Virginians worried about the effect of slavery on the industry of the white population. In the first half of the eighteenth century this line of thought continued despite the rapid growth of slavery as an institution. Slavery's initial exclusion from Georgia was intended in part to prevent the idleness of the white population there. William Byrd, who himself owned many slaves in Virginia, observed that slaves "blow up the pride and ruin the industry of our white people, who seeing a rank of poor creatures below them detest work for fear it should make them look like slaves."[40]

The same thought appeared often in the writings of the revolutionary generation of southerners. Jefferson, Arthur Lee, Richard Henry Lee, and George Mason repeatedly voiced their objections to slavery. On occasion these objections took the form of an economic argument. Richard Henry Lee felt that "some of our neighboring colonies, though much later than ourselves in point of settlement, are now far beyond us in improvement." He attributed this state of affairs not to nature, which had given Virginia fertile soil and ample sunshine, but to the slave trade.[41]

A borrowed Puritanism haunted the southern condemnation of slavery. While slavery might yield profits in the short run, its effects on the morals of the whites undermined their energy. In Jefferson's famous discussion of the "manners" of Virginia, he outlined in a compelling fashion the links among slavery, social psychology, and economic activity. "The whole commerce between master and slave is a perpetual exercise of the most boisterous passions, the most unremitting despotism on the one part, and degrading submissions on the other. Our children see this and learn to imitate it. . . . The man must be a prodigy who can retain his manners and morals undepraved in such circumstances. . . . For in a warm climate, no man will labour for himself who can make another labour for him."[42] It was industriousness, he declared, that distinguished more balanced economies from that of Virginia. Slavery engendered the laziness of the South and kept the colony from being a well-rounded society.

This same line of reasoning had previously been used to advocate the suppression of the slave trade. In 1772 the Virginia Assembly sent an address to King George III stating that "some of your Majesty's subjects in Great Britain, may reap emoluments from this sort of traffic; but when we consider that it greatly retards the settlement of the Colonies with more useful inhabitants, and may, in time have the most destructive influence, we presume to hope, that the interest of a few will be disregarded."[43]

The Revolution pointed up inconsistencies that at least some of its leaders recognized. While these revolutionaries hoped that a separation from England would create a more just society, few of them directly agitated against slavery. An ambivalence about slavery permeated revolutionary leadership in the South. Even into the early period of the republic, men who personally opposed the institution went to great lengths not to make it a central issue of their politics. Jefferson did not object when Charles Pinkney assured slaveholders of South Carolina:

> There are men who will tell you Mr. Jefferson is an unsafe president for you; he whose whole estate is exactly like that of your own planters, who owns two hundred negroes himself, and who, in order to remove all doubts upon the subject, has explicitly authorized his friends to declare as his assertion: "That the Constitution has not empowered the federal legislature to touch in the remotest degree the question respecting the condition or property of slaves in any of the states, and that any attempt of that sort would be unconstitutional and a usurpation of rights Congress do not possess."[44]

For the revolutionary generation criticism of slavery remained largely a theoretical affair. In the nineteenth century, southerners who questioned the institution carried the debate into politics. During the tariff controversies, the argument emerged that slavery, and not trade regulation, lay behind the South's economic problems. Not surprisingly, these issues came to the fore in Virginia, where slavery was of dubious profitability. While the discussion simmered throughout the 1820s, it reached a boil in the debates held during the 1831–32 session of the Virginia legislature. All parties agreed that these debates hinged on economic considerations.

The representatives from western Virginia advanced the basic argument that slavery as an institution had slowed the economic development of the eastern part of the state and thus limited the markets and exports of the western half. Argued Thomas Marshall, "[slavery is] ruinous to the whites; retards improvements; roots out our industrious population; banishes the yeomanry from the country; and deprives the spinner, the weaver, the smith, the shoemaker, and the carpenter of employment and support."[45] Pointing to the slow growth of Virginia in comparison to the North, antislavery forces concluded that slavery explained the state's relative decline. The western Virginians conducted their economic attack on slavery in a straightforward and unrhetorical manner. While making comparisons to the North, they did not invoke the colonial analogies common to their planter adversaries. It remained the task of Hinton Rowan Helper to turn the rhetoric of the slaveholders' colonial refrain against slavery itself.

Helper was born in Rowan County in the backcountry of North Carolina.[46] His father died while he was still an infant. Although his father had owned a slave family, Helper grew up on the edge of impoverishment. He managed to complete his schooling at a local academy but lacked the financial resources to attend college. He worked as an apprentice to a nearby storekeeper. In 1850 he went north to New York City and in 1851, at the age of twenty-two, he went west to seek his fortune in the California gold fields. Helper returned to North Carolina disillusioned with both the West and the South. Intent on a literary career, he first wrote an exposé of the gold rush. Then he composed his famous critique of slavery, *The Impending Crisis of the South.*

A staunch racist throughout his life, Helper advocated abolition only to advance the economic position of poor whites.[47] His book became a major piece of Republican campaign literature in the 1860 election and a cause célèbre. Like *Uncle Tom's Cabin, The Impending Crisis* played a major role in shaping northern opinion and provoking southern intransigence. Unlike Harriet Beecher Stowe's work, *The Impending Crisis* reflected longstanding southern themes of regional dependency.

Helper combined the traditional upcountry hostility to slavery with the colonial critique characteristic of the low country. In his version of a favorite stock piece of southern newspapers, Helper showed his skill for intertwining these powerful themes. This piece usually dramatized southern dependency by toting up the purchases a typical southerner made from northern businesses. It employed a repetitive rhythm that underscored the region's predicament. Consider this example from an Alabama paper:

> At present the North fattens and grows rich upon the South. We depend upon it for our entire supplies. We purchase all our luxuries and necessities from the North. . . . The Northerners abuse and

denounce slavery and slaveholders, yet our slaves are clothed with Northern manufactured goods, have Northern hats and shoes, work with Northern hoes, ploughs, and other implements, are chastised with a Northern-made instrument, are working for Northern more than Southern profit. The slaveholder dresses in Northern goods, rides in a Northern saddle, . . . sports his Northern carriage, patronizes Northern newspapers, drinks Northern liquors, reads Northern books, spends his money at Northern watering places. . . . The aggressive acts upon his rights and his property arouse his resentment—and on Northern made paper with a Northern pen with Northern ink, he resolves and reresolves in regard to his rights![48]

Now consider the twist that Helper put to the argument:

What about Southern Commerce? Is it not almost entirely tributary to the commerce of the North? Are we not dependent on New York, Philadelphia, Boston and Cincinnati, for nearly every article of merchandise, whether foreign or domestic? Where are our ships, or mariners, our naval architects? Alas! echo answers, where? Reader! would you understand how abjectly slaveholders themselves are enslaved to the products of Northern industry? If you would, fix your mind on a Southern "gentleman"—a slave breeder and human-flesh monger, who professes to be a Christian! Observe the routine of his daily life. See him rise in the morning from a Northern bed, and clothe himself in Northern apparel; see him walk across the floor on a Northern carpet, and perform his ablutions out of a Northern sewer and basin . . . [and so on]. See him when you will, where you will, he is ever surrounded with the industrial products of those whom, in the criminal inconsistency of his heart, he execrates as enemies, yet treats as friends. His labors, his talents, his influence, are all for the North, and not for the South; for the stability of slavery and for the sake of his own personal aggrandizement, he is willing to sacrifice the dearest interests of his country.[49]

Taking the basic notion of dependency from the colonial critiques Helper derived it from a totally new premise. Thus, a profligate South, although rich in natural resources, purchased almost all manufactured goods in the North; southern cities, although well situated, carried on a negligible commerce; and the region, although home to prosperous planters, remained impoverished. These paradoxes of dependency had a simple explanation: slavery.

The causes which have impeded the progress and prosperity of the South, which have dwindled our commerce, and other similar pursuits, into the most contemptible insignificance; sunk a large majority of our people in galling poverty and ignorance, rendered a small minority conceited and tyrannical, and driven the rest away from their homes; entailed upon us a humiliating dependence on the Free States; disgraced us in the recesses of our own souls, and brought us under reproach in the eyes of all civilized and enlightened nations—may all be traced to one common source, and there find solution in the vocabulary of human economy—*Slavery!*[50]

In his explanation, Helper relied heavily on the basic argument of Daniel Goodloe, who, in 1841, had written a tract entitled *Inquiry into the Causes Which Have Retarded the Accumulation of Wealth and Increase of Population in the Southern States.* In a passage quoted by Helper, Goodloe took the old argument concerning density, which had long been used to criticize the extensive pattern of southern agriculture, and linked it to the institution of slavery. According to Goodloe the "history of the United States shows, that while the slave States increase in population less rapidly than the free, there, is a tendency in slave society to diffusion, greater than is exhibited by free society. In fact, diffusion, or extension of area, is one of the necessities of slavery. . . . This arises from the almost exclusive application of slave labor to the one occupation of agriculture, and the difficulty, if not impossibility of diversifying employments."[51] Both Goodloe and Helper held that slave labor, because of its low productivity, required a specialization in agriculture. Where Fitzhugh had seen specialization as the product of a short-sighted reckoning of comparative advantage, Goodloe and Helper saw it as the necessary corollary of a slave labor system. Goodloe viewed the result as merely slow growth; Helper understood it as colonial dependence.

Helper truly hit his stride when discussing the importance of urbanization and diversification. His chapter "Commercial cities—Southern commerce" begins with a visionary statement:

Our theme is a city—a great Southern importing, exporting, and manufacturing city . . . where we can carry on active commerce, buy, sell, fabricate, receive the profits which accrue from the exchange of our own commodities, open facilities for direct communication with foreign countries, and establish all those collateral sources of wealth, utility and adornment, which are the usual concomitants of a metropolis, and which add so very materially to the interest and importance of a nation.[52]

But this city could arise only on the ashes of slavery.

Several historians have argued that Helper represented not so much the poor white farmers of the South as a potential business class.[53] Helper did place considerable emphasis on industrial diversification and urban growth, anticipating the campaigns of Henry Grady, champion of the New South after the Civil War. Helper's business outlook also surfaced in his willingness to draw a relatively flattering picture of the North. While he found the colonial analogy compelling, he clearly thought that the South's escape lay in emulation of the North, in urbanization and industrialization. Slavery had produced the differences between the South and the North. With slavery abolished, the South would enjoy a prosperity equal to that of the North. Southern dependency would disappear once the region imitated northern institutions.

Where Fitzhugh, ever cautious of what he perceived as the excesses of a New York or a London, argued for a careful introduction of urbanization, Helper gave up all restraint, all claim to doing better than the North. In this respect he ran the risks of the compradore. In attacking the ruling class of the South and blaming them for what he saw as the colonial position of the South, he opened the doors to the Trojan Horse of northern capital. For example, in his discussion of Abbott Lawrence, the New England industrialist, Helper glorified the benefits the South might reap from increased investment of northern capital in southern manufacturing. Helper avoided the possible implications of such interregional borrowings. While purchasing manufactured goods from the North represented regional dependency, apparently, southerners could use northern capital without fear of a new colonialism. Here, too, Helper anticipated elements of the business creed of the New South.

Helper's invitation to northern absentee capital seems naive, if not disingenuous, in an attack on regional dependency. Given the power of the slaveholding class at the time, Helper perhaps saw no other course. Advocates of the New South, who made much the same mistake in judgment in an age when the realities of the concentration of northern capital were much clearer, may deserve harsher criticism.

Helper sympathized with business, even northern business; but he still spoke for the southern yeomanry, his stint as a store clerk in the South hardly qualifying him as a capitalist. He attacked the slaveholding class. He compared them to the ruling class of the North and found the slavemasters wanting. Rightly or wrongly, he felt that a southern business class, or even the northern one, would do better by the majority of southern whites, who owned no slaves. Unlike the New South publicists of the postwar period, Helper had no direct involvement in urban or industrial development. All told, he tried to represent the interests of the mass of "non-slaveholding whites." And while his basic argument had much in common with the slaveholders' own colonial critique, he viewed the South's dependency as a result and not a cause of slavery.

Understandably, many northerners saw much sense in the Goodloe-Helper theme. The idea that slavery lay behind the ills of the South long had been commonplace in the North and provided a basic component in the broader attack on slavery. The northern version of the argument, however, went out of its way to deny the colonial position of the South. In particular, northerners denied that their region derived any significant benefit from the South's predicament. Slavery, they said, was an inefficient system that created no significant profits for the South and hence none for the North. George Weston, the abolitionist historian, whose *Progress of Slavery* appeared in 1857, berated southerners: "Refusing to see the true cause of their own misfortunes, and eager to attribute them to every cause but the right one, they insisted that they alone were the real producers of wealth, and that the North was thriving at their expense."[54] Weston went on to observe, "It has, without doubt, become the settled conviction of large numbers of persons in the slave States, that in some way or other, either through the fiscal regulations of the Government, or through the legerdemain of trade, the North has been built up at the expense of the South." According to Weston, the self-serving rationalizations by southerners avoided the obvious fact that the system of slavery, itself, caused southern poverty. Essentially, a slave society could only engage in agriculture and could not diversify into the promising areas of commerce and manufacturing. Weston concluded that eventually the higher efficiency of free labor would crowd the slave system into a small geographic area and greatly reduce its economic and political importance.

In a similar vein, Frederick Law Olmsted, after his southern sojourns between 1852 and 1854, vigorously denied the charge that northern business exploited the South. Olmsted asked, "How comes this capital, the return made by the world for the cotton of the South, to be so largely in the hands of northern men? The true answer is, that what these get is simply their fair commercial remuneration for the trouble of transporting cotton, transporting money, transporting the total amount of home comfort, little as it is, which the South gets for its cotton, from one part of the country to the other." Then Olmsted, in the fashion of some modern economist making light of neocolonial charges from the Third World, asked why, if northerners made exorbitant profits off the southern trade, "do not the planters transfer capital and energy to it from the plantations?" He concluded that northerners received only fair profits on a dispersed and hence costly trade.[55]

Olmsted emphasized that in the North profits were reinvested in machinery, while in the South profits on capital went back into buying more slaves and land. Sellers of slaves and land might have made productive investments with their proceeds, but Olmsted thought this unlikely. Most sales in the older slave states went to cover substantial debts. "The planters of the southwest are then, in fact, supplying the deficit of eastern production, taking their pay almost entirely in negroes," Olmsted argued, while by contrast, "the free West fills the deficit of the free eastern cereal production, but takes its pay in the manufactured goods, the fish, the oil, the butter and the importations of the free East."[56] For Olmsted, the fault lay not in the market system but in southerners' irrational attachment to slavery. He cautiously endorsed gradual emancipation.

Olmsted, like Helper, argued that slavery had eroded southern productivity. Fitzhugh agreed that southern productivity lagged behind that of the North, but he placed the blame on free trade itself. All three writers believed that a more diversified and urbanized economy was critical to the South's long-run growth. All argued that the immediate profitability of slavery provided a poor guide to the "comfort" of the community, but only Fitzhugh and Helper characterized the resulting situation as essentially colonial and dependent in nature. Despite his careful sociological explanation, Olmsted stopped short of agreeing. Unlike Fitzhugh and Helper, he saw no reason to label as unequal an exchange freely entered into.

King Cotton

In the 1850s, in sharp contrast to all those who argued about the sources of the South's economic difficulties, there stood a growing band of both southerners and northerners who essentially denied that the South had a problem. This school started with the claim that there was a new southern prosperity, which belied colonial arguments. They went on to offer a theoretical explanation based on the gains achieved through interregional dependency.

Somewhat surprisingly, it was a northerner, Ellwood Fisher of Cincinnati, who produced the most impressive example of this argument. His essay "The North and the South," published in *DeBow's Review* in

1849, received wide circulation in both regions. Fisher started virtually in the colonial vein, recounting how the tariff had decimated southern commerce: "The harbors of Norfolk, of Richmond, of Charleston and Savannah have been deserted for those of Philadelphia, New York and Boston; and New Orleans is the only Southern city that pretends to rival its Northern competitors. The grass is growing in the streets of those cities of the South."[57] Fisher then noted that northerners often equated this state of affairs to impoverishment and placed the blame on slavery: "The North and even many in the South, have assumed a decline in manufactures and commerce to be a decline in general prosperity. This is an error. The policy of the Federal government and the domestic institutions of the Southern States have indeed been unfavorable to the latter in those pursuits, but the agriculture of the South has maintained and advanced in prosperity beyond that of any other people."[58] He went on to anticipate the modern positive evaluation of the productivity of slave labor: "It has been through negro slavery that agriculture has been made, for the first time in the history of the world, so profitable and attractive as to render rural life the favorite of wealth as well of the mass of the people."[59] Fisher also added that a meaningful calculation of the per capita income of the South must consider only the white population. Finally, he claimed that inequality among whites was no greater in the South than in the North.

The editors of the *Southern Quarterly Review* also denied the poverty of the South: "Hitherto [planters] have devoted themselves exclusively to the more congenial occupation of agriculture, and not unwisely, since it has netted them fifteen per cent per annum on their capital. . . . In agriculture there is no charlatanry. We publish no seductive calculations. We build neither palaces nor cities; no subsidized press proclaims our feats."[60]

These defenders of southern prosperity asserted that slave labor provided an effective way to accumulate capital in a land-rich and labor-scarce country. Ironically, this claim followed nineteenth-century thinking on colonial relations. Edward Wakefield, the most prominent British economist to consider the matter, argued that in a land-rich colony people would, if left to themselves, disperse widely, creating a disorganized subsistence agriculture. To avoid this result and to generate a surplus, labor had to be concentrated geographically.[61] This surplus then could form the basis for the accumulation of capital. While not an advocate of slavery, Wakefield gave the South high marks for overcoming the major obstacle to capital accumulation in a new colony.

In his "Memoir on Slavery" Chancellor Harper, perhaps the best-known defender of slavery, made use of Wakefield's argument.

> In early states of society when people are thinly scattered over an extensive territory, the labor necessary to extensive works cannot be commanded. Men are independent of each other. Having the command of abundance of land, no one will submit to be employed in the service of his neighbor. No one, therefore, can employ more capital than he can use with his own hands, or those of his family, nor have an income much beyond the necessaries of life. There can, therefore, be little leisure for intellectual pursuits, or means of acquiring the comforts or elegances of life. It is hardly necessary to say, however, that if a man has the command of slaves, he may combine labor and use capital to any required extent, and therefore accumulate wealth.[62]

Harper went on to explicitly cite Wakefield's claim that "no colonies have been successfully planted without some sort of Slavery." This observation explained why only in the South had agriculture produced significant concentrations of wealth.

Following Wakefield, Harper argued that despite its low population density, the slave South had concentrated labor and accumulted capital. Far from being an impoverished colony, the South had created great wealth. Indeed, Harper suggested that the wealth of the South had made possible the development of the North. Southern slave labor had produced more than two-thirds of the nation's exports, which in turn had provided employment to northerners engaged in transport and finance, and the slaveholding states formed "the great market" for all northern industries. Harper concluded that northern prosperity and civilization had been "for the most part created by the existence of Slavery."[63]

This picture of the South as a prosperous region and the source of northern wealth led naturally to viewing the relation between North and South as one of mutually beneficial interdependence. Such an argument drew heavily on the classical interpretation of free trade. As sectional tensions mounted, this old argument became a favorite of Unionists, North and South.

Encouraged by the prosperity of the 1850s, some southerners went so far as to suggest that the tables had been turned. The denial of southern dependency prompted an assertion of northern dependency. This claim had always been just below the surface of certain versions of the colonial position. If the South, although exploited, supported the North, then the North had grown dependent on the South and not vice versa. And, by an easy extension, the argument might cover the cotton manufacturers of Great Britain as well. At least in the libertarian-agrarian version of the colonial critique, the injunction to resist dependency and seek independence had always presumed the substantial, even if exploited, strength of the region's producers. Such ideas easily drifted, with a little prosperity, into exaggerated notions of southern power.

Advocates of this new position had to deny many of the South's favorite complaints. First, they had to attack the argument that the region's staples could be grown easily elsewhere in the world. The success of southern cotton in the 1850s and the South's virtual monopoly of the world cotton market tended to support this claim. If no other region or nation could competitively grow cotton, then the northern and British manufacturing sectors could not exist without the South's cotton. James H. Hammond, who in the 1840s had so bewailed the colonial position of the South and especially of South Carolina, confidently told the North in 1858, "You dare not make war upon cotton. No power on earth dare make war upon it. Cotton is king."[64] As British experiments with cotton production in India and elsewhere proved problematic, southerners increasingly maintained that the manufacturers' efforts to find other sources of supply would prove futile.

A small shift in the ratio of supply to demand can greatly alter perceptions about power relations. The cotton planters, (like businessmen everywhere) extrapolated long-term trends from rather skimpy short-run data. Their theme of a wealthy and a potentially independent South continued to gain advocates throughout the 1850s, despite the region's past experience with volatile staples markets that should have made southerners more cautious.

Northern businessmen with commercial interests in the South became genuinely alarmed at the growing political tension between the two sections. In their plea for reconciliation they repeated many southern claims. In 1860 Thomas Kettell, a journalist and representative of New York's merchant and financial community, asserted that the North needed to appease the South. In his short work *Southern Wealth and Northern Profits,* he argued that while production occurred in the South, capital accumulated in the North. Kettell claimed that virtually all northern capital was derived from slave labor. Starting with the premises that "labor is the source of all wealth" and that "capital, in whatever shape it exists, is the surplus of production over consumption," Kettell, firmly in the vein of Wakefield, asserted, "The unaided labor of a man can produce for him very little more than his own requirements." From these propositions Kettell jumped to a startling conclusion: "all the wealth or capital existing has been the result of slave-labor, or of the working of capital originally derived from slave-labor."[65] Slaves worked intensely and consumed little. In Kettell's world no mystery surrounded the origins of an economic surplus; the surplus emerged from a simple matter of caloric arithmetic.

Echoing the colonial critique, Kettell catalogued the many mechanisms used by Great Britain and the North to tap the surplus produced by southern slavery. Before the Revolution, British regulations and British merchants had guaranteed that the American colonies kept little of the produce of American slavery. "The moment separation took place, however, New England became, to the South and slave-labor, what Britain had been"; and the recaptured capital provided the basis of manufacturing in New England.

According to Thomas Kettell the momentum of economic power had shifted. Manufacturing in both New England and Britain continually required the cotton of the South, grown with slave labor. Kettell saw no likely substitutes for southern cotton in the short run. He had no doubt that if the South closed off its commerce with the North it could achieve a great deal on its own. Just as the Revolution had created the incentive to domestic manufacturing in the North, so a separation of North and South would stimulate manufacturing in the South. While in the past the North had exploited the South, an important change loomed on the horizon, he said: "The South has commenced to make capital work at home. . . . In addition to its strength of position and natural resources, it is rapidly gaining wealth, and by so doing, creating a defence to the operation of Northern capital."[66]

This same theme of the awakening of a colonial South appeared in David Christy's famous 1860 essay, *Cotton Is King: or, Slavery in the Light of Political Economy.* Although Christy had acted as the Ohio agent of the American Colonization Society and presumably questioned the legitimacy of southern slavery, he nevertheless argued that slavery should not be destroyed. Cotton manufacturing had made southern slaves the driving force of much of the national economy. "The institution of slavery, at this moment, gives indications of a vitality that was never anticipated by its friends or foes," he declared. The South controlled the cotton supply, so crucial to textile manufacturing and this "monopoly" guaranteed the viability of slave agriculture.[67]

Christy contended that the staple-crop agriculture of the slave South provided a market for the agricultural produce of the North and West. Slavery, not the northern economy, constituted the driving, dynamic force in the country. This position gave to slavery a great power. "American slavery, though of little force unaided, yet properly sustained, is the greater central power, or energizing influence, not only of nearly all the industrial interests of our own country, but also of those of Great Britain and much of the Continent; and . . . if stricken from existence, the whole of these interests, with the advancing civilization of the age, would receive a shock that must retard their progress for years to come."[68]

The prosperity of the 1850s wedded northern and western farmers to cotton and slavery. This marriage of convenience required a continuing territorial expansion of the cotton culture to maintain its monopoly in expanding foreign markets. Restriction of American supplies could only encourage competition through high prices. From this logic came the cry for both new slave land and a reopened slave trade. In a curiously fatalistic manner, Christy concluded that, under the circumstances, the nation must allow this engine of "Christian civilization" to continue on its course. It was too late to turn back. The slaves must wait until the prosperity produced by their own enslavement had grown enough to allow "the universal elevation of the barbarous tribes."[69]

Kettell and Christy described an energetic and expansive southern economy, an assessment in sharp contrast to Olmsted's picture of a lethargic and unproductive society. These contradictory northern appraisals of the South reflected contradictory themes in the colonial critiques themselves. For years agrarians had claimed that wealth originated in the productive activities of agriculture. The exploitation the agrarians described robbed the productive classes for the benefit of the moneyed interests. On the other hand, the fear that dependency necessarily led to marginalization had an even longer history in the colonial critique. Olmsted and Beverley might easily have agreed on the shortcomings of southern agriculture. Thus, northern disputes about the productivity of the southern economy reflected longstanding southern uncertainties. The mercantilist version of the colonial critique had always argued that the South had to break with the staples economy and its traditional agriculture to increase productivity and reduce its dependency. From the beginning, however, the libertarian version had maintained that the South was productive, and had aimed its fire at northern manipulation of government and finance.

Throughout two centuries southerners had disputed the productivity of their economy. In the boom of the late 1850s southern confidence increased markedly. Not surprisingly, the arguments of Kettell and Christy met with considerable favor in the South, while Olmsted's aroused hostility. Despite the continuing growth of the industrial North, the years before the Civil War in the South and, especially, in the Southwest brought a new perception of economic buoyancy. Of course, much of this shift reflected the more prominent position of the new Southwest. Planters there had become accustomed to prosperity, and they suffered a good deal less angst than did their cousins in the old seaboard states. Even allowing for this phenomenon, however, the South as a whole gave over to an increasing optimism. The southern economy again seemed capable of capital accumulation on a broad scale.

George Fitzhugh, who had put together one of the finest statements on specialization and colonial relations, suddenly came over to King Cotton. Thus, we find him, on the eve of the Civil War, writing that for fifty years the South "has been more usefully, more industriously, more energetically, and more profitably employed than any people under the sun. Yet all the while she has been envying and wishing to imitate the little 'truck patches,' the filthy, crowded, licentious factories, the mercenary shopkeeping, and the slavish commerce of the North."[70] In the heady days immediately preceding the Civil War, this testimonial to southern productivity came from the same Fitzhugh who had explained the process whereby agricultural states were entrapped by free trade in a deadening specialization.

As the South moved toward secession it pulled in on itself and became impervious to external criticism. Increasingly, anything that belittled the region was considered subversive and disruptive. Every colonial argument that disparaged the traditional agriculture of the region thus became suspect. The South became a victim of a paranoid political style.[71] This mind-set demanded the complete vindication of southern institutions, especially of the slave plantation. Among secessionists in particular, the sufficiency of southern agriculture became a critical proposition in the argument for political independence. This tenet led naturally to a reemphasis on the agrarian nature of the southern economy.

While debates over the "causes" of secession will continue long into the future, economic historians now concentrate on southern concerns over the value of slave property in a union where slavery had become both a political and an economic issue. Sectional harangues between North and South increased the uncertainty surrounding the future of slavery and hence the capitalized value of slave labor.[72] Presumably, slaveowners in an independent South would find their chattel considerably more valuable. There can be little doubt that much of the support for secession came from such reasoning; but just as surely, that support continued the tradition of viewing the South as separate from and exploited by the North, a tradition that went back at least to the Revolution. For many secessionists the preservation of slavery provided a pretense to fight for southern political and economic independence, while for others the promise of a more prosperous South could be used to support an institution they felt was imperiled.[73] Whatever the subtler motives, there can be no doubt that, as the libertarian colonial argument devolved into a faith in King Cotton, the self-deprecatory quality of much southern economic thought receded. The new ideology, based on a significant, but most likely transitory, improvement in material conditions, represented an important social psychological event. Whether self-delusion or not, the King Cotton perspective released impressive energy among southern whites of diverse social classes. The emerging leadership of the Confederacy claimed a real plan for "decolonization," a plan built on a belief in the emerging strength of the region.

Secession promised territorial expansion. Much has been made of the thesis that the cotton economy needed geographic expansion to survive. More recently, this idea has come under heavy fire from economic historians arguing that the basic slave economy had ample land for expansion within its borders.[74] Moreover, even in the 1850s, southerners disagreed over land policies for the West. In this context the mentality of southern expansionism may have been more important than any pressing need for land.

Looking back at nineteenth-century imperial Britain from the mid-twentieth century, Joseph Schumpeter, a famous economist, argued that imperialist policy often flowed from a need to cement internal class relations and not from any narrow economic gains. The nationalism stimulated by expansion has value to a ruling class, even when colonies drain the treasury. In the case of the South such concerns may have contributed powerfully to the imperialist rhetoric of secession. For years small farmers had quarreled with slaveholders. Only in Virginia did these conflicts eventually lead to the political dissolution of the commonwealth, but they appeared in almost every southern state. The alliance of slaveowners and small farmers that had fought the Revolutionary War in the South had drawn strength from the promise of opening lands to the west and protecting the frontier. In the early nineteenth century, political tensions within the South had become far more complicated. It is doubtful that the promise of cheap land could really have motivated the small farmers of the South into rebellion in 1861, but the imagery of westward expansion carried a symbolic value more important than any plausible gains to be achieved from such a policy.

Rejecting the role of colonial province and asserting imperial ambition, the dream of an independent South stirred spirits. In the United States the frontier, whatever its economic value, had always had great symbolic appeal. Americans had come to equate territorial expansion with confidence and opportunity, if not always prosperity. A policy which settled for something less than expansionism would have admitted the peculiarity of the South's institutions and the derivative and colonial nature of its economy. Expansionist sentiment in the South, first within the context of union and then in the secessionist movement, carried with it a strong denial of southern imperfection.

Those who earlier had decried southern colonial dependency often belittled the region for its extravagant and wasteful agriculture, even to the point of bemoaning the abundance of land that prompted profligate husbandry. The new confidence engendered in the 1850s turned this argument around. Many secessionists from the Southwest, like John Quitman, of Mississippi, argued that the South needed geographic expansion. They did not apologize for the region's profligate use of its resources. For them the spread of slavery represented fulfillment of the South's destiny, not a sign of its improvidence. Over the years, the South had participated eagerly in the country's mood of expansionism. With the Mexican War and the annexation of Texas the South's attitude had increasingly taken on a more regional emphasis. In the 1850s Quitman and his collaborators in southern imperialism attempted to accelerate this tendency. Their schemes to absorb Cuba, Mexico, Nicaragua, and other well-populated parts of Latin America conveyed an almost visionary quality, governed not by plausibility but rather by the sense of a destiny. Incorporating the broader national faith into a willful southern policy changed the world view of many southerners. The colonial analogies had urged southerners to look beneath expansionism, to decipher its true meaning in terms of the exploitation of the South. The new ideology of expansion did not so much deny this past as build upon it—the South could move from colony to colonizer.

As rebellion became more likely, the relation between secession and the various colonial critiques became ever more delicate. A good deal of ink had been spilt in the late 1850s in argument on behalf of the power and potential of the southern economy. In their new mood, southerners rejected the self-criticism implicit in the colonial analogy. Yet in a drive for independence they could refer to only one clear historical precedent for rebellion—the Revolutionary War. Early secessionists in South Carolina repeatedly compared their present with the revolutionary past. Claims of northern oppression allowed the secessionists to cloak themselves in the unquestionable rights of colonial subjects rebelling to achieve independence, to win self-determination. At once they mounted a moral refutation of the North and encouraged all southern whites to bind together. The secessionists mixed the colonial critiques with a celebration of southern power and vague promises of empire. This heady mixture proved just the thing to motivate thousands of poor whites to fight for a system that was actually of dubious value to them.

Chapter Four

A Conquered Province

In his inaugural address to the Southern Economic Association, in October of 1933, Tipton Snavely, the first president of that body, concluded that "during the last half of the last century the South did not contribute her fair share of economic writing or teaching, due to the devastated conditions which followed the Civil War."[1] Some years earlier, the historian William Dodd had reached a similar conclusion. He ascribed the sudden reversal in southern economic thought to the ravages of war. "Men who should have become active teachers and original students along advanced lines," wrote Dodd, "have been feeding and clothing themselves and their people."[2] No southern economist from this period earned even a footnote in the history of economic thought.[3] Postbellum southern economics became, even more than before the Civil War, the province of men of affairs—politicians, journalists, and businessmen.

For ten years or more after the Civil War, the bulk of southern social commentary dealt with the political issues of Reconstruction. The race problem dominated concerns. White southern critics of Reconstruction vilified the Republican party but avoided serious economic analysis of the southern predicament. This widely scattered literature demonstrated a flare for spirited denunciation of carpetbaggers and scalawags. While the rhetoric drew on the longstanding theme of colonial dependency, it made little use of the store of analytical insights recorded by earlier writers.

For their part, Republicans in the South often defended their railroad building and other expenditures as being in the interest of southern economic development. Accusing the slaveowners of having ruined the antebellum southern economy, the Republicans promised a great deal; "railroads, canals, factories, workshops, schools, family farms, cities, mineral development, and an influx of northern capital poured from Republicans' speeches."[4]

These claims won little support among the bulk of white southerners, who were obsessed with the desire to rid the South of carpetbagger and scalawag alike. But once the Democratic party had successfully achieved hegemony, the goal of achieving greater economic growth again commanded attention. Especially in the urban centers of the South, waking to commercial and industrial possibilities, a need for a well-articulated ideology emerged. In this environment a group of journalists, proclaiming faith in a "New South," aggressively advanced their own interpretation of southern dependency. These journalists, from Baltimore, New Orleans, Louisville, and Atlanta, addressed an audience that was largely urban and middle class. Earlier urban journalists had written on southern economic matters, most notably Jacob Cardozo, of Charleston. Unlike Cardozo and other antebellum editors, the advocates of the New South no longer took for granted that planters would provide the economic leadership. They did not believe that the future of their cities depended on the well-being of large landholders. Indeed, all of them campaigned for a new, urban-led South of modest diversified farms enriched by commercial and industrial development.

Henry Grady and the New Southern Dependency

Henry Grady, of the Atlanta *Constitution,* became the principal spokesman for the New South movement. Grady had just the right character to champion new ideas; as one not-so-friendly commentator has put it, "he had an intelligence superior enough to activate his contemporaries without being so profound or original as to baffle them."[5]

Grady inherited a background well suited to his chosen task. His father, William Grady, had been a successful businessman in Athens, Georgia, before the Civil War. Although the elder Grady had owned slaves, he had had no extensive agricultural investments and had opposed secession. Nevertheless, he organized a military company at the outbreak of the war, and he died of wounds received at the Battle of Petersburg in 1864. The soldier's son completed his undergraduate studies at the University of Georgia and did a year of graduate work at the University of Virginia. Although his family might have preferred a career in law and politics, Grady entered journalism. Grady's business activities always remained on a modest scale. While he lived comfortably, he did not amass a large fortune.[6] Despite all his writings in defense of the acquisitive spirit, Grady remained more of a worker than a dealer.

Henry Grady embodied the best traits of Victorian charity. According to Joel Chandler Harris, his colleague at the *Constitution,* Grady had "love and sympathy for the poor and lowly, for the destitute and the

forlorn." Grady could not understand "why, in the economy of Provi-
dence, some human beings should be rich and happy and others poor
and friendless."[7] This concern extended to the black population of the
South. "He was fond of the negroes because they were dependent, his
heart went out to them because he understood and appreciated their
position."[8] Harris did not suggest exactly why Grady should have developed this sensitivity to the "dependence" of the black South, but
throughout the region's history concerns over southern economic dependency had been intricately entwined with reflections on black
dependence.

Grady carefully nourished the memory of the antebellum South. His
co-worker Harris ably assisted this effort with his famous Uncle Remus
stories. In Grady's writings and speeches he never belittled or vilified
the slaveowning class of that earlier period, yet he explicitly attributed
the South's historic dependency to the region's commitment to slave
agriculture.[9]

Thus, in his famous speech to the New England Club of New York
in 1886, Grady proclaimed:

> The South found her jewel in the toad's head of defeat. The shackles
> that had held her in narrow limitations fell forever when the shackles
> of the negro slave were broken. Under the old regime the negroes
> were slaves to the South; the South was a slave to the system. The
> old plantation, with its simple police regulations and feudal habit, was
> the only type possible under slavery. . . . The old South rested every-
> thing on slavery and agriculture, unconscious that these could neither
> give nor maintain healthy growth.[10]

While ever respectful, the substance of Grady's position came quite
close to the radical arguments made by Hinton Helper before the war
and the Republicans after the war. Slavery had in practice enslaved the
slaveowners and their region; it had produced a specialized economy and
offered no way for industrial development to take hold.[11] The economic
drawbacks of slavery became a stock part of the New South ideology.
Hoke Smith, Grady's one-time friend and then rival in journalism and
politics, echoed Grady's line when he said: "Had it not been for the
institution of slavery . . . the South, with natural resources in its favor
in 1860, would have been the greatest manufacturing and mining, as
well as agricultural, section in the Union."[12] And Richard H. Edmonds,
the Baltimore chronicler of the New South movement, returned to this
theme again and again in his *Manufacturers' Record.*[13]

This argument, considered virtually treasonous before the war, now promised a quick resolution of regional problems. By attributing southern dependency to slavery, Grady and other New South advocates argued that the major barriers to southern development had fallen with the old regime. The Civil War became a blessing in disguise. In Grady's view, the demise of slavery unfettered the native energies of the region. He told of an "old gentleman" from the Sea Islands who prided himself on the quality of the turkeys he grew. When Grady suggested that the turkeys must have produced a considerable income, the man responded, "Income! Why, my young friend, no southern gentleman ever sold poultry!" But Grady claimed to have heard from the old gentleman's son: "Sell poultry? Well I should say so! He sells the eggs, then he sells the meat, then he sells the feathers, then he has the soil of the poultry-house scraped up and sold."[14] Grady never tired of such contrasts. In this he represented a logical extension of the long tradition of southern jeremiads against the laziness of the region. Like many before him, including Jefferson, he held that slavery had undermined ambition and energy. This regional lethargy had left the South open to exploitation.

Ultimately, its proponenets felt, the New South's prosperity would depend on the development of modern industry. The economic impact of slavery had prevented the South from participating in the growth of manufacturing, despite the region's possessing all the resources necessary. Here Grady harked back to that favorite antebellum theme, the stock southern lament of extravagant importation from the North. No one portrayed southern industrial dependency with better humor than Henry Grady. In describing a funeral in Pickens County, he bemoaned:

> They buried him in the midst of a marble quarry: they cut through solid marble to make his grave; and yet a little tombstone they put above him was from Vermont. They buried him in the heart of a pine forest, and yet the pine coffin was imported from Cincinnati. They buried him within touch of an iron mine, and yet the nails in his coffin and the iron in the shovel that dug his grave were imported from Pittsburgh. They buried him by the side of the best sheep-grazing country on the earth, and yet the wool in the coffin bands and the coffin bands themselves were brought from the North. The South didn't furnish a thing on earth for that funeral but the corpse and the hole in the ground.[15]

Proponents of the New South argued that all this dependency could be changed. The bountiful resources of the region, the improved transportation system, and most importantly the demise of slavery would now allow a wholesome development of manufacturing. First among industries, the South would bring the textile mills to the cotton fields.

At the center of his political economy was Grady's belief that the South could use northern capital to finance its new departure. Before the Civil War some southerners had hoped to secure financing from Europe in order to develop direct trade. Grady envisioned a much more extensive process of economic development based on outside financing. He invited northerners to invest in transport, resources, and manufacturing. Although he continually celebrated the achievements of southern industrialists, he clearly thought that southern capital accumulation would by itself prove insufficient to sustain rapid regional growth.

In the latter half of the nineteenth century, interregional and international capital mobility had expanded greatly as absentee capital financed a host of direct industrial investments around the world. Most notably, southerners observed the constructive role eastern capital played in the economic development of the Midwest. Yet, inviting northern capital to exploit the South surely entailed serious risks. The New South's effort to lure outside capital to the region made sense only if the growth induced in this fashion would ultimately free the South of its longstanding dependency. This now-classic question in economic development haunts many Third World countries today. The New South advocates faced it at a time when capital mobility for industrial investment was still new.

Of course, Grady's strategy could proceed only if the New South did actually attract northern capital. Grady aggressively courted northern financiers and industrialists. When in the North, he explicitly based sectional reconciliation on mutual interest in a northern-financed program of southern economic development. He believed that far into the future the return on industrial capital would remain significantly higher in the South than in the North. With the North now presumably freed of prejudice against the South, northern capital would naturally flow toward Dixie. "We have . . . hung out latchstring," said Grady, "to you and yours."[16]

In the South, Grady gave this argument a different twist, shifting the emphasis from reconciliation to a new regional competition, in which the South would have the advantage of drawing on both its own and northern capital. The South would use the North's capital to reclaim its rightful position in the Union.[17] Grady predicted that northern-financed industrial development would stimulate urban growth.[18] The cities of the South would finally provide a market, encouraging southern agricultural diversification. As rural areas prospered, they would in turn provide markets for southern industry. A new more independent South would emerge.

In all of their speculations, Grady and his colleagues suppressed any fears they may have had of a new dependency. They avoided any suggestion that foreign capital might exploit domestic labor. The colonial critiques on which they built had focused on exploitation through unfair taxation, unequal exchange, and exorbitant service charges. Advocates of the New South saw in the increasing mobility of capital an important opportunity to raise regional productivity and create regional markets. They hoped that an industrialized economy, even if industrialized with northern capital, would prove robust and dynamic.

While Grady and his friends optimistically viewed the prospects of attracting northern capital, they could not avoid acknowledging the deepening plight of southern agriculture. When cotton's hold on the region's farms did not subside over the years, but rather intensified, the New South enthusiasts had to consider an embarrassing reality. They reluctantly concluded that the increased importance of cotton production reflected the insufficiency of agricultural credit and threatened a renewed dependency. Farmers in the postwar South had little collateral. They could obtain credit only from small merchants, who themselves commanded credit only with difficulty. Rural banks were virtually nonexistent. As a result southern agriculture had to adjust to an extremely conservative insistence that farmers and tenants commit themselves to the cash crop. High cotton prices immediately after the war had encouraged this trend, but as prices slumped farmers had greater and greater difficulty extricating themselves from the credit trap.

This interpretation of southern agricultural developments appeared in the press throughout the New South. The basic story still commands wide respect as an explanation of the persistent problems of southern agriculture between the Civil War and World War II.[19] New South advocates linked this analysis to renewed calls for crop diversification. Grady contrasted Lancaster County, Pennsylvania, with North Carolina. A farmer in Lancaster County identified the secret of its prosperity as tobacco, while a farmer in North Carolina told Grady that tobacco had cursed the state. According to Grady, "the difference was that in Carolina, tobacco was made the sole crop. In Lancaster it is made the crown and money crop of a diversified agriculture. The one crop system never made any people prosperous."[20]

The call for diversification yielded little in the way of practical results. Although uncomfortably aware of the problem, Grady failed to perceive concrete solutions. Without a new system of financing, the notion of turning the impoverished tenants of the South into diversified general farmers remained chimerical at best. In desperation, the New South writers even suggested the old and unlikely remedy of self-sufficient farms producing for their own consumption. More often, they reassured the farmers with the promise that eventually the development of urban centers would guarantee them large and diversified markets. As the 1890s approached, few farmers could have taken such promises seriously.

The fundamental problem of southern agriculture, identified by Grady and others, often got lost in the torrent of New South boosterism. In Grady's habitually cheerful speeches the darker truths percolated through only with difficulty. In the midst of a highly optimistic discussion of the South's future, Grady fell into the following observation:

> The Comstock lode is, perhaps, the richest spot of the earth. And yet, all about it is bleakness and misery. Its teeming riches have gone to build up distant cities and carry great currents, of which the miners, gasping in its depths, hear but dim report. The cotton field is a new Comstock lode. And for years the farmers fought in destitution, as the miners fight, while the bales of cotton, as of silver, went to enrich the cities beyond their horizon.[21]

Grady concluded that at last farmers had "learned how to catch the ebbing sea at the edge of the patch, and throw its enriching flood back on their own fields." Despite this optimistic pap, the haunting metaphor of the miners' struggle testified to Grady's appreciation of rural dependency.

In the story of the Pickens County funeral Grady had suggested that rural markets could provide a significant stimulus to southern industrialization, but now it seemed clear that an impoverished agricultural sector could generate little demand if any. Quite the contrary, prosperity on the farm had to await the growth of urban markets. Without strong regional demand, prospects for development obviously were worse. The intensifying dependency of southern agriculture in the late nineteenth century raised a challenge that journalists only reluctantly acknowledged.

Grady and proponents of the New South were left open to the embarrassing charge that they were merely fronting for northern capital, which was out to loot the region further. In this view, the New South spokesmen, far from struggling against southern dependency, had forged an ideology that accepted dependency.[22] The New South writers made an easy target for such agrarian criticisms. Their boosterism grated. Their promises never materialized. They underestimated the dangers of northern investment in the South and overestimated the South's ability to retain an increased portion of its surplus. The level of analysis in the New South writings, including those of Grady in Atlanta, Henry Watterson in Louisville, and Walter Hines Page in North Carolina, written largely for newspapers and magazines, fell considerably below the best economic writings of the antebellum period. Propagandizing a new world view, they had little time to work out the subtleties of the argument.

Despite its often disingenuous Victorian simplicity, a striking quality remains in these writers' work. As much as they attempted to force the harsh realities of a continuing dependency into neatly packaged and uplifting ideas, the harshness of those realities only became clearer by contrast. For all their claim that southern dependency had disappeared with the demise of slavery, their own observations showed a renewed dependency coupled to the new, highly exploitative labor and credit system. The best of them, like Henry Grady, acknowledged and spoke out against this new burden.

Populism: The Belated Economics of Agrarianism

In the 1880s champions of the New South took a conciliatory, although ambivalent, attitude toward their old enemies in the North and East. Southern populists of the 1890s left no doubt about their ties to an older agrarian tradition and its analysis of regional dependency.[23] "The Eastern States have always been against Jeffersonian principles," the firebrand Tom Watson of Georgia announced. "They have always been for Hamilton and Federal doctrine; they have always been for money legislation as against manhood legislation; they have always been in favor of bonds and banks, and for special protection of capital; they have always been in favor of legislation that increases the debt and makes it harder to pay; which diminishes the money and thereby adds to its value."[24]

In the Northeast, they understood that such speeches embodied a new sectionalism. Frederick Emory Haynes, of the Harvard economics department, concluded in 1896 that "we need not be surprised at the appearance of a cleavage between the sections whose relations are mainly those of debtor and creditor."[25] Haynes went on to argue: "In the influence of the policy of the federal government, in the industrial relations of the East with the West and South, and in the economic changes that have come from the closer settlement of the West and the industrial transformation of the South, we have the principal influences that have produced the new sectionalism."[26] Haynes felt he had ample evidence on which to base his conclusion, most notably the geographic distributions of Populist electoral successes. And, although Haynes did not find it necessary, he might have easily drawn on the fiery Populist denunciations of Wall Street and the eastern plutocracy.

The core of populist thought harkened back to the old agrarian distinction between producers and nonproducers. The populists knew, just as John Taylor had suspected, that the division between these two broad classes still fell along regional lines. Southern populists had little patience with complicated theories of unequal exchange. Quite simply, the wealth of the North had been stolen from the agrarian regions through the use of the federal government. Again, Tom Watson:

> Use your eyes. Look about you. See things as they are. Where is the bulk of the wealth of the nation? In that portion of it which nature did the least for — New England. How did bleak, barren New England come to be so rich? She made the laws to suit herself, and these laws took the prosperity of the South and West and gave it to the capitalists of the East and North.[27]

Of course, the tariff played a significant role in this transfer of wealth. The flag of the first farmers' alliance in Texas had as one of its mottos "Free Trade."[28] But the populists had identified another, even more important source of rural problems. They strongly believed that the banking and monetary system impoverished the farmer. Just as the financial interest after the revolutionary war had forced the federal assumption of otherwise devalued paper, the bankers of the East after the Civil War had maneuvered the country back onto a gold standard, thus deflating the currency, constraining credit, and intensifying the real burden of rural indebtedness. In the *National Economist*, the short-lived organ of Populist political economy, farmers read, "There is now, and has been for over a quarter of a century, a steady transfer of the values produced in the West and South to the East and North; . . . the agricultural sections are being systematically robbed by a false financial system for the benefit of the protected sectors."[29]

Despite their criticism of the Northeast, the populist movement had no interest in challenging that region for industrial supremacy. Indeed, the populists explicitly rejected the New South dream of bringing the factories to the fields. As Tom Watson suggested, they consciously drew their inspiration from the agrarian economics of Jefferson. They accepted, indeed welcomed, a worldwide division of labor. Southern populists had little interest in mercantilist efforts to balance their regional economy. They desired to improve the channels of commerce.

Populists eagerly sought national and international markets for their cash crops. They explicitly denied the South suffered because of economic specialization. They felt that it was dependence on monopolized transport and finance, not an imbalance of the regional economy, that left farmers prostrate. If farmers could tame these monsters, through either cooperatives or the agency of the federal government, then they could achieve an idyllic agrarian community, untainted by the evils of urban, industrial society. In 1891 Leonidas F. Livingston, president of the Georgia State Alliance, contributed a piece entitled "The Needs of the South" to *The Farmers' Alliance History and Agricultural Digest,* a compendium of populist writings. Livingston stated that "the development of the South" meant the development of "rural sections." Nature limited that development to the pursuit of agriculture. In Livingston's view, those who argued that the manufactories of the world could or should be transferred to the South made a serious mistake. Livingston went on to give a solid free-trade argument that southern classicists, like Cooper and Dew, would have endorsed heartily: "God never intended that one simple section of this world should ever be independent of other sections. We are tied together thus by nature, and the largest amount of happiness and prosperity depends upon the freedom and interchange of ideas and products."[30] Livingston did call for a modest diversification of southern agriculture, but only because the greedy controlled transportation and commodity speculation. "When absolute control by the government of the transportation of this country can be had, then an interchange of products, with the greatest possible profit to the producer, with no gambling or speculative prices to the consumer, will demonstrate that the products of the one section so peculiarly adapted thereto can be exchanged with other sections at a profit."[31]

Harry Tracy, editor of the *Southern Mercury,* made an even more explicit argument: If cotton farmers diversified their production, then how would wheat, corn, and hog producers be able to buy cotton? Diversification represented a move away from civilization. Commerce made possible a productive division of labor. State and national policy must aim at perfecting commerce, not destroying specialization.[32]

The southern populists knew that the world needed cotton. In this respect they, like the secessionists, firmly believed in King Cotton. While modest diversification might be useful, it could not provide a basic solution to southern problems. If a prosperous agriculture required a valuable cash crop, why were cotton farmers in such difficulty? The populist response centered characteristically on the exploitation of producers by nonproducers. The nonproductive sectors of the economy, especially transportation and finance, should exist only to aid producers, but railroad monopolies and financial speculation had subverted these handmaidens to "Industry."

The capitalists of the Northeast told the farmers that they had simply produced too much; hence, agricultural prices had fallen. The populists hotly denied this theory of overproduction. As long as honest men desired to work and stood willing to exchange their produce for that of other honest workers there could be no overproduction. The problem lay not in production but in distribution. The artificial monopolies of finance and transport robbed the people, reduced their purchasing power and led to underconsumption. W. Scott Morgan, of Arkansas, made the basic case in his *History of the Wheel and Alliance and the Impending Revolution*:

> Over-production is impossible so long as the wants of the human family are unsupplied. Rather call it under-consumption. It is the proper term. The product of one thing creates a demand for another, inasmuch as the producer desires to exchange it for something else which he needs. This creates a demand for a medium of exchange and means of transportation. Medium of exchange and facilities for transportation are the two principal agents of distribution. These agents should exist in proportion to production. A proper system of distribution will overcome so-called "over-production."[33]

The Southern Alliance hit on one way to improve the channels of distribution: cooperatives. Throughout the South the Southern Alliance launched a major effort to build cooperatives.[34] By replacing "the middlemen," the alliance hoped to free its farmer membership from the exorbitant interest and charges of the multiple intermediate exchanges that characterized commerce in the South. Yet, the cooperatives never delivered on their promise. The practical problems of running large-scale businesses, the hostility of the financial community, and a serious national economic downturn undermined the cooperative movement.[35] After achieving only minor gains for their members, suballiance cooperatives found themselves forced to close.

Frustrated in the effort to construct its own system of distribution, the Alliance, led by Charles W. Macune, reasoned that the banks and the gold standard had produced the cooperatives' financial problems, and those of the farmers themselves. Macune, Tracy, and others now argued that only a complete overhaul of the financial system could make possible a free and uninhibited commerce, which would in turn guarantee rural prosperity. The Populists went beyond a symbolic hostility to financial institutions. They began by building on widely circulated, if not academically approved, economic theories of the day. They supported bimetallism—allowing silver as well as gold to act as a base for expanding the money supply. They called for the abolition of the national banks, because those banks had unduly restricted credit. Finally, they moved to rebuild the financial system of the country on a novel plan aimed at linking the issue of money not to the business conditions of the city but to those of the country. They tried also to alter the crop lien system that the New South editors could only bewail.

Dr. Charles W. Macune, although not born a southerner, had come to Texas as a young man. He took up the practice of both law and medicine. Macune, a first-rate organizer, quickly rose through the ranks of the Texas Alliance. As president of the Southern Alliance, formed in 1887, he launched the major campaign that organized the cotton belt. He had been one of the founders and the business manager of the Texas Alliance Exchange and knew from first-hand experience the difficulties of financing cooperatives. He consistently held that the alliance must address the needs of all farmers, including the poorest. He had wanted to allow the Texas Alliance Exchange to extend credit to poorer farmers, but this plan had failed because the alliance had been unable to raise the required capital funds. As a result, Macune came to believe that the goals of the alliance could be achieved only if the federal government put its powers to the service of the farmers.[36]

In 1889 at the St. Louis meeting of the Southern Alliance, the Northern Alliance, and the Knights of Labor, Macune's "Committee on the Monetary System" (consisting exclusively of southerners) presented a subtreasury plan that Macune had designed with the particular concerns of the South in mind. The subtreasury approach attempted to link the nation's money supply to the need for agricultural credit. The committee report, echoing John Taylor of Caroline, asserted: "The Financial Policy of the General Government seems today to be peculiarly adapted to further the interests of the Speculating Class, at the expense and to the manifest detriment of the Productive Class." By that policy "a privileged class can, by means of the power of money to oppress, exact from Labor all that it produces except a bare subsistence."[37]

More specifically, the committee found that in the harvest months the supply of money generally proved insufficient to sustain the large increase in agricultural transactions at that time of year. "The class that controls the volume of the Circulating Medium desire to purchase these Agricultural products for speculative purposes, so they reduce the volume of money by hoarding, in the face of the augmented demand, and thereby advance the exchangeable value of the then inadequate volume of money." The need for money rose in the fall, but the money supply contracted. With little money in circulation, agricultural prices declined sharply. Farmers under heavy debts regularly found themselves forced to sell at low prices, oppressed by the power of money. Speculators bought farm products cheaply to sell in the winter for high prices.[38]

According to Macune and the committee, the answer lay in linking the quantity of money in circulation to the "actual addition to the wealth of the Nation presented by Agriculture at harvest time." The government, recognizing the insufficiency of the supply of gold, already allowed banks to expand the money supply in their own interest. The subtreasury plan instead would base the expansion of the money supply firmly on the productiveness of agriculture. Every county with more than half a million dollars—worth of agricultural produce each year would become the seat of a subtreasury, along with required warehouses and elevators for storage. Farmers would be able to store their crop and receive storage certificates and a one-year currency loan against 80 percent of the stored crop at 1 percent annual interest plus modest handling charges. Thus, farmers could arrange to sell their crop at the most advantageous time and still pay off pressing debts.

The headline in the *National Economist,* the newspaper of the Southern Alliance, modestly announced: "EUREKA! Key to the Solution of the Industrial Problem of the Age."[39] A large part of the membership agreed. The subtreasury plan clearly addressed the traditional southern concerns with both the paper interest and financial indebtedness, concerns extending back to the eighteenth century and earlier. The plan's southern focus riled midwestern populists, whose greatest debts were farm mortgages, not crop liens. They had to lobby within the alliance to extend the subtreasury plan to include real estate as collateral.[40]

Even before the Civil War, southerners had noted an apparent insufficiency of ready money to handle the marketing of the cotton crop. Like Macune they had concluded that the financial interests of the North and East manipulated the scarcity of funds for their own purposes. Thus, in 1852 a member of the Virginia House of Delegates complained, "The price, the worth, the market value of all we and the people we represent own of every kind of property, is dependent upon the speculative pleasure of the Merchants, the Bankers, and Brokers of New York. And why? Because Wall Street can depress the money market when it pleases." The subtreasury plan attacked this old dependence in the late-nineteenth-century context of crop liens and falling cotton prices. Macune and his associates meant the new system to be revolutionary. They meant to give back control of financial institutions to the people. Once freed of speculative manipulations, the independent farmers would be able to rebuild the agrarian republic.[41]

Southern farmers studied political economy in order to understand how the Wall Street financiers were robbing them. And Macune gave them plenty to study. The *National Economist* ran a regular feature on political economy with articles devoted to mercantilism (bad), Adam Smith on free trade (good), and John Stuart Mill on property (good). Jeffersonian Republicans had known that the national debt and banks worked against producers, but they had not known how to construct a monetary system to work for that class. The subtreasury plan spoke directly to this question.

The subtreasury plan and other examples of the populist concern with monetary reform grew out of an abiding faith that the root cause of rural difficulties lay in financial manipulation. Populists wanted to rebuild the financial system to support their own specialized commodity production. Moreover, they believed that these revolutionary changes would ultimately benefit urban workers as well. Despite misgivings among their allies in the Knights of Labor (selling no final product, the Knights feared that an expanded money supply would raise the cost of living without raising their wages), populists argued that the urban activities of manufacturing and commerce were dependent on rural productivity and prosperity. William Jennings Bryan, in his famous "Cross of Gold" speech in 1896, offered sentiments shared by the vast majority of southern populists: "The great cities rest upon our broad and fertile prairies. Burn down your cities and leave our farms, and your cities will spring up again as if by magic; but destroy our farms and the grass will grow in the streets of every city in the country."[42] In an agrarian version of a trickle-down theory the populists held that all would prosper if agriculture could be strengthened. Where New South advocates looked to industrialization to stimulate agriculture, the populists eagerly plotted to aid agriculture for the common good.

While, in their agrarian view, cities depended on the country side, populists nevertheless acknowledged the impressive efficiency of urban production. They generally denied that a regional redistribution of manufacturing would achieve any higher efficiency or prosperity. Given their strong faith in competitive market forces, populists had little reason to question the geographic distribution of productive economic activity.

Southern populists totally ignored the arguments of Fitzhugh and other southerners as to the limited potential for productivity growth in southern agriculture. Focused on combating various theories of "overproduction," they had little reason to consider problems of insufficient productivity. The dependency they spoke of was a dependency on eastern finance and monopoly, nurtured by corrupt (meaning sectionally favoritist) government. They saw a program of limited nationalization and financial reform as sufficient to the task. Here, as elsewhere, populists struggled to find solutions within a basic market economy.

Given that the southern populists' goals were regional, their proposal to nationalize the country's railroads had a regional purpose. Southern agrarian hopes for prosperous regional specialization had always rested on cheap transportation. Where Jefferson had looked to open and cheap transoceanic shipping to maintain American agriculture, the populists took much the same stance toward the railroads, which by the 1890s had laid over forty thousand miles of track in the South. The fathers of populists had hoped that subsidies to private railroads would suffice, but the populists discovered that the railroads, like the merchants and the banks, took their pound of flesh.

The problems of rural isolation involved more than just getting goods to market. Populists sought to build rural communities. As W. Scott Morgan put it: "Few who have not been residents of the country can rightly understand the monotony of the farmer's life. . . . The Order [the Farmers' Alliance] proposes to change this state of affairs, and render the farmers and their families one of the greatest services towards making his life happy that can be done for him. It offers them the means of improving their social intercourse, of adding to their pleasures, and of improving their condition mentally as well as socially."[43] The Southern Alliance built on local participation in regular biweekly meetings. Its leadership viewed the social aspect of the alliance as crucial. Part political rally, part school, with more than a dash of religion thrown in, suballiance meetings sought to bind together the rural farmers in a celebration of their economic role as producers.[44] Some of the populist leaders may have regarded these social activities as merely a useful base for economic and (subsequently) political organizing. In general, however, the populist commitment to a caring and ethical community seems to have been genuine. The membership at large viewed the golden rule and other Christian moral notions as the foundation for the populist social and economic program.

The ethical sentiment and sincerity of the populist movement notwithstanding, the populist conception of community ultimately remained a shallow one. While emphasizing cooperation, southern populists remained highly individualistic. They sought no community of interdependence. Their cooperatives related to consumption and sales, not production. The southern populists explicitly denied the ability of the local community to support a full division of labor. In contrast to the early mercantilists and George Fitzhugh, their acceptance of regional specialization left a localism based on similarity, not reciprocity. While it must seem a rather far-fetched comparison, the populist community shared elements with the modern suburban municipality. Producing for distant markets, southern farmers, like metropolitan suburbanites, shared consumption but not labor.

This theme, of course, haunted all the libertarian versions of the colonial critique. The South might be exploited as a whole, but it struggled for the economic independence of individuals. Curiously, the conditions of the late nineteenth century demanded that the projected agrarian independence be sustained by a powerful federal government capable of nationalizing railroads and warehousing the staple crops of the country. Perhaps, as some contemporaries claimed, the populist political program amounted to a contradiction; but if so, there had already been hints of this contradiction in Jefferson's Louisiana Purchase and Calhoun's Bonus Bill.

That the southern populist theme, contradictions and all, proved appealing to western farmers simply underscored the basic logic of the older agrarian position. Freed of the defense of slavery, southern farmers sought to complete the western alliance they had so long desired. That alliance lasted long after the populist movement had passed. From a people's party it declined into an agricultural lobby. Although the farmers of the South and West finally obtained many of the programs the Populists sought, their gains did not form the base of a renewed agrarian republic but only underscored their increasingly dependent position in the national economy.

From Populism to Demagoguery

The decline of southern populism paved the way for those extreme forms of demagoguery that have plagued the region for the better part of the

twentieth century. Disenfranchisement of African-Americans represented the most tragic consequence of this unholy alliance. Angered by
the continuing advance of urban-industrial America, the rural South
took great pleasure in their demagogues' excoriating of Yankee business.
Rejecting the promises of New South spokesmen, those demagogues made
use of populist rhetoric and, through that vocabulary, the libertarian
versions of the colonial critique. Indeed, in critical respects they even
made contributions to it.

No single individual better personified the shift from populism to
demagoguery than Tom Watson of Georgia. Once a leader of a powerful
movement of social reform, Watson ended his life glorying in southern
racism, anti-Catholicism, and anti-Semitism. Strangely, the rhetoric of
dependency stood him in good stead throughout this long voyage.

Watson had early decried the penetration of northern capital into
the southern economy. By the turn of the century the South had actually
begun to experience some of the social dislocations of industrialization.
When the South did manage to establish a textile industry, Tom Watson
saw little to celebrate.

> Sometimes our editors go into ecstasies because a New England cotton
> mill has come down South—the northern capitalist has brought his
> money South and built another cotton mill down here and, oh, they
> go into raptures, jubilating! What difference does it make to you whether
> the northern manufacturer comes down South to rob you or stays up
> yonder and robs you! I believe if robbery's . . . to go on at all, I would
> prefer for him to stay in the North, where he would grind up his own
> little children into dividends and not come down here to the South,
> where our corrupt legislatures allow them to grind up our own children
> into dividends.[45]

This new direct exploitation of the region by northern capital, far
from providing meaningful economic development, simply robbed an
agrarian people of their traditional way of life. Only a few southerners
profited, and their profits gave further proof of the colonial status of the
region. More explicitly than most of his contemporaries, Watson focused
on the role of the southern compradores in furthering northern business
interests.

> Just as the English maintain their conquest of India by taking into
> copartnership with themselves a certain percentage of Hindus, so the
> North holds the South in subjection by enlisting southern capitalists
> and politicians. They put money into our daily newspapers; they sub-

sidize such organs as *The Manufacturer's Record*; they buy up our
railroads; they capitalize our mills; they finance our street railways;
they supply our banks, — always taking southern men in with them
to a certain extent, and they appoint some of our politicians to good
positions. United themselves, the northern capitalists divide the southerners, and thus rule and despoil the South.[46]

Sure of the basic productivity and value of agricultural work, Watson
saw no reason to support the industrialization of the South and certainly
no reason to encourage the migration of northern capital southward. But
he offered no plan to arrest such development. Like other populists,
he felt that once the unfair systems of tariff, finance, and monopoly
had been dealt with, the country—with the possible exception of the
Northeast—would return to agrarian pursuits.

Even if all of the populist demands had been won, the expansion of
American industry would not have been checked. Watson and other
southerners raised on the agrarian faith confronted major predicaments.
The industrial society they had so feared and hated continued to expand
all around them. The farmers they had championed found themselves
reduced to a minority of the labor force. The institutions of an industrial
society invaded the South and West, bringing many of the problems
agrarians had predicted. The colonial character of the southern economy
intensified as northern capital penetrated the region. Yet even as the
truth of their broader arguments became clearer and clearer (even winning over major urban support in the form of the progressive movement),
the relevance of their program receded.

Between 1900 and 1920 the labor force employed in agriculture in
the United States declined absolutely, while the total labor force grew
by more than a third and manufacturing employment almost doubled.
By 1920 manufacturing workers actually outnumbered agricultural workers. Even in the South, eight of the fourteen states experienced declines
in their agricultural labor forces over these two decades. As a share of
the U.S. labor force, agriculture had moved to a minority status; in the
South agriculture commanded a declining proportion.[47]

Watson and many of his colleagues in the populist movement had
anticipated a national government dominated by agrarian interests, which
the simple arithmetic of industrialization militated against. Before the
Civil War the population of the South had fallen behind that of the
North. By the early twentieth century the southern populist strategy of an
agrarian revolution, already late in the 1890s, had become an anachronism.

What can revolutionaries do when revolution is no longer possible? Well, of course, they might turn to reform; and surely, in the first two decades of the century, southern agrarians turned to reform with a vengeance. Many of the populist proposals, first suggested as the foundation for a new commonwealth, proved well suited to the more modest purposes of reform. The radicalism of the 1890s, appropriately domesticized, became the liberalism of the Progressive Age.

This transition from revolution to reform reached completion in the legislative whirlwind of the Wilson administration. Woodrow Wilson, a southerner by birth and a conservative by temperament, had little fondness for radical populism. Yet, in his administration, southern congressmen helped progressives from around the country to address virtually every populist issue from a reformist perspective. Tariff reduction, the progressive income tax, bank reform, anti-trust measures, railroad regulation, and agricultural credit all commanded attention.

Ironically, many of the staunchest Democratic opponents of the Populist party in the South fought to legislate the populist economic program. Thus, Senator James K. Vardaman, "the white chief" from Mississippi, declared himself in favor of "government ownership of utilities; an elastic currency; long-term credit for farmers; a strong graduated income tax; postal savings banks and the expansion of parcel post; the initiative, referendum and recall; and the ending of speculation in agricultural commodities."[48] This from a man who had worked conscientiously to subvert the Populists during the critical years of the early 1890s.

The southern progressives drew heavily on radical populism, but the programs they helped to enact attempted no revolution. They accepted industrialism and tried to give it a human face. Rather than projecting a new independence for the region and its large mass of farmers, they worked to make the terms of dependency less oppressive.

While progressive Democrats adopted the bulk of the populist program, the bulk of the Populists returned to democracy. By 1910 even Tom Watson had announced his return, which actually had been accomplished a number of years earlier.[49] Although Watson could never generate much enthusiasm for Woodrow Wilson, no longer did he plot revolution.

While the complaint against industrialism and Yankees remained strong, along side it came a new harsher vituperation. Racism, anti-Catholicism, and anti-Semitism had a long history in the South. The same white farmers who felt threatened by their dependency on a changing and unpredictable commercial world, felt threatened by blacks, Catholics, and Jews. The agrarian world had been hopelessly upset by the advance of industrialism. The populist dream of restoring a Jeffersonian yeomanry to the South had run aground. More than ever, dependency was the character of individual experience. If the economic dependency could no longer be challenged directly, then at least imaginary threats to independence—the threat of black rule, of Popish ensnarement, and Jewish conniving—could be battled.

To homes where Tom Watson's warnings against eastern trusts and northern railways had been read, Watson's racist diatribes now carried warnings of new dangers to southern independence. C. Vann Woodward has suggested that this shift represented a diversion from the frustration of the populist experience.[50] Surely the demagoguery that Watson adopted and many southern politicians perfected provided a circus-like relief for white farmers, but an element of entertainment had always infected populist attacks on the industrial menace. Nor did the demagoguery represent just an attack on the strange and the foreign. Perhaps the hostility toward Catholics and Jews fell into this category, but white southerners had known black southerners for a long time.

For southern whites, demagoguery represented a convoluted striving for independence, an inverted empowerment. It created dangers and then succeeded in destroying them. It required no complicated economics, no correspondence between political program and theoretical understanding. The populist thread in American thought often has been labeled anti-intellectual, yet the southern populists, in their economic program, had attempted an intellectual analysis of their dependency. Ultimately this analysis, however true, had failed to deliver. The racism of the demagogue delivered every time. Whatever legislation the New Freedoms (or, at a later date, the New Deal) might generate, the southern farmer would remain poor and dependent on the capital and industry of the North. By the end of the populist period, most southerners understood that painful fact. The southern agrarian economy would never be independent. But the unholy success of the demagogues won a half-century of a terrible independence for southern agrarian culture.

Chapter Five

Endings

Throughout the early twentieth century, the more aggressive elaborations of the colonial critique were buried under the rhetoric and racism of demagogic populism. The liberal alternative, Progressive reform, had a bit of the Yankee tinge to it. After World War I, a new generation of southern intellectuals emerged, a group raised on modernism and, like their northern contemporaries, hostile to the nation's bourgeois culture. Not surprisingly, these young southerners balked at the region's peculiar accommodation to northern values and northern economic power. In exploring the history of southern thought, they found serious regional themes to build upon and fashioned a reassessment of the South that led—interestingly enough—in two different directions. In Chapel Hill, North Carolina, a new "southern sociology" reinvigorated the mercantilist critiques with a gospel of planning. In Nashville, Tennessee, a group of poets rediscovered Old Republican values and the political economy of John Taylor. For all their differences, however, these two schools of southern thought began from a shared appreciation of regional dependency.

The Self-conscious Agrarians

Normally poets do not take up the study of political economy, but the 1930s in the United States hardly qualified as normal times. The Great Depression had the look of an Armageddon. Radical intellectuals in the North pointed to the Soviet Union and its new society as an alternative to decadent capitalism. Observing this turmoil from below the Mason-Dixon line, southerners drew energy from this radical attack on mammon. But to parallel it they had to create, as had the Marxists, a programmatic alternative. Southern intellectuals began to rummage through the various traditions of the region's colonial analogy. The Nashville Agrarians made a particularly serious effort. Eager to claim for themselves a tradition hostile to northern capitalism but distinct from northern

Marxism, they reinvented the colonial analogy. Starting with a romantic defense of traditional southern values, the Nashville Agrarians moved on to denounce their region's dependency and call for fundamental change.

Led by John Ransom, Donald Davidson, and Allen Tate, the Nashville Agrarians developed out of the literary circle that in the 1920s had produced the *Fugitive,* a poetry magazine with a distinctly southern cast. Although familiar with rural life, most of them came from just those middle-class elements that had strongly endorsed the New South creed. Moreover, they had been attracted to Vanderbilt University by Edwin Mims, head of the English department there and a staunch advocate of an enlightened New South.[1] Yet these intellectuals from the postwar generation made much of rejecting just that industrial society which the New South advocates embraced.

Poets and literary people accounted for the majority of these urban-based agrarians. A few social scientists provided leavening. Not surprisingly, their major collective effort, the famous set of essays entitled *I'll Take My Stand,* had the hallmarks of a fine literary work. Their writing skills surely account in part for the still-considerable interest that volume commands. Motivated by a concern to develop a more human environment, these agrarians ascribed an almost spiritual quality to southern culture. However, given their hostility to northern materialism, the fundamentally materialist analysis that characterizes their writing comes as something of a shock.

The Nashville Agrarians asserted that the dangers facing southern culture originated in the dangers facing southern agriculture. They had little sympathy for Marxism, but the notion that a society's economic base strongly influenced its culture appealed to these southern poets. Since they knew that some time previously northern industrialism had destroyed any promise of northern culture, it followed that southern culture must have benefited from the economic and social organization of their home region.

To restore the South's "humanism" necessarily meant to deal with the region's material conditions. Their position, as Ransom put it in the introduction to *I'll Take My Stand,* was, "We cannot recover our native humanism by adopting some standard of taste that is critical enough to question the contemporary arts but not critical enough to question the social and economic life which is their ground."[2] In emphasizing simultaneously their alienation from industrial society and their southernness, the Nashville poets sought to explain in concrete terms how southern society had avoided for a long time the excesses of industrialism.

The answer seemed clear: southerners had not been employed in industry and had not lived in crowded cities, because they had been employed in agriculture and had lived on rural farms. Being southern meant having a close connection to the land. This agrarian assertion echoed populist and Old Republican themes. The Nashville Agrarians, like both Tom Watson and John Taylor, feared that the South's rural life faced nefarious enemies.

The essayists of *I'll Take My Stand* knew that the danger came from the North. In the nineteenth century, northerners had created an industrial society propelled by technological progress. Northern industrialism had inevitably sought to use the power of the central government for its own ends and thus had brought on the Civil War, a conflict between an agrarian (not a slave) society and an industrial one.[3]

After the war the South found itself reduced to dependency. According to Herman Nixon, the political scientist of the group, the Civil War left

> no effective check to an industrial dominance in national public policy, particularly in tariff matters. It partially terminated and partially modified the distinctive plantation system, making southern agricultural diversification and industrial recovery difficult for lack of physical goods and capital. It forced a dependence in the South on the one-crop system, temporarily reinforced by unusually high prices for cotton. . . . It created a southern vacuum for an economic invasion, with the region becoming a suppliant for outside aid and yielding much control of its economic destiny.[4]

Not surprisingly, Nixon called for a diversification of southern agriculture.

The most complete development of the dependency theme in *I'll Take My Stand* came in the essay by Andrew Lytle, entitled "The Hind Tit." Sensitive to the dynamics of the cash nexus, Lytle retraced the spread of the cotton economy after the Civil War to the back hills of the South. Lytle argued that an increasing reliance on the market economy had robbed the small farmer of his independence. Citing the rise of farm tenancy in the South, Lytle went on to ridicule the notion that increasing use of new machinery and methods would untangle the rural South. Increased productivity led only to overproduction and greater debt.

Where populists, farmers themselves, had struggled to find a program that would allow them to continue to specialize in commercial crops, Lytle planned a retreat toward self-sufficiency. "To avoid the dire consequences and to maintain a farming life in an industrial imperialism, there seems to be only one thing left for the farmer to do, and particularly for the small farmer. . . . [H]e must deny himself the articles the industrialist offers for sale."[5] The results of such denial would be a positive reassertion of community. "Throw out the radio and take down the fiddle from the wall. Forsake the movies for the play-parties and the square dances."

Diversification alone would not suffice, Lytle argued; indeed diversification into multiple cash crops only complicated matters. "The farmer is no better off when he has two or three money crops, if they are all over-produced, than he is with one. He has three crops instead of one to worry with."[6] Lytle based his program on diversification intended to increase self-reliance. Stopping short of a call for complete self-sufficiency ("So long as the industrialist remains in the saddle there must be a money crop to pay him taxes"), Lytle argued for a diversification that allowed a reduction of money needs. "Let him [the southern farmer] diversify, but diversify so that he may live rather than that he may grow rich."[7]

Lytle's argument harkened back to Jefferson's flirtation with a self-sufficient agriculture. For hundreds of years southerners had advocated similar steps, but never had so dramatic a case been made. Lytle eloquently demonstrated that the cash nexus involved more than a question of simple exchange. The overhead of the commercial economy, according to Lytle, was both expensive and emotionally deadening.

> [The southern farmer] will be told that [avoiding cash markets] is not economical, that he can buy clothes for much less than he can weave them, and shoes for half the labor he will put into their creation. If the cash price paid for shoes were the only cost, it would be bad economy to make shoes at home. Unfortunately, the matter is not so simple: the fifteen-hundred-dollar tractor, the thousand-dollar truck, the cost of transportation to and from town, all the cost of indirect taxation, every part of the money economy, enters into the price of shoes. In comparison, the sum he hands over to the merchant is nothing more than a war tax.[8]

Like George Fitzhugh, Lytle looked behind the immediate mutual advantage of market exchange and discovered the threat of a deep dependency. Where Fitzhugh had emphasized the dangers of complacency, Lytle underscored the broad costs of participating in a market. Independent farmers could not pick and choose their opportunities from a distance; markets engulfed them, changing their tastes and needs. Lytle's profound point challenged the core of traditional political economy, which, while maintaining the efficiency of markets in satisfying wants, stubbornly refused to consider the origins of people's preferences.

In their eagerness to return to a more pristine economy, the Nashville Agrarians accepted the basic overproduction argument. They had little sympathy for the commercial orientation of the populists. They denied the effectiveness of either crop controls or diversification into other commercial crops. The basic solution to the South's dependency lay in a return to the stable and simpler economy of agrarian self-sufficiency.

If they differed with the populists as to method and faith in progress, the agrarians surely agreed with the populists as to the importance of local, rural community. Like the populists they envisioned this community largely in terms of its social consumption. In their romantic way, the Nashville Agrarians saw little need or desire for a division of labor even within that community. Ironically, this group of urban academics, so dependent on others for their support, called for a withdrawal from an extensive division of labor.

Observers noted that the manifesto of *I'll Take My Stand* produced a strong denunciation of industrialism but only a hazy explication of an agrarian program. H. L. Mencken accused the authors of committing the error of "social reformers at all times and everywhere": they had invented utopia and then invited people to "move in tomorrow." Blinded by their own enthusiasm, they had failed to appreciate the chimerical nature of their proposals. Mencken went on to assert that the South "is tied to the industrial system so tightly that any cutting loose would have the effect, not of mere revolution, but of cataclysm, and out of cataclysm nothing could emerge save chaos."[9] Mencken even suggested that the agrarians' attack on industrialism amounted to "banal borrowings" from such radical journals as *New Masses* and the *New Republic.*

As the Depression continued, several of the Nashville Agrarians attempted to fill out their political economy. Simultaneously they began a search for political allies on the broader national stage. For example, in 1932 John Ransom published an article entitled "Land!" in *Harper's Monthly Magazine.* Starting from the idea of overproduction, Ransom told a story of a new dependency. With the rise of "big business," towns had been trapped in the national business cycle. As a result, each town had "scarcely any control over its own economic life. It is only an outpost of empire."[10] Farmers had followed along the same path, ever more caught in the commercial network. Ransom suggested "to the patriots and economists that they try to reestablish self-sufficiency as the proper economy for the American farm." Pointing to the abundance of American land, he argued that resettling many of the urban unemployed on farms made good economic sense. But of course these new farmers must give priority to self-sufficiency, approaching the market gingerly. Ransom couched his argument completely in terms of agrarianism versus industrialism. He made no reference, here, to the conflict between North and South. Rather, he advanced his principles in a broad theoretical fashion with little concern for geographical particulars. This new agrarianism, like that of Jefferson, aspired to a national role.

To spread their new political economy, Ransom, Tate, and Davidson committed themselves to a fledgling journal, *American Review,* published by Seward Collins of New York. Collins saw a natural alliance between the southern agrarians and a host of other groups hostile to industrialism. He included in his list the English distributists, who, like the agrarians, were few in number and relied heavily on literary skills—in this case, those of Hilaire Belloc and G. K. Chesterton. The distributists argued that only a broad distribution of productive property could protect democracy from socialism and fascism. To maintain such a system would in turn require considerable state involvement, since, as Belloc contended, the Marxists were correct that unbridled competition led inevitably to bigness.[11]

Among the Nashville Agrarians, Allen Tate found distributist economics particularly appealing. He saw in it an ideology based on a human scale. In *American Review,* he wrote, "The joint-stock corporation is the enemy of private property in the same sense as communism is."[12] Small property owners were only tricked into siding with big business because they could not "imagine another kind of property." Tate drew on the Marxist categories of use-value and exchange-value to emphasize that true property ownership required that the owner be able to choose between selling and using. In this choice lay the very essence of liberty. "As the freedom to 'use' disappears, liberty begins to disappear," wrote Tate. "There has never been a society in which use-value has been the exclusive kind of value; no such society is being recommended now. But it must remain the basis of liberty."[13] Echoing the concerns of Thomas Carlyle and his disciple John Ruskin, Tate drew a distinction between economics and political economy. Tate asserted that the first was only the study of wealth, while the second was concerned with human welfare. To achieve improved well-being of the people, he said, "we have got to add politics to economics in order to get a sum that we may, perhaps, call free citizens."[14] In the distributists, Tate saw clear echoes of the Old Republicans.

While the association with *American Review* continued, the Nashville Agrarians began to cooperate with Herbert Agar, a strong advocate of economic and political decentralization. This association culminated in a second volume, *Who Owns America,* that was jointly edited by Tate and Agar and included a geographically diverse group of contributors. However, it contained essays by eight of the original "twelve southerners." *Who Owns America* had all of the fire of the earlier work. In it the southerners continued to generalize and nationalize the critique they had made. Not surprisingly, this effort led them back toward the longstanding southern hope of an alliance with the West. For example, Donald Davidson, in his essay, argued, "The Northeast has been the imperial capital region, and the other regions, including even the West, have been the colonial dependencies from which it bought cheap and to which it sold dear."[15]

In attempting to universalize the southern critique, Davidson advocated "political regionalism." He drew on Frederick Jackson Turner's belief in the importance of "physiographic provinces" and W. Y. Elliott's "system of regional commonwealths." Davidson suggested that strong safeguards had to be offered the regions against "imperialism at two points: first in their economic pursuits . . . and second, in their cultural and social institutions." With respect to economics, Davidson, quoting Frank Owsley, argued that regions should have "an equal share in making of the tariff." Beyond such an arrangement the regional commonwealths needed the power to tax and to regulate "foreign" enterprises and "to control to some degree credit and even money." The Middle West and the Deep South had a right to prevent absentee ownership of farm lands "by Wall Street speculators or by their own expatriates." Reaching out in a novel way for a southerner, Davidson even suggested that the Northeast should have the power to protect its union labor against low-wage southern labor.[16] In his effort to establish a broad regionalism anchored in abstract principles, Davidson self-consciously drew on the thought of Calhoun.

All of the Nashville Agrarians saw themselves as attempting an intellectual restoration. They repeatedly echoed the libertarian versions of the colonial critique. They claimed that the theories of the first generation of agrarians were still relevant to the nation as a whole. This claim appeared most sharply in an essay by Andrew Lytle entitled "John Taylor and the Political Economy of Agriculture," which was serialized in three parts in *American Review*. The articles formed a paean to that early agrarian. According to Lytle, the worst fears of Taylor had come to pass. The country had been overwhelmed by "that abstract slavery" wherein a financial hierarchy centralized power in the hands of New York and London financiers, "those private rulers of the public credit"[17]

To see the origins of this predicament, we must go back to the very beginnings of the Republic. Taylor, like many of his contemporaries, faced a "predicament" produced by "conservative instincts and desires coupled with liberal intellectual principles."[18] For Lytle, the American War of Independence represented not a radical revolution but an attempt to restore traditional British values threatened by an aristocracy of money. This essentially conservative action had gotten itself tied up with the liberal rhetoric of the Enlightenment, thus creating considerable confusion. Despite Taylor's own inconsistencies, his "principles and his analysis of the evil forces working like false yeast in the wine of American life became the complete guides for future conservative action."[19]

The worst effects of the paper aristocracy's corruption had been postponed by repeated waves of westward movement, opening new and rich resources; but conservative agrarians like Taylor understood that the day of reckoning could not be postponed indefinitely. The Great Depression demonstrated the truth of his prediction. The paper aristocracy had squandered the wealth of the nation and lost it to European financiers. When the American papercrats "turned to replenish the gambling purse, they found exhausted fields, exhausted moral character, hungry mobs, and banks stacked full of paper." With the real wealth gone, the country could see this paper "in its true light, in the character given it by old Taylor a hundred-and-twenty-five years ago." Paper only served as a means for transferring wealth. Once the wealth had been transferred back to Europe, the remaining paper stayed useless and idle.[20]

Lytle concluded that from the first years America had needed "leaders of a counter-revolution" to restore the traditional values threatened by the aristocracy of money. At their best, he wrote, the leaders of the War of Independence had stood not for radical revolution but for conservative British values.[21] These values and not liberal principles held the best hope for America. This realization had motivated the southern conservatives—Taylor, Calhoun, and Fitzhugh among them—who finally saw the need to drop the liberal baggage of Jeffersonian agrarianism.

Lytle knew that the old system of northern capitalism had come to an impasse. He envisioned a conservative romantic regionalism as a solution. Recognizing the depths of the crisis in American life, he reverted to an older republican vision—a vision hopelessly outdated. Desperately hostile to the industrialism of the twentieth century, he confused it with the paper economy attacked by Taylor and other agrarians in the early nineteenth century. The other Nashville Agrarians agreed with him, pointing to the economic chaos of the 1930s as proof. Although acutely (and eloquently) aware of the price exacted by the mass-production economy, they offered little guidance for controlling the power of industrialism.

Not many Americans at the time seemed eager to follow the agrarians' backward-looking path. Indeed the agrarians themselves had little stomach for it. Unable to win popular support and overwhelmed by their careers, the majority of the Nashville Agrarians lost interest in this campaign after the Depression. Ransom and Tate retreated into the elitist culture of the literary reviews. Donald Davidson, the agrarian who maintained the strongest connection to the region, increasingly defined his political action in terms of defending racial segregation. Frank Owsley became enmeshed in a superficial racism and Red-baiting.

The racism of the Nashville Agrarians comes as a particular shock when contrasted with the sensitive poetry and obvious humanism of the group. They almost went out of their way to assert their fundamental acceptance of white southern racial attitudes. In their advocacy of all things southern there is a desperation among these literary fugitives, a desperation to root their identity in the region's folk culture. Their emphasis on "separate but equal," their endorsement of Booker T. Washington's program of black vocational education, and their assertion of the superiority of rural race relations to urban ones all suggest a search for superficial solutions to inherently radical problems. At least Robert Penn Warren realized from the start that the South required some accommodation between the races. In one of the most perceptive statements in *I'll Take My Stand,* Warren cautioned against the proposition that industrialism would necessarily guarantee black independence. Industrialism in the South, as in the North, was fond of pitting black against white. Warren argued, "If this industrialism is to bequeath anything except the profit of the few, the conscious or unconscious exploitation of racial differences, and a disastrous rancor, an enlightened selfishness on the part of the southern white man must prompt him to encourage the well-being and possibly the organization of negro, as well as white, labor."[22] Both Warren and Nixon went on to make their peace with American liberalism. Nixon in particular worked hard to give democratic content to the agrarian vision. But he could not do this in the context of southern agrarianism; he had to defect to the liberal camp from Chapel Hill.

A Colonial Apology

The improbability of implementing the agrarian program during the 1930s measured the extent of the victory that had been won by the very forces the agrarians feared. At the time they were writing, however, the terms of the South's final surrender had yet to be defined. While the Nashville Agrarians represented a rear-guard action, the Chapel Hill sociologists hoped to negotiate a favorable peace. In presenting the South's case, they often cited their version of the colonial critique as evidence of mitigating circumstances.

Critics described the agrarians as romantic dilettantes, aesthetes dabbling in political economy. No such charge could be leveled at the band of sociologists who collected at the University of North Carolina in Chapel Hill. The central figure in the group, Howard Odum, became the southern champion of a broadly conceived regional planning. As his life's work, Odum brought a serious and scholarly social science to the South. At the same time, he led a group, including his protégé Rupert Vance and a host of students, that identified themselves with liberal national politics. No unreconstructed poets, the Chapel Hill sociologists advocated a progressive science. One could hardly imagine two academic schools with more different styles.

The University of North Carolina's sociology department and its journal, *Social Forces,* represented a new departure in southern intellectual life. Odum audaciously held the South and its institutions to a critical scrutiny.[23] He and his colleagues all had solid southern credentials. Both Odum and Vance came from modest southern rural families. More clearly than the Nashville Agrarians, they could claim an attachment to the folk of the South whom the Vanderbilt poets so celebrated. Nevertheless, the Chapel Hill sociologists sought an honest appraisal of southern society. With strong faith in the ability of social science to prescribe beneficial social reform, they went about their work with a certain methodical optimism.

Odum and Vance each produced an encyclopedic book on the southern economy.[24] These volumes marshalled armies of statistics and maps to describe the South as it had never been described before. Vance's *Human Geography of the South* included 47 tables. Perhaps a little embarrassed, Odum did not number the 272 tables and charts in his *Southern Regions of the United States,* which included measures of virtually everything. In the second part of the work, each of the six major chapters begins with "Samplings of Indices Relating to . . . ." None of the six lists contains fewer than one hundred items. Little wonder that Gordon Johnson, one of Odum's collaborators, felt compelled to gloss Odum's study for the general reader.

The Chapel Hill sociologists defended such obsession for measurement as a necessary antidote to southern rhetoric. With an eye toward the Nashville Agrarians, they went to great pains to distinguish their form of regionalism from unreconstructed sectionalism. For Odum, regionalism considered "the nation first, making the national culture and welfare the final arbiter," while sectionalism emphasized "political boundaries and state sovereignties." Regionalism "by the very nature of its regional, interregional, and national cooperative processes" implied "more the designed and planned society than sectionalism, which is the group correspondent to individualism." Sectionalism invited a coercive federalism, whereas regionalism avoided such confrontations.

The agrarian Donald Davidson suggested that Odum's exercise itself appeared "rhetorical and a little anxious."[25] While suspicious of Odum's enthusiasm for planning, he made his most telling point by noting that the "regionalist" school simply lacked a power base in either the South or the nation. As a result, Odum had adopted an almost plaintive tone. He had "proved, up to the hilt, the South's old contentions as to its disadvantaged condition," but he could only hope that the North might accept regionalism in "a change of mind, amounting almost to religious conversion."[26] The romantic agrarians, showing a certain slyness, accused their well-connected New Deal countrymen of being utopian. Still, their point was well taken. One must wonder at the naiveté with which Odum looked forward to a nationally cooperative spirit of planning. "Instead of the old and recent recurring questions, will the South or the West 'fight,' there would be substituted the inquiry as to whether the South or the West or any other region will plan and work together for the mutually better ordering of the common good."[27]

Obviously, the Chapel Hill sociologists and the Vanderbilt agrarians took considerable exception to each other's political programs. Nevertheless, it would be a mistake to emphasize too strongly the differences between their analyses of the southern predicament. Rupert Vance put together the most persuasive version of the colonial critique written during the twentieth century. One recent commentator (a Chapel Hill sociologist to be sure) has concluded that the agrarians actually took their analysis of the South's colonial economy from Vance's work.[28]

Vance's discussion "The South, A Colonial Economy" deserves serious study, for it provided the ultimate statement of the colonial analogy. Combining the traditional themes of the colonial critique with important insights from twentieth-century sociology and economics, Vance came close to defining a new and serious political economy of regions.

It seems clear that Vance approached the colonial theme with considerable reluctance. Not until page 467 of the *Human Geography of the South* did he pose the classic question that had haunted the region for close to three centuries. With more statistical justification than anyone had gathered before, he "surprisingly" reached "the conclusion that, without drastic changes in its natural resources or in its human elements, the South might have attained a much higher state of material well-being." He went on to ask, "After geography and biology, what factors remain to account for a region's economic position?"[29]

Vance, like his colleagues at Chapel Hill, took a far more critical attitude toward the South than was customary (or prudent) in the region's academic institutions. They criticized the region's race relations, labor relations, churches, schools, and local governments. But when confronting the central question of how one explained the economic plight of the South, Vance reached the same conclusion that so many southerners had for so many years: "the South remains largely a colonial economy."[30]

Vance emphasized that all of America began as a "colonial economy," forced to extract and export staple products to the mother country and then to reimport the same products after fabrication. "Thus the high level of a complex commercial and industrialized culture is stabilized for the mother country, while the colony can support its increasing population based on an extractive economy only by fresh and continuous excursions into the storehouse of nature." This need to plunder natural resources pushed on the ever-expanding frontier.[31]

The emergence of cotton as a world force in the early nineteenth century seduced the South into maintaining a colonial economy rather than following the commercial and industrial strategy of the East. Commenting only in passing on the evils of the tariff, Vance placed greater emphasis on the internal dynamic of the colonial economy. Such an economy "leads to the over-exploitation of natural resources without the accumulation of capital goods to take their place."[32] The cash-crop, cotton, appeared as a means "to escape from the frontier economy," but it forced an overspecialized commercialism.

The colonial economy always remained a debtor economy, said Vance. "It begins as an investment on the part of the mother country; it accumulates little capital of its own; it lacks the organization of credit,

and as economic opportunities arise on the frontier, they must be financed from outside the area. The surplus returns are exported as profits
and interest to outside business men in command of capital."[33] Ultimately, talented people looked elsewhere for opportunities while the
drain of dividend exports continued.

For Rupert Vance, as for George Fitzhugh, the South's dependence
on agriculture greatly limited the application of modern machinofacture.
"Energy is not multiplied nor is time telescoped in a vegetable civilization." Here Vance saw a major difference in the ability of agricultural
and industrial societies to generate technological progress and the con-
comitant productivity growth. Vance did note that wheat farmers had
been able to mechanize, but offered no explanation of why the cotton
farmers had not. Elsewhere in the same volume, Vance suggested that
the development of a practical mechanical cotton-picker could rationalize
the industry but would imply corporation farming and the massive dis-
placement of cotton tenants.[34]

Like the agrarians, Vance accepted the overproduction argument.
He even offered an explanation: Agriculture and industry differed in
their responses to declines in demand. Industry laid off workers and
reduced output, thus limiting supply to reduced demand. "Agriculture
chooses another way. It continues to over-produce, it accepts chronic
agricultural surpluses with low prices for staples, and the whole economy
endures a period of poverty."[35]

Vance acknowledged that the colonial economy, with its surplus
labor, could attract some industrial activities, but he claimed that such
industrialization would produce little improvement in living standards.
"The advance of industry into this region then partakes of the nature,
let us say it in all kindliness, of exploiting the natural resources and
labor supply of a colonial economy."[36] But the "threatening hordes on
the farm assert themselves" and keep wages well below those for similar
work elsewhere. Given low levels of income, the better educated migrated
out of the region sapping the potential leadership of the South. Finally,
Vance argued that the colonial economy necessarily kept average edu-
cational levels low. The segregated school system of the South further
complicated regional problems of education with its great inefficiencies.

This argument provided the most sophisticated treatment of the
South's colonial analogy ever written. Vance ably outlined the natural
evolution of the colonial predicament. Like Fitzhugh before him, he
needed no conspiracies to explain the South's plight. The rich resource
endowment encouraged an extractive economy that perpetuated colonial

conditions long after they had outlived their usefulness. While Vance made passing reference to tariffs and other traditional hobgoblins of various colonial critiques, these occupied only the periphery of his story. He emphasized, instead, the difficulty of sustaining high income levels through competitive and traditional staple agriculture in the midst of a technologically sophisticated economy dominated by large oligopolistic corporations.

Vance drew heavily on traditional colonial thought, but he balked at the sectional animosity common to that tradition. Instead of an attack on the Northeast as the dominant national power, he held out the promise of federally endorsed regional planning. This optimistic attitude toward national beneficence provoked considerable criticism from the Nashville Agrarians. Davidson objected that Vance had not identified "the exploiting agent."[37] In a way, Vance had produced a *Hamlet* without an evil uncle. As Davidson suggested, Vance and Odum avoided the hard edges of power.

The Chapel Hill sociologists constructed a plea for the South. They brought the region's case to the nation. Offering in their social science an apology for the South, they could hardly take on a bitter tone. Their version of the colonial critique presented a mechanistic and automatic colonialism that left the South a victim but required no particular region or class to play the role of villain. In advocating national concern for regional problems, Vance, Odum, and their associates believed that an apology for the southern economy served better than an indictment of the northern one. While careful to avoid vituperative rhetoric, they focused on the problems of maintaining the "love of native place and native folk" in an ever more complicated world. Their plans for regional reconstruction left little doubt of their fundamental concern for the agrarian culture, if not the agrarian movement.

Howard Odum, in his proposals for agricultural reform, basically accepted the thrust of the agrarian position, even if he criticized its sweeping generalizations. Sympathetic to the "dream of a revitalized agrarian culture in the Southeast," he warned that this goal could be achieved only through planning that was "very realistic, practical, subregion by subregion."[38] Odum's plans for the rural South put emphasis on new commercial crops and urban generated markets. Nevertheless, like the Nashville Agrarians, he acknowledged a need for increased self-sufficiency. And, when Odum came to conclude his chapter "An Agrarian Country," he offset his criticism of agrarian oversimplification with the perennial southern call for a leavening of industrial society by older rural culture.[39]

Less distance divided the Chapel Hill sociologists and the Nashville Agrarians than either group would have liked to think. Both drew heavily on the basic colonial analogy of a region exploited. Both criticized strongly the New South's quest for an unbridled industrialism, and both projected a reconstruction of the rural base of the region. They differed not so much in analysis as in prescription, and even here one suspects a greater affinity than their mutual denunciations might suggest. Their fight concerned proportions. The agrarians wrote a manifesto, the social scientists an apology. Both accepted the inevitability of industrial America.

Black Thought and the Colonial Analogy

To write an apology for the South required more than just explaining the poverty of the region. The Chapel Hill sociologists also had to address the longstanding issue of southern race relations. The white liberals of Chapel Hill sought black participation in their research on the black community. In various cooperative projects in the social sciences, white and black scholars worked together at analyzing the problems of southern black poverty and underemployment. In these joint efforts, black and white academics minimized differences in their intellectual traditions. But differences there were. Not the least of these concerned the nature of the southern economy.

Starting with Frederick Douglass, black southerners had written on the economy of their region. African-American writers only reluctantly endorsed white southern claims of economic dependency. For many white southerners, the colonial analogy had formed part of a broader justification of southern society. Even for the Chapel Hill sociologists it supplied an apology for the region. Given these connotations, perhaps we can appreciate that black southerners have seemed rather cool to the main thrust of the colonial argument. Understandably concerned with the immediate problems of economic survival and civil rights, southern blacks had little interest in the subtleties of the various colonial critiques. They were painfully aware of the power that southern whites wielded over their lives, and they made a rather unreceptive audience for critiques that painted the South as victim. Indeed, not until the 1930s did such an idea win any significant support among African-American intellectuals. While white southerners created a colonial critique of the South's position relative to the commercial and industrial power of the North, black southerners saw their own economic exploitation not as a regional phenomenon but rather as a racial phenomenon with an increasingly national dimension. Despite their differences, each of these traditions emphasized the concept of dependency. Given that the history of blacks in the United States has been so entwined with that of the South, we can reasonably ask whether black and white interpretations of those histories have interacted in any serious fashion.

Antebellum black writings on the southern economy uniformly adopted the abolitionist view of the slavocracy. Frederick Douglass in particular drew a picture of a powerful slave oligarchy working its will in cooperation with a tainted Constitution and an all-too-pliant federal government. Douglass did argue that slavery took a heavy toll from the land, but he put this idea forward as an explanation of the internal pressures promoting the geographic expansion of slavery not as a sign of colonial exploitation. Douglass also suggested that slavery did little for non-slaveowning whites. Nevertheless, he generally showed respect for the economic strength of slavery and argued that "prosperity" had blinded the moral sense of the South.[40]

Douglass, of course, spent most of his adult life working in the North and addressing northern audiences who were very likely to be hostile to the South. Like the white abolitionists, he found it useful to portray the South as an expanding power, and surely southern political maneuvering in the 1840s and 1850s gave considerable support to this position. While the abolitionists undoubtedly held their views sincerely, they obviously would have been unlikely to adopt the colonial analogy popular among southern whites.

Douglass continued to write about the South after the Civil War, but he changed his economic thinking little. For a time he suggested that African-Americans might gain great power in the South because of the central importance of their labor to the region's economy. Even after the collapse of Reconstruction, in an address to the American Social Science Association, Douglass argued that "the dependence of the planters, landowners and old master-class of the South upon the Negro, however galling and humiliating to southern pride and power, is nearly complete and perfect."[41] He went on to suggest that this leverage could eventually win southern blacks both economic security and political rights. He based this optimism on his conviction that the southern staples were of continuing value. However, as conditions for blacks continued to deteriorate in the South with the solidification white supremacy, Douglass essentially moved back to his earlier interpretation of the region's economy. He took an active part in protesting the ever-widening restrictions of Jim Crow and the atrocity of lynching. For Douglass these abominations were proof of the reemergence of the slaveowner class.

"The old master class are wise in their day and generation. They know if they can once divest the Negro of the elective franchise and nullify his citizenship, the partition wall between him and slavery will no longer exist, and no man can tell where the reaction will stop." Or again: "The landowners of the South want the labor of the Negro on the hardest terms possible. They once had it for nothing. They now want it for next to nothing."[42]

Douglass answered these problems in an essentially political fashion. Feeling that the South had to be reshaped by political means, he paid no attention to the New South call for industrialization. That call saw the answer to southern dependency in the building of an urban industrial sector. Douglass seems not to have even considered the implications of the New South analysis. While he advocated black economic cooperation, his central emphasis remained on civil rights. If African-American rights could be protected, prosperity would follow. Presumably fair and honest dealings would allow blacks to share in the richness of the region's agricultural resources. There was nothing wrong with the southern economy that the Fourteenth and Fifteenth amendments and a little self-help could not cure.

At first glance, Booker T. Washington's economics seem to contrast sharply with Douglass's. Washington played an important role in the new economics of the region. Indeed, he became the black spokesman for the New South movement. Newspaper editors around the country interpreted Washington's speech at the Atlanta Cotton Exposition of 1895 as a broad endorsement of New South goals and as an acceptance of the disenfranchisement of southern blacks. There can be little doubt that Washington stood willing to settle for the limited racial accommo-dation that formed a cornerstone of the New South program. Moreover, parts of Washington's economic message did reflect New South thinking. The argument that blacks should develop practical mechanical skills, while politically opportune, paralleled the general New South criticism of the Old South's fascination with leisure. Washington's glorification of businessmen recalled the praise which Henry Grady and the other editors of the South lavished on these new men.[43]

Washington made his most explicit endorsement of the New South view in an 1891 speech in Washington, D.C. At that time he quoted at length from Henry Grady, contrasting the South's early industrial de-pendency with the growth and diversification it was then experiencing. Washington argued that the new economic development was opening up opportunities for black business in the South. Indeed, he suggested,

"With all the disadvantages presented by the South we can find our way to the front sooner through southern prejudice than through northern competition."[44]

Despite all these connections to the New South movement, Booker T. Washington never adopted the core of their economic analysis of the South. While careful to present a romantic picture of the Old South, the New South publicists saw the origins of the region's economic plight in the overspecialized agriculture dictated by the slave system. However, Washington, like Douglass, emphasized the productivity of slavery and the continuing productivity of southern agriculture. Apart from his 1891 address, he did not make the dependent status of the region a major theme. He repeatedly argued that slavery had taught the black man how to labor. Washington clearly felt that blacks should remain in the rural South with agriculture their primary pursuit.[45] While he championed the spread of industrial training and the growth of a skilled black labor force, he always argued that African-Americans could, if fairly treated, find opportunity in southern agriculture.

Perhaps Washington's position reflected his awareness that many New South spokesmen advocated industrial employment for poor whites only. Seeking such jobs for blacks could easily have upset his moderate role in the region. But we should note that Washington consistently objected to the exclusion of blacks from trades like carpentry and brick-laying. Washington advanced a considerably more aggressive civil rights position in private than he did in public. Thus, Washington may truly have shared the common southern distrust of cities and things industrial. He saw black out-migration from southern rural areas as a problem to be answered by agricultural education. In his writings he always pointed to black land ownership as the single most important index of progress. In these matters he may genuinely have been part of the agrarian South. If this was the case, it adds another note of irony to Washington's skill in manipulating his New South allies.

All things considered, the idea of the South as an exploited region played no major role in Washington's thought. He tended to interpret most southern problems, including southern poverty, as originating in the tremendous adjustments demanded by emancipation. While this position may have been politic both in the North and the South, Washington saw an optimistic future for southern agriculture.

Booker T. Washington's most significant critic was W. E. B. Du Bois. Like Hinton Rowan Helper, Du Bois subscribed to the thesis that slavery had hindered the South's development. Helper had blamed slavery for restricting the opportunities open to the majority of white southerners who owned no slaves. Du Bois fashioned an interpretation that was broader and free of Helper's crude racism. In 1907, when Du Bois was teaching at Atlanta University, he and Washington gave a series of lectures entitled "The Negro in the South." Washington's lectures presented his usual plea for industrial education. Du Bois, however, attempted a serious look at the South's economy. Citing Olmsted and Helper, Du Bois argued that "at the very time when the South ought to have been increasing in intelligence, law and order, the use of machinery, industrial concentration, and the intensive culture of land with the rest of the world, she lost a half century in a development backward toward a dispersing of population, extensive rather than intensive land culture, increased and compulsory ignorance of the laboring class, and the rearing of a complete system of caste and aristocracy." Du Bois clearly subscribed to the nineteenth-century American conviction that density and industrial diversity played crucial roles in economic development. The concentration produced by urban industrialization led to "a wonderful contact of man with man which sharpened mind and sharpened thought."[46]

On the issue of whether others had forced the South into its poverty, Du Bois equivocated. On the one hand he blamed southern leadership for failing to establish the Jeffersonian ideal of small independent farms. If such farms had dominated the southern economy, the rise of cotton might have led to a "development which would have been the wonder of the world."[47] On the other hand, Du Bois asserted that "the forward forces of industry . . . fastened slavery on the South." This position suggested a version of the colonial critique popular with southern whites, but Du Bois may have meant only that the industrial North and Britain shared in the moral responsibility for the perpetuation of slavery. In fact, Du Bois did not emphasize the dependency of the southern economy even in the post Civil War period. While he mentioned the influence of northern capital in the industrialization of the South, he drew no menacing inferences.

Perhaps Du Bois came closest to the colonial analogy in his romantic novel, *The Quest of the Silver Fleece,* written between 1904 and 1906. A major subplot of the novel concerned the manipulations of northern capitalists trying to assemble a cotton trust that would monopolize the industry from fields to finished product. Wall Street comes in for considerable criticism. Thus, as southerners began to rejoice over increasing cotton prices, "far away to the north a great spider sat weaving his web."[48]

Despite these hints of southern dependency, the novel portrays rich and decadent cotton planters actively participating in the financial speculation. While Du Bois highlighted the distrust between northern and southern capital, the latter at worst takes the role of junior partner. Du Bois did not define the South as a colonial dependency of the North. Instead, he took as his central motif the manipulation of the racism of poor whites by prosperous whites. Focusing on the options open to the African-American community under such conditions, Du Bois emphasized self-help and hard work. He only hinted at the possibility of a coalition with poor whites.

Many years later, during the Great Depression, Du Bois returned to live in the South. At that time he came in contact with the new generation of white liberal sociologists from Chapel Hill and elsewhere in the region. In a speech to the fifth annual meeting of the Southern Sociological Society, Du Bois still made little effort to incorporate the South-as-colony view popular with many of those assembled. Instead, he maintained that southern "industry including agriculture" had organized around "the mudsill theory of society: namely, that it was to the advantage of the State and to all persons in the State to have at the bottom of society a mass of laborers with the lowest standards of living, the most curtailed wage and with periodic unemployment. Industry thrived on this dogma and industry ruled politics and the State."[49] If he had wanted to, Du Bois could easily have identified southern industry as essentially a compradore class controlled largely from outside the region. Such an idea would have appealed to Du Bois's audience and would have fit rather naturally into his analysis. Du Bois, however, seemed almost to go out of his way to avoid this colonial interpretation.

Du Bois's avoidance of the southern colonial thesis cannot be attributed to any lack of familiarity with its basic outline. He had read widely in southern history and written on both the antebellum and the Reconstruction South. At the same time, Du Bois obviously knew better than most southerners the broader theories, both Marxian and liberal, of colonial relationships. Indeed, his own description of the black community as a "negro nation within a nation" parallels many of the same economic ideas that white southerners had used in their critiques. In 1935 Du Bois explicitly called for the development in the United States of "an economic nation within a nation, able to work through inner cooperation, to found its own institutions, to educate its genius." He went on to say, "By letting Negro farmers feed Negro artisans, and Negro technicians guide Negro home industries and Negro thinkers plan

this integration of cooperation, while Negro artists dramatize and beau-
tify the struggle, economic independence can be achieved."[50]

All told, the work of Douglass, Washington, and Du Bois resisted
the white southern identification of a colonial South. Douglass and
Washington saw no particular reason to label the southern economy
unproductive. In their own way, they maintained the myth of King
Cotton. While Du Bois, a younger man, emphasized the inefficiency of
both slavery and tenancy, he stopped considerably short of blaming the
North for the South's economic problems. Eventually, Du Bois defined
the black community as a colony. For him, blacks formed a nation within
the United States, but the South had no such status. Accepting the
colonial analogy for the South would have implied at least a partial
endorsement of the white southern conception of the southern community.

With the close of World War I, black radicalism in the United States
began to reach out to a broad mass audience. Per force this required an
analysis of the southern economy. Southern apologies had little appeal
to these activists. Black radicals eagerly included capitalism in the crimes
of the South. However, like Du Bois, they did not consider the region's
penetration by northern (as opposed to southern) capital as particularly
objectionable or oppressive. Whenever the new radicals made a regional
distinction, it served only to underscore the greater opportunism and
hypocrisy of southern capital.

When, in 1919, A. Philip Randolph, then co-editor of the self-
proclaimed radical Negro magazine, *The Messenger,* discussed the problems of black labor in the South, he used Marxian categories, not the
colonial analogy. Randolph reviewed the ills of the South: debt peonage,
child labor, and lynching. In each case he traced the problem to the
interest of a powerful capitalist class, but he emphasized the native
character of that class. Thus, when he discusses child labor and how it
forced white children of the South to compete with their parents for
employment, Randolph concludes, "This is how much the southern
white gentlemen capitalists care about white children whom they prate
[about] so much."[51]

Rather than single out northern capital as particularly aggressive,
black radicals found it more important to emphasize the continuing
danger of a powerful old order. Echoing Frederick Douglass and the
abolitionists, radicals continued to warn against the dangers of southern
political power in the nation. In 1920 William Colson wrote in *The
Messenger,* "Confederate-Americanism has gained such headway that it
now threatens to become the dominant Americanism. It dominates the

present Federal Administration . . . The President of the United States and his Cabinet are largely Confederate-American . . . Confederate-Americanism dominates Congress."[52]

Black radicals often combined this theme of the continuing power of the South with an evaluation of the slave South closer to Douglass's than Du Bois's. Abram Harris, a noted economist and, at the time, a militant advocate of working-class solidarity, argued that slave labor had made the antebellum southern economy a wealthy one. He explicitly claimed that southern slavery had been profitable.[53] Harris did allow that the southern economy had languished in the aftermath of the Civil War, and that in this period corporate capital had consolidated its power in the national economy.[54]

In the mid-1930s, Ralph Bunche, then a militant in the civil rights movement, outlined a position quite similar to Randolph's. Bunche argued that "large white land-holding and industrial groups in the South are determined to keep the Negro in a servile condition and as a profitable and almost indispensable labor supply." Black labor competed with white labor much to the advantage of "the employing class, which is not insensitive to the merits of the policy of *divide et impera* in labor-employer relationships."[55]

In general, then, black radicals of the interwar period saw no reason to emphasize the dependent position of the southern economy. They observed white southern intransigence but avoided interpreting that intransigence in the context of a colonial apology. For them, the South contained property owners and workers of two races and that sufficed to explain its dynamic.

It remained for southern black sociologists to take up seriously the colonial theme. This willingness emerged from the increased contact between black and white academics in the South. During the 1920s the development at Chapel Hill of a liberal sociology department under the leadership of Howard Odum and Rupert Vance and the emergence of the Atlanta-based Commission on Interracial Cooperation created openings for the southern black community that had not existed before.[56] At the same time a number of African-American scholars were training at the University of Chicago sociology department under Robert E. Park. Park, who had worked for many years as Booker T. Washington's publicist, eagerly sent his students into the South. African-American sociologists actively participated in the creation of the new version of the colonial critique that explained and to some extent excused racial problems in the region as a manifestation of poverty and economic dependency.

Interestingly, the most direct statements of a colonial critique on the part of black writers appeared when they collaborated with white colleagues. The first important such collaboration produced *The Collapse of Cotton Tenancy*, by Charles S. Johnson, Edwin R. Embree, and Will W. Alexander. Johnson, a black sociologist, was among those who had trained with Park at the University of Chicago. This slim book summarized the field studies conducted by Johnson's own students at Fisk and Rupert Vance's students at North Carolina. At the time, this type of interracial collaboration represented a revolutionary development in the South.

While primarily concerned with the immediate problems of southern tenants, the report contained clear references to the colonial analogy. Quoting Louis XIV of France to the effect that "credit supports agriculture, as the cord supports the hanged," Johnson and his co-authors went on to make a scathing critique of the financial system of the South. In the best southern tradition, they noted that "even under slavery the chief capital supporting cotton cultivation was not available in the South, a situation which kept the whole area in a secondary slavery to the capital of the North."[57]

Other portions of the book emphasized how the South's reliance on cotton had worked to the disadvantage of the region. In classic critique style the authors called for a program to extend land ownership to millions of landless southerners, black and white. Indeed the basic argument of the report took an almost agrarian spirit. Asserting that "the cities and their industries are already over-crowded," Johnson and company argued for a diversified and self-sufficient agriculture. They acknowledged that "small farm owners will not be stopped from growing their quota of cotton or of any other commercial crop, since they must have some income to buy clothes and shoes, and shelter and food beyond what they themselves can produce."[58] Nevertheless the "chief efforts of these new homesteaders will be toward growing foodstuffs for their own consumption and making things for their own use."

The Collapse of Cotton Tenancy, virtually indistinguishable in its philosophy from the work of the Chapel Hill group in the 1930s, built on a perception, shared by Johnson and his colleagues, that the South had reached this economic impasse largely as the result of its unbalanced and dependent economy. These themes appeared even more explicitly in a second collaboration between white and black sociologists.

Arthur F. Raper, one of Odum's students from Chapel Hill, employed by the Commission on Interracial Cooperation, and Ira De A. Reid, a black professor from Atlanta University, co-authored *Sharecrop-*

pers All, a serious effort at investigative sociology. In the introduction to the book, Raper and Reid offered the reader a new version of the stock story of southern dependency on goods created elsewhere: "Nowadays the bright tin roof on the cotton tenant's cabin epitomizes the South's place in the nation. It reflects the exhaustion of local forests from which shingles were once rived; it emphasizes the unbalance between urban and rural economies, for the tin roof was made on machines driven by fossil fuels but paid for by cotton grown in the sun by hand. The price of the roof decreased scarcely one fifth during the depression, cotton over half—the price of the roof was protected by monopoly and tariff, the price of cotton by neither." In this same vein they went on to say that even if the tin roof had been made in the South, "the ownership and control of the operation most likely would be centered outside the region, with tribute siphoned off in the form of interest and profits."[59]

Argued Raper and Reid, "For decades the city dwellers have been buying farm products cheaply and selling the farmers town-made goods and town-administered services dearly. This unbalance, most aggravated in the cotton South, is not unrelated to the tariff, differential freight rates and hand processes which handicap the cotton growers."[60] They denounced the emergence of a class of "regional overseers" who represent the national corporations largely controlled by "financial interests outside the South."

The sociologists who took up the colonial analogy had been sensitized by their direct observation of the collapse of southern agriculture. This dramatic event underscored the community of interest between white and black farmers. African-American writers emphasized the shared plight of rural blacks and whites. This idea, already evident in the work of the white Chapel Hill sociologists, took on prominence when they collaborated with black scholars. The addition of racial discrimination, segregation, and violence to the long list of problems generated or exacerbated by the South's dependent economy represented an important emendation of the colonial analogy. This expanded understanding of the South as victim provided an important bridge between southern white liberals and the region's expanding black leadership during the interwar period. The collaborations of these two groups resulted in one of the sharper ironies of southern intellectual history: a doctrine that had been developed largely as a defense of a slave society was transmuted into a program for interracial cooperation.

Black commitment to the various versions of the colonial critique should not be exaggerated. In the post–World War II period, African-

American scholars have not built seriously on this line of thought. The work of the historian John Hope Franklin is representative. Born in Oklahoma in 1915 and a student at Fisk University in the 1930s, Franklin must have been exposed to the colonial idea early in his career. Nevertheless in his classic work, *From Slavery to Freedom: A History of American Negroes,* originally published in 1947, Franklin made only passing reference to the region's dependency when discussing the post–Civil War period: "While the white leaders of the South were preoccupied with questions of Negro suffrage and civil rights, northern financiers and industrialists took advantage of the opportunity to impose their economic control on the South, and it has endured to the present day."[61]

While the colonial analogy has won only scattered support from black writers, the economic thinking behind that analogy relates closely to a major theme of African-American thought. Stretching back to the nineteenth century, the idea of a group economy has played a prominent role in the black community. Essential to this view has been the achievement of conscious cooperation between blacks of different occupations and classes, with the purpose of reducing an exploitative dependence on the larger economy. This idea comes very close to the prescriptions advanced by many white southerners as part of their colonial critique. The injunction to build up black businesses through selective patronage runs exactly parallel to the campaign to "buy southern." The theory of the "double-duty dollar" might just as easily have been put forth by Henry Grady as by black minister-journalist Gordon B. Hancock.[62]

In its most dramatic form, the internal colony thesis has played a part in the black nationalist call for independent black sovereignty. This theme appeared in the political programs to achieve African colonization, the establishment of all-black communities such as Mound Bayou, Mississippi, the attempt in the 1890s to make Oklahoma a black territory, and even the Communist party proposal for an African-American nation to be carved out of the deep South.[63]

The idea of a group economy has also characterized the economic thinking of many black intellectuals who stopped short of or were even hostile to the nationalist position. In one form or another, it shows up in Douglass, Washington, Du Bois, and even among the radicals of the interwar period.[64] More recently, colonial interpretations of the ghetto economy dominated black economic thought in the 1960s. The writings of Stokely Charmichael, Charles Hamilton, Roy Innis, and Eldridge Cleaver all took this theme as central. In his 1974 review of the economics of ghetto development, Bennett Harrison concluded that "while the concept of black (or 'ghetto,' or 'minority,' or 'urban community') economic development may have been new to white America [in the 1960s], it was anything but new to black intellectuals and black political leaders." Harrison argued that a continuous if varied tradition linked these writers to the late nineteenth century.[65]

Advocacy of a group economy for the black community left little room for African-Americans to endorse a colonial analysis of the southern economy. Even the appreciation by many black intellectuals of the economic exploitation of the region did not provide a sufficient base for accepting the South as a colony. Virtually all colonial arguments incorporate important cultural components. Racism played too central a role, in the white South to allow many black thinkers to celebrate their links to southern culture. On this score, the competing concept of a black colony had far more appeal.

While many African-American intellectuals knew the colonial analogies used by white southerners, they generally avoided invoking these arguments in their own analysis of the South. For some, the South always remained an economic power dominated by the former slaveowning class. As the twentieth century unfolded, the economic weaknesses of the South became clearer and clearer. The penetration of northern capital could not be ignored. However, for many black writers, the North, despite its own hypocrisy, represented a progressive force in the South's economy.

Whatever the analysis of the southern economy, any appeal to southern solidarity had to be met with disbelief by blacks, who daily witnessed the racism of that region. The tradition that emphasized the colonial nature of the relation between black and white economies seemed far more compelling than the one based on geography.

The major exceptions to these generalization came in the writings of black sociologists working in the South during the interwar period. A hallmark of the liberal sociology of the 1920s and 1930s held that racism represented an aberration nourished by ignorance and poverty. The same sociology emphasized the importance of community and civic participation. These reformers, black and white, eagerly anticipated a sense of community between whites and blacks throughout the South. In the midst of the shared catastrophe besetting the region's agriculture, the South as an exploited colony seemed a natural theme to support such a reform agenda. Given the national shame over Depression conditions in the South, it seemed at least possible to the black sociologists that southern blacks might gain from a stronger, less dependent regional economy.

As the South has converged with the rest of the country, the notion of the South as an internal colony has lost much of its immediacy. The idea of the African-American economy as a distinct and dependent entity still continues to be timely. Perhaps this justifies the position of many black intellectuals, who, over the years, saw little reason to view the South as a colony. At least it suggests that the colonial dependency that many of them did see in the relation between black and white economies has proved a good deal more intractable than the geographic dependency that white southerners were so fond of denouncing.

The Demise of Critical Thought

The prosperity that began in the South with the coming of World War II prompted southerners once again to reconsider their society and economy. In the 1930s the colonial analogy had become a virtual apology for the South. The great majority of serious social thought done in the South since 1940 has taken a sharply self-critical tone. Raper and Reid's *Share-croppers All* had perhaps already crossed that boundary. Of course southerners had criticized their region before, and the colonial perspective had more than once played a role in such self-criticism. Southerners had attacked the overspecialization in cotton, the low level of urbanization, and even the peculiar institution of slavery in the context of the colonial analogy. But all these discussions had begun from the premise that the South had a unique and special character worthy of preservation. Thus, when Henry Grady told southerners to be more like Yankees, he at the same time assured them that they would always be different. The glorification of the Old South, the emphasis on the continuation of southern religion and culture, and the insistence on the subordination of black southerners provided ample evidence of the southernness of the New South program.

Starting in the 1940s, southern thought ventured into very different territory. Increasingly, southerners perceived the ills of their economy as directly related to a self-perpetuating and highly suspect regional culture. In intellectual circles the dependency apology no longer washed. One might expect that under such circumstances the colonial argument would disappear, but its grasp on the southern imagination proved far too strong. The new criticism accepted colonial status as historical fact but ruled it irrelevant. Colonial exploitation might explain the region's past but could not serve as an excuse for its present.

These ideas had already appeared in Raper and Reid. Although the region had been victimized in the past, Raper and Reid made clear that the South had done less than it might have to help itself out of its predicament. For them, this lack of activity no longer reflected a charming southern sluggishness. Rather, it provided evidence of the region's perverse obsession with race, an obsession that suggested a serious cultural pathology, for which the South had to take responsibility. Raper and Reid concluded that the South had been "handicapped less by the sharecroppers than by the heritage of the plantation system, less by outside opposition than by inside complacency, less by the presence of the Negro than by the white man's attitude toward him, less by the specter of class uprisings and Negro domination than by the fear of them." Retelling a folk story about "haunts," they moralized that the "most important thing about 'haunts' is what they make you do to yourself."[66]

A similar theme characterized Wilbur Cash's classic, *The Mind of the South,* published in the same year as *Sharecroppers All.* A journalist by profession, Cash was powerfully influenced by the reformist social science of the 1930s. *The Mind of the South* takes as given the early colonial position of the region. The "Old South had been pretty much in the position of a European colony," Cash wrote. It had been "set down in a nation side by side with, and forced by the tariff to buy everything it needed from, an economy with a much higher and continually mounting standard of living." Cash argued that "after the Civil War this position had been made greatly worse," at least in part because the "tariff gang had now got a completely free hand." If one had any doubt as to who exactly composed this gang, Cash told us that "the great banking interests of New York were an integral and in the last analysis probably the most essential, part of the tariff gang. . . . These banking interests were guilty of exploiting the South in other ways on their own private account," that is, through the region's usurious credit system. This all meant that in the end "a very great part of even such poor wealth as it could manage to create was being drained off to fatten the pockets of the masters of the North."[67] Now this is fairly tough talk. However, for Cash the fact of exploitation played only an incidental role in the region's history. Dependency might explain early features of the South's economic development, but it did not explain the region's character. The South's backwardness and narrowness had outlived by far its colonial past. Despite all the New South rhetoric, the southern character had long resisted the onslaught of progress and industry, undermining economic and social development. The southern middle classes, particularly shallow in their own aspirations, failed to play their historic modernizing role. This southern character, and not any ongoing southern dependency, had long ago become the stumbling block to a more appropriate development of the region.

Cash's sociology of the South held the region responsible for its own fate. The modern South labored under no special burdens; it just got in its own way. The thinking of academic economists in the region followed a somewhat different course to much the same conclusion. Southern economists in the twentieth century had never strongly advocated the colonial analogy, although they had maintained a perennial concern with the problem of achieving a more balanced regional economy. Starting in the 1920s, southern economists struggled to establish respectable departments in various universities of the region. Given the norms of the profession nationally, an espousal of unorthodox notions of regional exploitation would hardly have been the path to institution building. As was true in much of the North, southern economics departments became identified with a brand of serious conservatism uncongenial to speculations about colonial exploitation. Many in these departments strongly supported free trade, but they paid little attention to the more inflammatory arguments in their forbears' thought. Indeed, the contributors to the *Southern Economic Journal* produced no articles organized about the themes of dependency. While they dealt at length with North-South wage differentials, they never raised the charge of exploitation. Oriented toward the goals of the New South, southern economists adopted a course of traditional economics, drawing little on regional intellectual themes.[68]

Economic Resources and Policies of the South, a study by two economists from Duke University, Calvin B. Hoover and B. U. Ratchford, typified the orthodox approach to southern problems. This study, published in 1951, responded to a request by the National Planning Association Committee of the South. In many ways this volume provided an economic equivalent to the survey works by Odum and Vance from before the war, yet Hoover and Ratchford had far less sympathy than those sociologists for the spirit of the colonial critiques. Indeed, they saw it as their responsibility to criticize that time-honored southern genre. Warning that many explanations of southern backwardness had "been taken over as shibboleths or slogans," Hoover and Ratchford went on to seriously question several of the pillars of the colonial analogy. They described differential freight rates, absentee ownership, and even the tariff as mixed blessings and came to the verdict that southerners had given far too much emphasis to these forces. Indeed, while Hoover and Ratchford acknowledged that southern development lagged far behind the rest of the country, they seemed unwilling to give an explanation for this phenomenon. In the area of agriculture they looked favorably on trends toward diversification but had only limited sympathy for the notion of encouraging yeoman farmers. While eager to see industry expand in the region, they seemed convinced that market forces could do the job.

Hoover and Ratchford thus staked out a middle ground. Rejecting the larger claims of the economic critiques, they treated the South as just a poorer version of the rest of the country. And if they did not apologize for the South, they also refrained from attacking the South. Other economists—especially those focusing on the new subdiscipline of development economics—proved less aloof.

Victory in World War II placed the United States in a new and powerful international position. As a result, the country greatly expanded its relations with Third World nations, the majority of whom, newly emerging from colonial status, were undertaking their first conscious economic development programs. The United States had an obvious interest in encouraging them. Economists throughout the country began seriously to consider the economic problems of development. Not surprisingly, theorists largely committed to the free play of open markets found little use for neocolonial and other potentially radical theories of Third World dependency. In their place they offered a range of descriptive and explanatory propositions. These often involved a considerable concern with the psychological orientation of underdeveloped peoples. Some of this came perilously close to "blaming the victim."

In any event, a new wave of academic economists in the South took up development economics. Their experiences in their own region provided them with both an appreciation of agricultural economics and a sensitivity to the challenges of underdevelopment. Their basic conservatism, however, left them unsympathetic to neocolonial theories. Ironically, then, these sons of the South adopted an intellectual position hostile to precisely the thinking that had so long characterized their own region. Inevitably, some of these academics returned to evaluation of the South's own problems with economic development. The most distinguished economist in this group, William Nicholls, of Vanderbilt University, espoused his view of the South in an essay, *Southern Tradition and Regional Progress,* which provided one of the most telling attacks on southern traditions ever written by a white southerner. The essay particularly gained power from its gentle and concerned tone, an example of the finest southern form.

Nicholls began by emphasizing that "economists interested in eco-

nomic development cannot avoid concerning themselves with noneconomic factors." He cited his own work on underdeveloped countries and
suggested that development policies often went astray because of a lack
of sensitivity to the noneconomic. The same held true for the South.
Nicholls argued that "certain peculiar noneconomic factors in the southern tradition have offered formidable barriers to the material progress
of the region." Nicholls, a good southerner, allowed that the South began
as a "colonial or tributary economy."[69] But even in doing so he suggested
that this status had been favored by the planter interest, which actively
opposed a more diversified economy. Specialization, far from being forced
on the South, had been chosen. In the post–Civil War period, Nicholls
suggested, southerners had rejected a progressive program of economic
development despite the efforts of the New South people. He summarized
nineteenth-century southern economic history: "when the ante-bellum
agrarian South could have industrialized, it did not want to; when the
post-bellum prostrate South decided belatedly that it did want industrialization its sudden frenzied efforts to achieve it met with only limited
success; and when its limited success had become apparent, it tended
to return to the old agrarian values which had prevailed before the Civil
War."[70]

It is clear from Nicholls narrative that, whatever the origins of the
South's specialized agrarian economy, its perpetuation had fundamentally reflected the southern psyche and not any extrinsic economic barriers. He particularly criticized the Nashville Agrarians. "The Agrarian
program would have segmented a national economy whose major asset
had been its vast free-trade area; it would have revived and strengthened
the South's negative and destructive spirit of sectionalism; and it would
have reduced to an even slower pace the industrial-urban development
and agricultural progress which are essential if we are to solve the South's
serious problem of poverty."[71]

For Nicholls, northern domination had not straitjacketed the southern economy. Quite the contrary, the South's own agrarian values, rigid
social structure, undemocratic politics, conformity, violence, and lack
of social responsibility had held it prisoner. Where the agrarians, writing
in the midst of the Great Depression, had argued the impossibility of
the South's duplicating northern economic achievements, Nicholls asserted, "The South must choose between tradition and progress."[72] And
Nicholls had faith that in a free-market economy with a modest amount
of support from federal and state governments that the prize could be
won.

Subsequent developments in the South have surely borne out Nicholls' prediction that the region had the wherewithal to achieve higher per capita incomes. Just as surely, this development has eroded the traditional values Nicholls identified. However, one can reasonably ask whether these changes did not follow on a change in the way northern businesses participated in the South's economy. Rather than emanating from a southern conversion to progress, the South's prosperity may well have its roots in external changes. Northern corporations, facing reduced European immigration and, in the 1950s and 1960s, a relatively successful union movement, found the South far more attractive than they previously had. In addition, congressional legislation to raise minimum wages and control hours had helped to create in the South consumer markets that had never before existed.[73] From this perspective one might conclude that the South had been promoted from colony to province. Did the South's status change because of its rejection of its traditional values or because its time had come round at last?

Unequal Exchanges

For years now the South has been shedding its history. This process has produced real progress in a region that has been poor too long. But I am hardly the first to suggest that, in transformation, the South has given up much of the good with the bad. Self-critical social thought among southern intellectuals required courage, but the general acknowledgment of southern deficiency seems to have greatly dulled the southern critique of industrial society. The rich traditions of southern economic thought have largely disappeared. Admittedly, worse things have happened to the South. Yet the decline of the colonial analogy in the region's economic writings represents a serious loss to critical political economy.

Over quite a long time, southerners developed economic theories that sought out and attempted to identify the mechanisms of dependency. The South's initial concern with this topic, shared with the North in prerevolutionary times, developed into a uniquely regional body of thought. Rich with conflicting themes, these colonial critiques all focused on the meaning of dependency and the colonial relationship.

The southern concern with dominance and dependency surely derived from the mercantilist theories common in the seventeenth century, but the mercantilist vantage point had shifted to the colonial shore. From there it seemed natural to emphasize injunctions to develop well-ordered and diverse communities, rather than those mercantilist doctrines that allowed colonies only a role as providers of raw materials and plantation staples. This transformation of mercantilist thought itself came in conflict with a quite different analysis of the colonial predicament, one that emphasized freedom from a central government, not as a means of establishing local authority, but as an end in itself. Eventually drawing on the economics of Adam Smith, southerners asserted an almost libertarian theory of economic development.

These often conflicting critiques of the colonial situation coexisted in surprising proximity. Even gifted southerners like Jefferson and Calhoun failed to reconcile the underlying tension. Often their arguments degenerated into broad attacks on commerce as such. Such primitivism failed to provide a synthesis. In John Taylor's penetrating analysis of the paper system, the libertarian critique reached its nineteenth-century apogee. However, Taylor sidestepped completely the mercantilist vision, both economic and communitarian.

The first southern academics proved hardly ready for the task of synthesis. Their defense of free trade left little room to explore the subtlety of colonial dependency. Captured by the logic of classical political economy, these champions of laissez faire declared the perfect wisdom of Adam Smith's invisible hand. Oddly enough, even the most impressive formal analysis of the much-attacked tariff came from a politician, George McDuffie, not an academic.

The eccentric George Fitzhugh created the most perceptive nineteenth-century version of the colonial critique. More clearly than other southern writers, he diagnosed the ensnaring quality of modern staples markets and showed that short-run gains of trade could be damning in the long run. His theory of unequal exchange stands as a major achievement. In advocating a diversified local economy, he astutely challenged the logic of what would become known as mass production and also advanced an economic vision of community. Yet, Fitzhugh's obsession with the need to defend slavery as an institution forced him to adopt a cynical attitude toward individual liberty. His denial of individual rights limited his capacity to reach a meaningful synthesis of the mercantilist and laissez-faire critiques of dependency.

As the Civil War approached, Hinton Rowan Helper advanced the view that the southern colonial position derived from the slave order. Dangerously radical in the antebellum period, this thesis became a commonplace of the New South movement. The champions of that crusade, despite having considerable understanding of their region's economy, could only offer the hope that a new wave of "foreign" capital would prove far more helpful than had the credit so painfully acquired in the past.

The populists, like the academics of the antebellum period, hoped against hope that free markets would guarantee their prosperity. Yet in their experimentation with cooperative forms and monetary interventions, they seemed to recognize that freedom from dependency required something more than a laissez-faire national economic policy. Their discussion of overproduction anticipated major elements of Keynesian economics. At the analytical level, however, their thought remained muddled and provided an embarrassing touchstone for several generations of demagogues.

Like Fitzhugh, the Nashville Agrarians occupied an eccentric position. They represented the most impressive twentieth-century American effort to construct a meaningful conservative economics. The agrarians stood for conservativism in the European sense and not for a misnamed nineteenth-century liberalism. They looked to tradition to reconcile individual freedom and community needs. They subscribed to a seductive, romantic psychology whose appeal to southerners unsure of their regional identity proved considerable. Yet they never produced a political economy to match their social psychology. Like the populists, their concept of rural community lacked glue. During the Depression this shortcoming might be overlooked, since at that time the national economy seemed bankrupt. When the economy later boomed, the agrarian position became considerably harder to defend. Besides, the agrarians lacked commitment to their own cause. Having built their world view on the importance of place and community, they, like many of their southern forebears, turned out to be a mobile lot, only loosely tied to any particular community. Little wonder that they lost interest in their venture.

All this leaves us with the sociologists, the southern liberals. Surely, Rupert Vance contributed the best balanced presentation of the colonial analogy in this century. He provided the hints of a synthesis. Strengthened by an emerging understanding of the macroeconomics of depression, Vance could see a role for both individual initiative and regional planning. Indeed, like Keynesian liberals, Vance, Odum, and their colleagues consciously searched for a "third way," between unbridled capitalism and state socialism. But Vance dropped the colonial theme early in his career, and Odum always had approached it circumspectly. With some justification, agrarians taunted the sociologists for avoiding the radical implications of their own work. The southern liberal sociologists looked to the North for support. Critical of much in the South, their national ties provided intellectual confirmation and a measure of political protection. Their careers left them hardly eager to champion a militant South. Theirs was a supplicant South. In turning away from this stance they lost an opportunity to synthesize the colonial critique, but perhaps they understood better than anyone that, at least for the South, the time for such synthesis had passed.

What relevance do the southern colonial critiques have today? First of all they suggest an alternative to the dominant Panglossian orthodox political economy. Southern thinkers have always been more sensitive than northerners to the realities of force, inequality, and dependence. Even when willing, economists have largely failed to integrate these realities into the formalism of analytical economics. Southern writings provide a rich source of encouragement to this effort.

At the same time, southern economic critiques create a bridge to the varieties of dependency theory still popular among political economists in Latin America and the Third World. As C. Vann Woodward suggested long ago, the southern experience has much in common with the world outside the United States. Southern writings on dependency represent a little known body of work potentially of interest to many of these scholars. They also provide southerners and other Americans a background to use in understanding theories from abroad. It would be fascinating to undertake a comparative history of intellectual thought on dependency.

The rootlessness of most Americans has undermined our sense of place, our loyalty to community. Southern economic thought built squarely on just these values. Although ultimately unsuccessful in integrating them into a persuasive normative theory, the southern versions of dependency theory stand as eloquent pleas for a geographic conception of community. We have been so numb to our surroundings that few of us perceive ourselves as part of a community at all. In accepting the bounty of the national economy we have given up our place in it. This is surely an unequal exchange of the worst sort. Whatever our origins, the South's own political economy challenges us to again find a place for community in our political economy.

Notes

Chapter One Introductions

1. Adam Smith, *The Wealth of Nations* (London, 1776; New York: Modern Library, 1937), pp. 579–81, and book 4, chap. 7, passim.

2. Smith, *The Wealth of Nations,* book 3, "Of the Different Progress of Opulence in Different Nations," passim, esp. chap. 1. Also note the preference Smith held for the "agricultural system" of the physiocrats over the "mercantile system." Drew McCoy, in *The Elusive Republic: Political Economy in Jeffersonian America* (Chapel Hill: University of North Carolina Press, 1980), p. 175, discusses the appeal that Smith's theory of a natural sequence of economic development held for the Republicans, North and South, of the postrevolutionary period.

3. The natural protections created by transportation costs and uncertainties play a major role in Smith's analysis of economic development. They even appear in his famous argument for the invisible hand. See my "Invisible Hands," *Journal of Economic Perspectives* 3 (1989): 195–201.

4. Gustav von Schmoller, *The Mercantile System and Its Historical Significance,* trans. W. J. Ashley (New York, 1884; New York: A. M. Kelley, 1967).

5. For a particularly good introduction to the history of mercantilist thought, see the essays in D. C. Coleman, ed., *Revisions in Mercantilism* (London: Methuen, 1969).

6. Sir James Steuart, *An Inquiry into the Principles of Political Oeconomy,* ed. Andrew Skinner (London, 1767; Edinburgh: Scottish Economic Society, 1969), p. 203.

7. Henry Robinson, *England's Safety in Trade's Encrease* (London, 1641), quoted in Philip W. Buck, *The Politics of Mercantilism* (New York: Octagon Books, 1964), p. 114.

8. *Britannia Languens; or, A Discourse of Trade* (London: Tho. Dring, 1680), reprinted in *Early English Tracts on Commerce,* ed. J. R. McCulloch (London, 1856; Cambridge: Cambridge University Press, 1970), pp. 298–99.

9. Smith's argument has been recapped in the work of Robert Ekelund and Robert Tollison, *Mercantilism as a Rent-Seeking Society: Economic Regulation in Historical Perspective* (College Station: Texas A & M University Press, 1981).

Eli Heckscher authored the still-classic history *Mercantilism* (London, 1935; London: Methuen, 1969).

10. An important exception to this generalization is the fine book by Paul Conkin, *Prophets of Prosperity: America's First Political Economists* (Bloomington: Indiana University Press, 1980).

11. It is interesting to note that at the same time Carey was writing, the British economist Edward Wakefield reached similar conclusions concerning the sources of productivity growth. Of course both Carey and Wakefield were elaborating on mercantilist notions. Wakefield's ideas won endorsement from no less an economist than John Stuart Mill. However, as Mill emphasized, Wakefield eschewed protectionism in favor of high land prices in less developed regions and colonies. Presumably, the high land prices would encourage compact settlement. For his endorsement of Wakefield and his criticisms of Carey see John Stuart Mill, *Principles of Political Economy,* ed. W. J. Ashley (London, 1848; London: Longmans, Green, 1929), pp. 922–25, 965, 972–74.

12. Henry C. Carey, *The Past, the Present, and the Future* (Philadelphia, 1848; New York: Augustus M. Kelley, 1967), p. 388.

13. Friedrich List, *The National System of Political Economy,* trans. Sampson S. Lloyd (Stuttgart, 1841; London: Longmans, Green, 1928), p. 200.

14. Many discussions of dependency theory start with the work of Raul Prebisch and the Economic Commission for Latin America (ECLA) of the United Nations. Prebisch emphasized the distinction between center and periphery and the need for a program of import substitution. Major contributions were then made by Theotonio Dos Santos, Celso Furtado, and Andre Gunder Frank, among others. For an informative history of dependency theory and a full bibliography, see Magnus Blomstrom and Bjorn Hettne, *Development Theory in Transition: The Dependency Debate and Beyond: Third World Responses* (London: Zed Books, 1984). Also see Joseph Love, "Raul Prebisch and the Origins of the Doctrine of Unequal Exchange," *Latin American Research Review* 15 (1980): 45–72.

15. Andre Gunder Frank, *Lumpenbourgeoisie: Lumpendevelopment; Dependence, Class, and Politics in Latin America*, trans. Marion Davis Berdicio (New York: Monthly Review Press, 1972), p. 1.

16. James Caporaso and B. Zare, "An Interpretation and Evaluation of Dependency Theory," in *From Dependency to Development,* ed. H. Munoz (Boulder, Colo.: Westview, 1982), p. 49, and quoted in Wilfred L. David, *Conflicting Paradigms in the Economics of Developing Nations* (New York: Praeger, 1986), p. 174.

17. The failure of programs of import substitution in Latin America received particular attention from Celso Furtado and Andre Gunder Frank.

18. The parallels between Latin America and the southern United States have not escaped the *dependistas.* Andre Gunder Frank, in his *Lumpenbourgeoisie,* shows a special interest in this theme. However, D. C. M. Platt, in an influential review of dependency theory, claims the analogy is false. He concludes that the

South *was dependent,* while Latin America, at least in the early nineteenth century, was just ignored by the metropolitan powers. D. C. M. Platt, "Dependency in Nineteenth-Century Latin America: An Historian Objects," *Latin American Research Review* 15 (1980): 113–30.

19. The term "provincial mercantilism" was coined by John C. Rainbolt in *From Prescription to Persuasion: Manipulation of Eighteenth-Century Virginia Economy* (Port Washington, N.Y.: Kennikat Press, 1974).

20. Samuel Fortrey, *England's Interest and Improvement* (London: Nathanael Brook, 1673), reprinted in *Early English Tracts,* ed. McCulloch, p. 244.

21. Josiah Child, *A New Discourse of Trade* (London: John Evingham, 1693), reprinted in *Selected Works, 1668–1697* (Farnborough: Gregg Press, 1968), pp. 205–7. Parts of this discussion are quoted in David Bertelson's brilliant book, *The Lazy South* (New York: Oxford University Press, 1967), p. 85. More generally, the discussion in the text reflects Bertelson's treatment of early British mercantilist attitudes toward colonies.

22. For an insightful treatment of Berkeley and the influence of mercantilist thought among the colonial elite, see Rainbolt, *From Prescription to Persuasion.* The discussion below draws heavily on Rainbolt's interpretation of "provincial mercantilism."

23. William Berkeley, *A Discourse and View of Virginia* (London, 1662), p. 2.

24. Ibid., pp. 7–8.

25. On this point see Carville Earle and Ronald Hoffman, "The Urban South: The First Two Centuries," in *The City in Southern History: The Growth of Urban Civilization in the South,* ed. Blaine A. Brownell and David R. Goldfield (Port Washington, N.Y.: Kennikat Press, 1977).

26. See Rainbolt, *From Prescription to Persuasion,* for a full history of the plans to build up towns in late eighteenth-century Virginia.

27. Berkeley, *A Discourse and View of Virginia,* p. 7.

28. Robert Beverley, *The History and Present State of Virginia,* ed. Louis B. Wright (London, 1705; Chapel Hill: University of North Carolina Press, 1947), p. 316.

29. Ibid., p. 6.

30. This aspect of Beverley's writings (and those of many other southerners) is emphasized in Bertelson, *The Lazy South.* Bertelson puts a spiritual and religious meaning on these concerns, as opposed to the more political interpretation given below.

31. For evidence of these views among common planters in Virginia, see Rainbolt, *From Prescription to Persuasion.* Bertelson, in *The Lazy South,* describes similar views held by colonial farmers in South Carolina and Georgia. On the general lack of a coherent community structure in the eighteenth century, see Rhys Isaac, *The Transformation of Virginia, 1740–1790* (Chapel Hill: University of North Carolina Press, 1982).

32. See Joseph Dorfman, *The Economic Mind in American Civilization,* vols. 1–2, *1606–1865* (New York: Viking Press, 1961), for a survey of economic thought in the northern colonies.

33. Theories of slavery traditionally emphasize the land-to-labor ratio. The combination of a scarcity of labor and an abundance of land encourages the powerful to avoid the dilemma of high wages and low rents: see Evsey Domar, "The Causes of Slavery or Serfdom: A Hypothesis," *The Journal of Economic History* 30 (1970): 18–32. Clearly such theories presume that the powerful have something they can do with the surplus product. Thus the feudal lord must have a use for the serfs' grain. A commercialized agriculture always has an obvious use for slave-produced staple crops. Slavery emerged in Virginia and the rest of the South not only because of the high land-to-labor ratio but also because of the well-established commercial agriculture.

34. On the differences between southern agriculture and that of New England, see James Henretta, "Families and Farms: Mentalité in Pre-Industrial America," *William and Mary Quarterly* 35 (1978): 3–32. For a discussion of the debate this paper launched, see Edwin Perkins, *The Economy of Colonial America,* 2nd ed. (New York: Columbia University Press, 1988), pp. 67–74.

Chapter Two   Agrarianism and the Paper System

1. The still-standard work on early southern agricultural history is Lewis C. Gray, *History of Agriculture in the Southern United States to 1860,* (Washington, D.C.: Carnegie Institution, 1933). Particularly helpful on Virginia in the eighteenth century is T. H. Breen's *Tobacco Culture: The Mentality of the Great Tidewater Planters on the Eve of Revolution* (Princeton: Princeton University Press, 1985).

2. See Gray, *History of Agriculture,* also discussion in Joseph Dorfman, *The Economic Mind in American Civilization,* 5 vols. (New York: Viking Press, 1961), vol. 2, pp. 122–24.

3. For a discussion of planter mentalité and the meaning of debt in the eighteenth century, see Breen, *Tobacco Culture.*

4. For a discussion of early interest in opening western development, see Dorfman, *The Economic Mind,* vol. 2, pp. 124–25, and Charles Ambler, *Sectionalism in Virginia from 1776 to 1861* (Chicago, 1910; New York: Russell and Russell, 1964) pp. 16–22.

5. Breen, *Tobacco Culture,* p. 195.

6. Thomas Jefferson, "A Summary View of the Rights of British America" (1774), in *The Papers of Thomas Jefferson,* ed. Julian P. Boyd (Princeton: Princeton University Press, 1950), vol. 1, p. 122.

7. Ibid., p. 135.

8. This observation is made by Pauline Maier in her perceptive discussion

of Lee and his psychology, in *The Old Revolutionaries: Political Lives in the Age of Samuel Adams* (New York: Alfred A. Knopf, 1980).

9. Richard Henry Lee, "To James Madison," Aug. 11, 1785, in *The Letters of Richard Henry Lee,* ed. James Ballagh, 2 vols. (New York, 1914; New York: Da Capo Press, 1970), vol. 2, p. 383.

10. On the origins of this southern view of commerce in British "country ideology," see J. G. A. Pocock, *Virtue, Commerce, and History: Essays on Political Thought and History, Chiefly in the Eighteenth Century* (Cambridge: Cambridge University Press, 1985), p. 273, and T. H. Breen's *Tobacco Culture.*

11. Robert A. Rutland, ed., *The Papers of George Mason,* 3 vols. (Chapel Hill: University of North Carolina Press, 1970), vol. 3, p. 989. Mason proposed a two-thirds rule for passing commercial legislation until 1808. Rutland quotes Jefferson as eventually agreeing with Mason.

12. The role of Sheffield as an advocate of neocolonialism was suggested by William Appleman Williams in his provocative history of the United States, *The Contours of American History,* (Chicago: Quadrangle Books, 1966). Williams organizes much of his analysis around the tension between mercantilist and laissez-faire thought in the American context.

13. John Lord Sheffield, *Observations on the Commerce of the American States* (London, 1783; New York: Augustus M. Kelley, 1970), p. 193.

14. Ibid., p. 203.

15. Ibid., p. 5.

16. This discussion of Washington's involvement in river development after the Revolution is based on Ambler, *Sectionalism in Virginia,* pp. 47–48.

17. Ralph Ketcham, in *James Madison: A Biography* (New York: Macmillan, 1971), pp. 168–69, provides a discussion of Madison's activities on behalf of the port plan. William Appleman Williams, in *Contours of American History,* makes much of these early mercantilist leanings. On the other hand, notice that Drew McCoy dissents, in *The Elusive Republic: Political Economy in Jeffersonian America* (Chapel Hill: University of North Carolina Press, 1980). The most obvious conclusion is that Madison, like Washington, carried a considerable ambivalence on this score throughout his life.

18. For a discussion of southern (and northern) expectations about population growth and the likely loyalties of the West, see Staughton Lynd, "The Compromise of 1787," in *Class Conflict, Slavery, and the United States Constitution: Ten Essays* (Indianapolis: Bobbs-Merrill, 1967).

19. For a pithy treatment of sectional quarreling in the postrevolutionary period, see Joseph L. Davis, *Sectionalism in American Politics, 1774–1787* (Madison: University of Wisconsin Press, 1977). Also see Robert A. McGuire and Robert L. Ohsfeldt, "An Economic Model of Voting Behavior over Specific Issues at the Constitutional Convention of 1787," *Journal of Economic History* 46 (1986): 79–110. McGuire and Ohsfeldt conclude that "delegates who owned slaves or

represented slaveowning constituents were more likely to oppose issues favoring a national form of government."

20. See Staughton Lynd, "The Abolitionist Critique of the United States Constitution," in *Class Conflict,* for a defense of this radical interpretation.

21. Thomas Jefferson, *Notes on the State of Virginia* (Paris: privately printed, 1784), reprinted in *The Writings of Thomas Jefferson,* ed. Andrew A. Lipscomb and Albert Bergh, 20 vols. (Washington, D.C.: Thomas Jefferson Memorial Association, 1905), vol. 2, p. 229.

22. On the importance of virtue as a central concept of republican thinking, see Drew McCoy's very fine book, *The Elusive Republic,* pp. 69–80. McCoy emphasizes the importance of virtue to northern as well as southern republicans of the late eighteenth century.

23. For a discussion of the meaning of "virtue" and its opposition to (and sometimes compromise with) "commerce," see Pocock, *Virtue, Commerce, and History,* p. 235.

24. This point is made with respect to R. H. Lee's involvement in the Revolution by Pauline Maier in *The Old Revolutionaries,* p. 188.

25. Thomas Jefferson, "To Chastellux with Enclosure," Paris, Sept. 2, 1785, in *The Papers of Thomas Jefferson,* vol. 8, p. 468.

26. Jefferson, *Notes on the State of Virginia,* vol. 2, p. 226.

27. John Taylor, *The Arator* (Georgetown, 1813; Indianapolis: Liberty Classics, 1977), p. 66. For a comprehensive introduction to Taylor's life and philosophy, see Robert E. Shalhope, *John Taylor of Caroline: Pastoral Republican* (Columbia: University of South Carolina Press, 1980); Eugene Mudge's *The Social Philosophy of John Taylor of Caroline: A Study in Jeffersonian Democracy* (New York: Columbia University Press, 1939) provides a useful precis.

28. Thomas Jefferson, "To Jean Baptiste Say," Feb. 1, 1804, in *The Writings of Thomas Jefferson,* ed. Lipscomb and Bergh, vol. 11, p. 2. A similar point, but with less emphasis on the mutuality of benefit, is made by Jefferson in *Notes on the State of Virginia.*

29. On this dilemma, again see McCoy, *The Elusive Republic,* pp. 90–104.

30. This report is discussed in some length in Douglas C. North, *The Economic Growth of the United States, 1790–1860* (New York: W. W. Norton, 1966).

31. Thomas Jefferson, "Report on the Privileges and Restrictions on the Commerce of the United States in Foreign Countries," Dec. 16, 1793, *The Writings of Thomas Jefferson,* ed. Lipscomb and Bergh, vol. 3, p. 275.

32. Ibid., p. 276.

33. This position is advanced by William Grampp in his *Economic Liberalism* (New York: Random House, 1967), p. 152. Grampp distinguishes three stages in Jefferson's thought: agrarian self-sufficiency, market-oriented agriculture, and a balance of agriculture, commerce, and manufacturing.

34. On the differences between Jefferson and Madison, see Andrew W.

Foshee, "Jeffersonian Political Economy and the Classical Republican Tradition: Jefferson, Taylor, and the Agrarian Republic," *History of Political Economy* 17, no. 4 (1984): 523–50.

35. Thomas Jefferson, "To Benjamin Austin Esq.," Jan. 9, 1816, in *The Writings of Thomas Jefferson,* ed. Lipscomb and Bergh, vol. 14, pp. 391–92.

36. Several treatments of Taylor's life wrongly assert that he was left an orphan. In fact, after his marriage and purchase of a sizable estate, Taylor brought his mother to live with him; see Shalhope, *John Taylor of Caroline.* The biographical account presented here largely follows Shalhope's treatment.

37. The historian Loren Baritz has noted that "Taylor's statement was one of the first formal expressions of a schism between the northern and southern states in American history." John Taylor, *An Inquiry into the Principles and Policy of the Government of the United States,* ed. Loren Baritz (Fredericksburg, Va., 1814; Indianapolis: Bobbs-Merrill, 1969), p. xiii.

38. See discussion of this incident in Shalhope, *John Taylor of Caroline,* p. 101. For Madison's point of view, see Ketcham, *James Madison,* pp. 394–97.

39. Taylor, *The Arator,* p. 314.

40. See Paul Conkin, *Prophets of Prosperity: America's First Political Economists* (Bloomington: Indiana University Press, 1980), p. 56. This was an idea that Adam Smith, whom Taylor greatly admired, had rejected explicitly.

41. Taylor, *The Arator,* p. 94.

42. Ibid., p. 95.

43. Ibid.

44. Ibid., p. 115.

45. Ibid., p. 358.

46. Taylor, *An Inquiry,* p. 285.

47. Ibid., p. 286.

48. Ibid., p. 75.

49. Ibid., pp. 32–33.

50. Ibid., p. 60.

51. Ibid., p. 156.

52. As the historian Robert Shalhope has emphasized, Taylor used the term *capitalists* not in its modern sense or even in that used by the economist David Ricardo, a contemporary of his. Rather, he, like Marx at a later date, drew on the connotations established in the midst of the French Revolution, when the term suggested a heartless speculator obsessed with the rapid accumulation of his money. See the interesting discussion of this point in Shalhope, *John Taylor of Caroline,* p. 187. Shalhope observes that Taylor's usage was adopted from that of Arthur Young, the British agricultural reformer, who had toured France during the Revolution. He also suggests similarities to Adam Smith's use of the term *stockjobber.*

53. John Taylor, *Construction Construed and Constitutions Vindicated* (Richmond, 1820; New York: DeCapo Press, 1970), p. 242.

54. Taylor, *The Arator,* p. 87.

55. Taylor, *An Inquiry,* p. 219.

56. Ibid., p. 220. Implicit in these calculations is an interest rate of about 5 percent.

57. Ibid.

58. The influence of Taylor on the Jacksonians is particularly emphasized by Arthur Schlesinger, in *The Age of Jackson* (Boston: Little Brown, 1945), p. 115.

59. Taylor, *An Inquiry,* p. 253.

60. Ibid., p. 259.

61. Ibid., p. 273.

62. Shalhope, *John Taylor of Caroline,* pp. 191–92.

63. Quoted in ibid., p. 192.

64. See section 15 in Taylor's *Construction Construed.*

65. Letter by John Taylor, circa 1820, reprinted in *The Nation,* Mar. 30, 1911, p. 316, and quoted in Mudge, *The Social Philosophy of John Taylor,* p. 146.

66. Mudge, *The Social Philosophy of John Taylor,* p. 146.

67. This point is made by Joseph Dorfman, in *The Economic Mind,* vol. 1, pp. 135–41, in a section appropriately entitled "The Economics of Colonial Dependency."

68. Richard Walsh, *Charleston's Sons of Liberty: A Study of the Artisans, 1763–1789* (Columbia: University of South Carolina Press, 1959), p. 135.

69. See James H. Broussard, *The Southern Federalists: 1800–1816* (Baton Rouge: Louisiana State University Press, 1978), pp. 357–59.

70. Alexander Hamilton, *Report on Manufactures* (Philadelphia, 1791), reprinted in *Industrial and Commercial Correspondence of Alexander Hamilton Anticipating His Report on Manufactures,* ed. Arthur Cole (Chicago, 1928; New York: Augustus M. Kelley, 1968). Hamilton's report had not produced much in the way of serious policy in the 1790s, since Hamilton's major political backers, Northern merchants, were preoccupied with questions of commerce, especially with gaining access to British markets. See Williams, *Contours of American History,* p. 163.

71. Hamilton, *Report on Manufactures,* p. 286. Interestingly, Hamilton anticipated the development of the cotton industry in the southern states and saw this trade (and that in wool!) as potentially a strong bond between regions.

72. John C. Calhoun, Speech in the House of Representatives, Apr. 6, 1816, in *Reports and Public Letters of John C. Calhoun,* ed. Richard Cralle, 2 vols. (New York, 1851–56; New York: Russell and Russell, 1968), vol. 2, pp. 166, 172–73.

73. It is interesting to note that southern Federalists were hostile to the revival of Hamiltonian economics under the Republicans. On this point see Broussard, *The Southern Federalists,* pp. 183–92.

74. Indeed, the plan was too ingenious for many agrarians, including Madison, who, in a surprising move, vetoed Calhoun's bill. The ambivalent Madison suggested the need for a constitutional amendment, a position that Jefferson had held for quite some time, although neither man worked in any noticeable manner to realize such an amendment. My treatment of Calhoun's program and his "bonus bill" relies heavily on George Dangerfield, *The Awakening of American Nationalism, 1815–1828* (New York: Harper and Row, 1965).

75. Quoted in Russell Kirk, *John Randolph of Roanoke: A Study in American Politics, with Selected Speeches and Letters* (Indianapolis: Liberty Press, 1978), p. 112.

76. Melvin Leiman provides considerable biographical information in *Jacob N. Cardozo: Economic Thought in the Antebellum South* (New York: Columbia University Press, 1966), which also considers Cardozo's thought in detail. Also see discussion in Dorfman, *The Economic Mind,* vol. 2, pp. 551–65 and Conkin, *Prophets of Prosperity,* pp. 135–41.

77. See the excellent summary of Cardozo's scattered writings on tariffs in Leiman, *Jacob N. Cardozo,* pp. 69–93.

78. Thomas Dew, *Lectures on the Restrictive System* (Richmond, 1829; New York: Augustus M. Kelley, 1969), p. 39.

79. Thomas Cooper, *Lectures on the Elements of Political Economy* (Columbia, S.C., 1826; New York: Augustus M. Kelley, 1971), p. 234.

80. The details of Cooper's life crowd Dumas Malone's still serviceable biography, *The Public Life of Thomas Cooper, 1783–1839* (New Haven, 1926; Columbia: University of South Carolina Press, 1961), on which this account is based. See also Conkin, *Prophets of Prosperity,* pp. 141–52.

81. William Freehling, *The Nullification Era: A Documentary Record* (New York: Harper Torchbooks, 1967), p. 25.

82. George McDuffie, speech in *Annals of the Congress of the United States,* 18th Cong., 1st sess., 1823–1824 (Washington: Gales and Seaton, 1856), p. 2403.

83. Ibid., p. 2418.

84. Interestingly, this same device was used by Alfred Marshall in *Money, Credit, and Commerce.* This comparison is made by Earl R. Rolph in "The Economics of the Nullification Movement," *Western Economic Journal* 11 (1973): 381–93. Rolph's paper presents an excellent introduction to McDuffie's logic; however, Rolph does not explicitly consider the colonial character of the argument.

85. Rolph, "The Economics of the Nullification Movement," p. 382.

86. George McDuffie, *Register of Debates in Congress,* 1829–1830, pt. 2 (Washington: Gales and Seaton, 1830), p. 843.

87. An estimate by John G. Van Deusen in his *Economic Bases of Disunion in South Carolina* (New York, 1928; New York: AMS Press, 1970) puts the division of internal improvements from 1789 to 1860 at eight million dollars for the free states and $5.7 million for the slave states. Van Deusen commented,

"This is certainly in favor of the free section, though it is far from being an advantage of ten millions claimed by [the secessionist Robert B.] Rhett," p. 137.

88. John C. Calhoun, "Original Draft of the South Carolina Exposition, Prepared for the Special Committee on the Tariff," Dec. 1828, in *The Works of John C. Calhoun,* ed. Richard R. Cralle (New York, 1851–56; New York: Russell and Russell, 1968), vol. 6, p. 40.

89. George McDuffie, "Speech at Charleston, May 19, 1831," in *The Nullification Era,* ed. Freehling, p. 116.

90. Calhoun, "Draft of the South Carolina Exposition," p. 10.

91. McDuffie, "Speech at Charleston," in *The Nullification Era,* ed. Freehling, pp. 114–15.

Chapter Three   Unequal Exchange

1. For an informative treatment of the problems facing southeastern cities in the early nineteenth century, see Thomas J. Wertenbaker, *Norfolk: Historic Southern Port* (Durham, N.C., 1931; Durham, N.C.: Duke University Press, 1962).

2. For a history of commercial conventions, see John G. Van Deusen, *The Ante-Bellum Southern Commercial Conventions* (Durham, N.C., 1926; New York: AMS Press, 1970).

3. George McDuffie's speech was reported in *DeBow's Review* 4 (1847): 208–25.

4. Quoted in Wertenbaker, *Norfolk,* p. 154.

5. George McDuffie in *DeBow's Review* 4 (1847): 220.

6. Ibid., p. 222.

7. Robert Hayne, "Report by Committee of Twenty-One," from 1839 commercial convention in Charleston, reprinted in *DeBow's Review* 4 (1847): 339–56.

8. F. H. Elmore at the same Charleston commercial convention made a comparison of northern and southern markets for foreign goods. He claimed that the costs to country merchants ran about 10 percent less in Charleston and that, in addition, Charleston businesses would accept southern bank notes at par while New York merchants discounted them 1 to 3 percent. He also asserted that Charleston would actually extend better credit. See Hayne, "Report by Committee of Twenty-One."

9. M. F. Maury, "Direct Foreign Trade of the South," *DeBow's Review* 12 (1852): 126, reprinted from the *Southern Literary Messenger.*

10. On these various schemes, see Robert Russel, *Economic Aspects of Southern Sectionalism, 1840–1861* (Urbana, Ill., 1924; New York: Russell and Russell, 1960), and John G. Van Deusen, *Economic Bases of Disunion in South Carolina* (New York, 1928; New York: AMS Press, 1970).

11. George McDuffie in *DeBow's Review* 4 (1847): 224.

12. See Charles Ambler, *Sectionalism in Virginia from 1776 to 1861* (Chicago, 1910; New York: Russell and Russell, 1964), pp. 122–27, 175.

13. James Hammond, "Progress of Southern Industry," *DeBow's Review* 8 (1850): 503.

14. Ibid., p. 504.

15. William Gregg, *DeBow's Review* 11 (1851): 131.

16. See Carey's brilliant and quite readable work, *The Past, the Present, and the Future* (Philadelphia, 1848; New York: Augustus M. Kelley, 1967). For a stimulating discussion of Carey's place in American political economy, see Paul Conkin, *Prophets of Prosperity: America's First Political Economists* (Bloomington: Indiana University Press, 1980). For a presentation that emphasizes differences between North and South, see Allen Kaufman, *Capitalism, Slavery, and Republican Values: Antebellum Political Economists, 1819–1848* (Austin: University of Texas Press, 1982). Carey's emphasis on density had considerable appeal for a people faced with the expansiveness of this continent. The notion that energy could be easily dissipated over space must have seemed quite compelling at the time.

17. Thomas Cooper, *Lectures on the Elements of Political Economy* (Columbia, S.C., 1826; New York: Augustus M. Kelley, 1971), p. 295.

18. George Tucker, *Progress of the United States in Population and Wealth in Fifty Years* (New York, 1855; New York: Augustus M. Kelley, 1964), p. 200.

19. The bulk of the biographical information that follows comes from Harvey Wish's *George Fitzhugh: Propagandist of the Old South* (Baton Rouge: Louisiana State University Press, 1943).

20. George Fitzhugh to George F. Holmes, Apr. 11, 1855, Holmes Letters, Duke University Library; quoted by Wish in *George Fitzhugh,* p. 20. As Eugene Genovese has put it, Fitzhugh was a man "who wrote too much and read too little." Eugene Genovese, *The World the Slaveholders Made: Two Essays in Interpretation* (Middletown, Conn.: Wesleyan University Press, 1988), p. 128.

21. Thomas Carlyle, *The Nigger Question,* ed. Eugene August (London, 1849; New York: Appleton-Century-Crofts, 1971), p. 9.

22. On the appeal of Carlyle's thought to southern writers of the 1850s, see Louis Hartz's excellent treatment in *The Liberal Tradition in America: An Interpretation of American Political Thought since the Revolution* (New York: Harcourt, Brace and World, 1955), esp. chap. 6, "The Reactionary Enlightenment."

23. See Carlyle's discussion of political economy in his *Latter-Day Pamphlets* (Boston: Phillips, Sampson, 1850), esp. "The Present Time," and my piece "A Dismal Romantic" in *Journal of Economic Perspectives* 4 (1990): 165–72.

24. William Thompson, *Labour Rewarded* (London, 1827; New York: Augustus M. Kelley, 1969), p. 115.

25. Ibid., p. 25. Thompson argued that among other problems unequal remuneration encouraged workers not to share their knowledge and skill. Interestingly, this argument anticipated a modern theme of internal labor-market

analysis. Peter Doeringer and Michael Piore, in *Internal Labor Markets and Manpower Analysis* (Lexington, Mass.: Health, 1971), pp. 33, 83–84, suggest that this problem provides the major motivation for seniority pay provisions and, more generally, the insulation of internal from external markets.

26. Thompson, *Labour Rewarded,* p. 54.

27. Warren championed a scheme of "labor notes," a currency which would allow deferred payments according to the egalitarian formula of an hour's labor for the produce of an hour's labor. This effort built on the notion (borrowed from British socialists) that price must be based on cost and not determined by value. The frontispiece of Warren's slim volume, *Equitable Commerce* (New York, 1852; New York: B. Franklin, 1967), showed a labor note; it bore a statue of the blindfolded goddess of justice holding her scales, and over her head the motto: "Cost the Limit of Price."

28. Quoted in George Fitzhugh, *Cannibals All!; or, Slaves Without Masters,* ed. C. Vann Woodward (Richmond, 1857; Cambridge: Harvard University Press, Belknap Press, 1960), pp. 43–44.

29. Quoted in Fitzhugh, *Cannibals All!,* pp. 47–48.

30. George Fitzhugh, *Sociology for the South; or, The Failure of Free Society* (Richmond: A. Morris, 1854), p. 169.

31. Not surprisingly, Fitzhugh didn't draw out the contradiction between this position and a racist evaluation of the quality of black labor.

32. In this assertion Fitzhugh essentially anticipated a central proposition of the theory of unequal exchange. That theory as advanced by Arghiri Emmanuel and others asserts that Third World exports are cheap because Third World labor is priced below its true value.

33. Eugene Genovese insists that by "free-trade" Fitzhugh means capitalism in general. Yet, as Genovese himself admits, "unfortunately, Fitzhugh's attack on free trade sometimes becomes merely an attack on the policy of free trade, narrowly considered" (*The World the Slaveholders Made,* p. 165). I think the dependency interpretation taken in the text does a nice job of bridging this apparent gulf.

34. Fitzhugh, *Sociology for the South,* pp. 173–74.

35. Ibid., pp. 151–52.

36. Ibid., p. 152.

37. Ibid.

38. Incidentally, this idea reappears as a hallmark of modern dependency theories. See, for example, Andre Gunder Frank, *Lumpenbourgeoisie: Lumpendevelopment,* trans. Marion Davis Berdicio (New York: Monthly Review Press, 1972).

39. Hartz, *The Liberal Tradition,* pp. 147–48.

40. Quoted in David Bertelson, *The Lazy South* (New York: Oxford University Press, 1967), p. 97. Bertelson presents a broad picture of southern concerns over the eroding effects of slavery on individual initiative.

41. Quoted in Pauline Maier, *The Old Revolutionaries: Political Lives in the Age of Samuel Adams* (New York: Alfred A. Knopf, 1980), p. 190.

42. Thomas Jefferson, *Notes on the State of Virginia* (Paris: privately printed, 1784), reprinted in *The Writings of Thomas Jefferson,* ed. Andrew A. Lipscomb and Albert Bergh, 20 vols. (Washington, D.C.: Thomas Jefferson Memorial Associations, 1905), vol. 2, pp. 225–26.

43. Quoted in Richard MacMaster, "Arthur Lee's Address on Slavery," *Virginia Magazine* 80 (1972): 151.

44. Quoted in Charles Beard, *Economic Origins of Jeffersonian Democracy* (New York: Macmillan, 1949), p. 375.

45. Thomas Marshall in the *Wheeling Intelligencer,* Nov. 28, 1859, quoted in Ambler, *Sectionalism in Virginia,* p. 193.

46. The material below is drawn from Hugh Bailey, *Hinton Rowan Helper: Abolitionist-Racist* (University: University of Alabama Press, 1965). For an excellent evaluation of Helper's significance as a champion of white nonslaveholders, see Lawrence Shore, *Southern Capitalists: The Ideological Leadership of an Elite, 1832–1885* (Chapel Hill: University of North Carolina Press, 1986), chap. 2.

47. Helper's racism comes out quite strongly in two volumes he wrote after the Civil War, *Nojoque* and *Negroes in Negroland.*

48. Quoted in Russel, *Economic Aspects,* p. 48.

49. Hinton Helper, *The Impending Crisis of the South: How to Meet It,* ed. George Fredrickson (New York, 1857; Cambridge: Harvard University Press, Belknap Press, 1968), pp. 355–56. This comparison between Helper's passage and that in the previously cited newspaper piece is suggested by several authors including Shore, *Southern Capitalists,* pp. 217–18, and Avery Craven, *The Growth of Southern Sectionalism, 1848–1861* (Baton Rouge: Louisiana State University Press, 1953), pp. 249–50.

50. Helper, *The Impending Crisis,* p. 25.

51. Quoted in Helper, *The Impending Crisis,* p. 112. George Fredrickson emphasizes Helper's debt to Goodloe. The essence of the density argument reappears in the work of Eugene Genovese. See his *Political Economy of Slavery: Studies in the Economy and Society of the Slave South* (New York: Pantheon Books, 1965), pp. 163–65.

52. Helper, *The Impending Crisis,* p. 331.

53. See Fredrickson's introduction to Helper's *The Impending Crisis.*

54. Quoted in Russel, *Economic Aspects,* p. 197.

55. Frederick Law Olmsted, *A Journey in the Back Country* (New York, 1860; New York: Schocken Books, 1970), pp. 323–24.

56. Ibid., pp. 322–25.

57. Ellwood Fisher, "The North and the South," reprinted in *DeBow's Review* 7, no. 2 (Aug. 1849): 135.

58. Ibid., p. 137. Interestingly, Fisher's evaluation of the relation between

urbanization and industrialization reappears in the criticism of Hinton Helper offered by Fogel and Engerman in their influential study of slavery. Robert Fogel and Stanley Engerman, *Time on the Cross: The Economics of American Negro Slavery* (Boston: Little Brown, 1974), p. 166.

59. Fisher, "The North and the South," p. 141.

60. *Southern Quarterly Review,* July 1849, reprinted in *DeBow's Review* 8, no. 1 (Jan. 1850): 53.

61. Of course, Henry Carey offered a similar argument, but not as a defense of slavery.

62. Chancellor Harper, "Memoir on Slavery," in *The Pro-Slavery Argument* (Philadelphia, 1852; New York: Negro University Press, 1968), pp. 19–20.

63. Ibid., p. 20.

64. Quoted in Drew Gilpin Faust, *James Henry Hammond and the Old South: A Design for Mastery* (Baton Rouge: Louisiana State University Press, 1982), p. 346.

65. Thomas Kettell, *Southern Wealth and Northern Profits* (New York, 1860; University: University of Alabama Press, 1965), pp. 9–10.

66. Ibid., pp. 136–38.

67. David Christy, *Cotton Is King: or, Slavery in the Light of Political Economy,* in *Cotton Is King and Pro-Slavery Arguments,* ed. E. N. Elliott (1860; New York: Negro University Press, 1969), p. 56.

68. Ibid., p. 127.

69. Ibid., p. 129.

70. George Fitzhugh, writing in *DeBow's Review,* as quoted in Russel, *Economic Aspects,* p. 206.

71. Paranoid styles in American politics had a considerable history in both North and South. See David Brion Davis, *The Slave Power Conspiracy and the Paranoid Style* (Baton Rouge: Louisiana State University Press, 1969).

72. On this, see Gavin Wright, *The Political Economy of the Cotton South: Households, Markets, and Wealth in the Nineteenth Century* (New York: W. W. Norton, 1978).

73. See Russel, *Economic Aspects* for a fascinating discussion of this issue that has yet to be surpassed.

74. Again, see Wright, *Political Economy,* pp. 133–35.

Chapter Four A Conquered Province

1. Tipton R. Snavely, "Economic Thought and Economic Policy in the South," *Southern Economic Journal* 1 (1933): 6–7.

2. William Dodd, "Contributions of the South to Economic Thought and Writing," in *The South in the Building of the Nation,* ed. James Ballagh (Richmond: Southern Historical Publication Society, 1909), vol. 6, p. 546.

3. This assertion ignores the critical roles played by Johns Hopkins Uni-

versity and Richard T. Ely in shaping modern political economy in this country. Founded by Quakers in Baltimore—a city with a persistently ambiguous regional identity—Hopkins almost monopolized the production of Ph.D.'s in economics before 1890. The institution's spirit of intellectual inquiry and tolerance set a high standard for its imitators. While on the Hopkins faculty, Ely almost single-handedly founded the American Economics Association. A northerner by birth, Ely never identified with the South, although he showed sympathy for the populist cause. He left for the University of Wisconsin in 1892. See William J. Barber, "Political Economy in the Flagship of Postgraduate Studies: The Johns Hopkins University," in *Breaking the Academic Mould: Economists and American Higher Learning in the Nineteenth Century*, ed. William J. Barber (Middletown, Conn.: Wesleyan University Press, 1988).

4. Laurence Shore, *Southern Capitalists: The Ideological Leadership of an Elite, 1832–1885* (Chapel Hill: University of North Carolina Press, 1986), p. 141.

5. John Donald Wade, "What the South Figured: 1865–1914," *The Southern Review* 3 (1937–1938): 360–67, p. 366. Wade, a member of the Nashville agrarian movement, was less than sympathetic to the New South program.

6. Raymond B. Nixon, *Henry W. Grady, Spokesman for the New South* (New York: Alfred A. Knopf, 1943), passim.

7. Joel Chandler Harris, ed., *Life of Henry W. Grady, Including His Writings and Speeches* (New York, 1890; New York: Haskel House, 1972), p. 21.

8. Ibid., p. 22.

9. Jonathan Wiener has persuasively argued that the endorsement by Grady (and other New South advocates) of the Old South myth showed their weakness vis-à-vis the still powerful planter class. See Jonathan Wiener, *Social Origins of the New South: Alabama, 1860–1885* (Baton Rouge: Louisiana State University Press, 1978), pp. 215–21.

10. Henry W. Grady, "The New South," speech, in *Life of Henry W. Grady*, ed. Harris, p. 90.

11. Grady's view of slavery had been anticipated in the late 1860s by Zebulon Vance, of North Carolina. See discussion in Shore, *Southern Capitalists*, pp. 116–18.

12. Hoke Smith, "The Resources and Development of the South," in *North American Review* (Aug. 1894): 130–31, quoted in Dewey Grantham, Jr., *Hoke Smith and the Politics of the New South* (Baton Rouge: Louisiana State University Press, 1958), p. 67.

13. See discussion of the analysis of slavery by New South advocates, especially by Edmonds, in Paul M. Gaston, *The New South Creed: A Study in Southern Mythmaking* (New York: Alfred A. Knopf, 1970), pp. 54–63.

14. Henry W. Grady, *The New South* (New York: Robert Bonner's Sons, 1890), p. 256.

15. Harris, ed., *Life of Grady*, p. 205.

16. Ibid., p. 88.

17. This contrast is particularly emphasized by Patrick Hearden, in *Independence and Empire: The New South's Cotton Mill Campaign, 1865–1901* (DeKalb: Northern Illinois University Press, 1982), p. 46. In discussing North-South relations Hearden uses the colonial analogy much more extensively than do other historians.

18. As a newspaper editor whose own profits responded strongly to Atlanta's population growth, Grady must have understood the ways that urbanization could enhance the prospects of southern businesses—what economists today call a regional multiplier effect.

19. See for example: Gavin Wright, *Old South, New South: Revolutions in the Southern Economy since the Civil War* (New York: Basic Books, 1986), chap. 4.

20. Grady, *The New South,* p. 209.

21. Ibid., p. 268.

22. For an evaluation of this charge, see Gaston, *The New South Creed,* p. 219.

23. Throughout this section the supporters of the People's Party as well as the Farmers' Alliance will be referred to as populists or southern populists.

24. Thomas E. Watson, speech given in August 1896, in *Life and Speeches of Thomas E. Watson* (Thomson, Ga.: Jeffersonian Publishing, 1911), p. 150.

25. Frederick Emory Haynes, "The New Sectionalism," *Quarterly Journal of Economics* 10 (1896), reprinted in George B. Tindall, ed., *A Populist Reader* (New York: Harper Torchbooks, 1966), pp. 171–83.

26. Ibid., p. 177.

27. Thomas E. Watson, speech given in summer of 1907, in *Life and Speeches,* p. 277.

28. This rather cluttered banner included two other inscriptions. The first, in simple utilitarian form, held for "The most good for the most PEOPLE." Some of the populists' later critics might have been surprised to learn the other motto on the flag: "Wisdom, Justice & Moderation." See photograph in N. A. Dunning, ed., *The Farmers' Alliance History and Agricultural Digest* (Washington, D.C.: Alliance Publishing, 1891), frontispiece.

29. *National Economist, Devoted to Social, Financial and Political Economy,* Apr. 6, 1889, p. 43.

30. L. F. Livingston, "The Needs of the South," in *The Farmers' Alliance,* ed. Dunning, pp. 285–86.

31. Ibid., p. 286.

32. See discussion in Bruce Palmer, *Man Over Money: The Southern Populist Critique of American Capitalism* (Chapel Hill: University of North Carolina Press, 1980), p. 118.

33. W. Scott Morgan, *History of the Wheel and Alliance and the Impending Revolution* (Hardy, Ark., 1891; New York: Burt Franklin, 1961), p. 513.

34. See Lawrence Goodwyn, *Democratic Promise: The Populist Moment in America* (New York: Oxford University Press, 1976), p. 122.

35. See Goodwyn, *Democratic Promise,* pp. 145–46, 169–70, for a discussion of why the cooperatives failed. See also Robert C. McMath, Jr., *Populist Vanguard: A History of the Southern Farmers' Alliance* (Chapel Hill: University of North Carolina Press, 1975), pp. 118–22, 147–48.

36. Biographical data and early background from Goodwyn, *Democratic Promise,* chaps. 3, 5.

37. Thomas E. Watson, *The People's Party Campaign Book, 1892* (Washington, D.C., 1892; New York: Arno Press, 1975), p. 112.

38. Ibid., p. 114.

39. *National Economist, Devoted to Social, Financial and Political Economy,* Dec. 28, 1889, p. 225.

40. See discussion in Goodwyn, *Democratic Promise,* p. 110. Also note that by time of the Ocala Platform, in December of 1890, real estate mortgage loans had been included.

41. Mr. Wheeler, of Portsmouth, in the *Richmond Enquirer,* Dec. 7, 1852, quoted in Robert Russel, *Economic Aspects of Southern Sectionalism, 1840–1861* (Urbana, Ill., 1924; New York: Russell and Russell, 1960). Russel, normally quite sympathetic to southern arguments, ascribed the decline in price at harvest time only to the unintended insufficiency of funds. He also suggested that New York business interests favored high cotton prices, since their sales to the South improved under such circumstances.

42. William Jennings Bryan, "Cross of Gold" speech, reprinted in George B. Tindall, *A Populist Reader,* pp. 203–11. Also see discussion of the southern populist view of cities in Palmer, *Man Over Money,* p. 200.

43. W. Scott Morgan, *History of the Wheel and Alliance,* pp. 247, 249. It is noteworthy that Morgan's volume includes an entire chapter entitled: "Social Features of the Union."

44. See McMath, *Populist Vanguard,* pp. 64–76, for a discussion of the Alliance as a community.

45. Thomas E. Watson, "How the Law Controls the Distribution of Wealth," in *Life and Speeches,* p. 263.

46. Thomas E. Watson, from Watson manuscripts, quoted in C. Vann Woodward, *Tom Watson, Agrarian Rebel* (New York, 1938; New York: Rinehart, 1955), p. 350.

47. Data from Harvey S. Perloff, Edgar S. Dunn, Jr., Eric E. Lampard, and Richard F. Muth, *Regions, Resources, and Economic Growth* (Baltimore: Johns Hopkins University Press, 1960), app. tbls. A1–A7, pp. 622–35.

48. William Holmes, *The White Chief: James Kimble Vardaman* (Baton Rouge: Louisiana State University Press, 1970), pp. 270–71. For a broad overview of the role of southerners in the Wilson administration, see George B. Tindall,

The Emergence of the New South, 1913–1945 (Baton Rouge: Louisiana State University Press, 1967), chap. 1.

49. Woodward, *Tom Watson, Agrarian Rebel,* pp. 408–9.

50. Ibid., pp. 418–19.

Chapter Five Endings

1. For biographical information on the agrarians and a sympathetic critique of their ideas, see Paul Conkin, *The Southern Agrarians* (Knoxville: University of Tennessee Press, 1988). For a discussion of their somewhat tense relation with Mims, see Michael O'Brien, *Rethinking the South* (Baltimore: Johns Hopkins University Press, 1988), chap. 6.

2. Twelve Southerners, *I'll Take My Stand: The South and the Agrarian Tradition* (New York: Harper Brothers, 1930), p. xvi.

3. See essay by Frank Owsley, "The Irrepressible Conflict," in *I'll Take My Stand,* by Twelve Southerners.

4. Herman C. Nixon, "Whither Southern Economy," in *I'll Take My Stand,* by Twelve Southerners, p. 188.

5. Andrew Lytle, "The Hind Tit," in *I'll Take My Stand,* by Twelve Southerners, p. 244.

6. Ibid., p. 239.

7. Ibid., p. 244.

8. Ibid., p. 245.

9. H. L. Mencken, "The South Astir," *Virginia Quarterly Review* 11 (1935): 52.

10. John Crowe Ransom, "Land," *Harper's Monthly Magazine,* July 1932, p. 218.

11. This treatment of the distributists and their relation to the agrarians draws heavily on Conkin, *The Southern Agrarians,* chap. 4.

12. Allen Tate, "Notes on Liberty and Property," *The American Review* 6, no. 5 (March 1936): 599.

13. Ibid., p. 600.

14. Ibid., p. 609.

15. Herbert Agar and Allen Tate, eds., *Who Owns America?: A New Declaration of Independence* (New York: Houghton Mifflin, 1936), p. 118.

16. Donald Davidson, "That This Nation May Endure: The Need for Political Regionalism," in *Who Owns America,* ed. Agar and Tate, pp. 130–32.

17. Andrew Lytle, "John Taylor and the Political Economy of Agriculture," *The American Review* 3 (1934): 438.

18. Andrew Lytle, "John Taylor and the Political Economy of Agriculture, Part 2," *The American Review* 3 (1934): 633.

19. Ibid., p. 638.

20. Andrew Lytle, "John Taylor and the Political Economy of Agriculture, Part 3," *American Review* 4 (1934): 92.

21. Ibid., p. 95.

22. Robert Penn Warren, "The Briar Patch," in *I'll Take My Stand,* by Twelve Southerners, p. 258.

23. For a solid discussion of Odum's program, see Daniel Joseph Singal, *The War Within: From Victorian to Modernist Thought in the South, 1919–1945* (Chapel Hill: University of North Carolina Press, 1982).

24. Howard Odum, *Southern Regions of the United States* (Chapel Hill: University of North Carolina Press, 1936), and Rupert Vance, *The Human Geography of the South: A Study in Regional Resources and Human Adequacy* (Chapel Hill: University of North Carolina Press, 1932).

25. Donald Davidson, "Social Science and Regionalism," in *The Attack on Leviathan: Regionalism and Nationalism in the United States* (Chapel Hill: University of North Carolina Press, 1938).

26. Ibid., p. 52.

27. Odum, *Southern Regions,* p. 259.

28. John Shelton Reed, "For Dixieland: The Sectionalism of *I'll Take My Stand,*" in *A Band of Prophets: The Vanderbilt Agrarians after Fifty Years,* ed. William C. Havard and Walter Sullivan (Baton Rouge: Louisiana State University Press, 1982), p. 49. Reed goes on to say that Vance "seldom used the phrase 'colonial economy' again and largely avoided the subject altogether. When I asked him why, he told me that his analysis gave aid and comfort to 'sectionalists.' But he never said his analysis was *wrong.*"

29. Vance, *Human Geography,* p. 467.

30. Ibid., p. 467.

31. Ibid., p. 468.

32. Ibid., p. 469.

33. Ibid., p. 470.

34. Ibid., p. 497.

35. Ibid., p. 471.

36. Ibid., p. 474.

37. Davidson, "Social Science and Regionalism," p. 48.

38. Odum, *Southern Regions,* p. 425.

39. Ibid., p. 430.

40. For example, see *Frederick Douglass Papers,* ser. 1, *Speeches, Debates and Interviews,* 3 vols., ed. John W. Blassingame (New Haven: Yale University Press, 1979–85), vol. 1, p. 122; vol. 3, p. 114. The latter citation is from a speech entitled "Aggressions of the Slave Power."

41. Frederick Douglass, "The Negro Exodus from the Gulf States," *Journal of Social Science* 11, May 1880, reprinted in Philip Foner, ed., *The Life and Writings of Frederick Douglass,* 5 vols. (New York: International Publishers, 1950-), vol. 4, p. 326. For a provocative treatment of Douglass's thought, see Waldo E. Martin, *The Mind of Frederick Douglass* (Chapel Hill: University of North Carolina Press, 1984).

42. Frederick Douglass, "Why Is the Negro Lynched," in *Life and Writings of Frederick Douglass,* vol. 4, pp. 504, 516.

43. For a discussion of the relation between Washington and the New South movement, see Paul M. Gaston, *The New South Creed: A Study in Southern Mythmaking* (New York: Alfred A. Knopf, 1970), pp. 208–14.

44. Booker T. Washington, "The South as an Opening for a Business Career," in *The Booker T. Washington Papers,* ed. Louis R. Harlan, 8 vols. (Urbana: University of Illinois Press, 1974), vol. 3, pp. 184–94.

45. August Meier, in *Negro Thought in America: 1880–1915* (Ann Arbor: University of Michigan Press, 1963), p. 105, points out that this aspect of Washington's thought "has ordinarily been overlooked."

46. W. E. Burghardt Du Bois, "The Economic Revolution in the South," in *The Negro in the South: His Economic Progress in Relation to His Moral and Religious Development* (New York: Citadel Press, 1907), pp. 82, 80.

47. Du Bois, *The Negro in the South,* p. 81.

48. W. E. B. Du Bois, *The Quest of the Silver Fleece: A Novel* (Chicago, 1911; College Park, Md.: McGrath, 1969), p. 193. Also see the discussion of this novel in Manning Marable, *W. E. B. Du Bois: Black Radical Democrat* (Boston: Twayne, 1986), pp. 66–67.

49. W. E. B. Du Bois, "The Federal Action Programs and Community Action in the South," in *Writings by W. E. B. Du Bois in Periodicals Edited by Others,* ed. Herbert Aptheker, 4 vols. (New York: Kraus-Thomson Organization, 1982), vol. 3, pp. 126–31.

50. W. E. B. Du Bois, "A Negro Nation within the Nation," in *Writings by Du Bois,* ed. Aptheker, pp. 5–6.

51. A. Philip Randolph, "Lynching: Capitalism Its Cause; Socialism Its Cure," *The Messenger,* March 1919, pp. 9–12, reprinted in Francis Broderick and August Meier, *Negro Protest Thought in the Twentieth Century* (Indianapolis: Bobbs-Merrill, 1965), p. 74.

52. William N. Colson, "Confederate-Americanism," *The Messenger,* Feb. 1920, pp. 9–10.

53. Abram Harris, "Economic Foundations of American Race Division," *Social Forces* 5 (1927): 468–78.

54. Sterling D. Spero and Abram L. Harris, *The Black Worker: The Negro and the Labor Movement* (New York, 1931; New York: Atheneum, 1968), chap. 2, "The Aftermath of Slavery," written primarily by Harris.

55. Ralph Bunche, "A Critical Analysis of the Tactics and Programs of Minority Groups," *Journal of Negro Education* 4 (1935): 308–20, reprinted in *Negro Protest Thought,* ed. Broderick and Meier, p. 164.

56. For a discussion of white liberal southerners and the role of the Commission on Interracial Cooperation, see John B. Kirby, *Black Americans in the Roosevelt Era: Liberalism and Race* (Knoxville: University of Tennessee Press, 1980).

57. Charles S. Johnson, Edwin R. Embree, and W. W. Alexander, *The*

Collapse of Cotton Tenancy (Chapel Hill: University of North Carolina Press, 1935), p. 25.

58. Ibid., p. 67.

59. Arthur F. Raper and Ira De A. Reid, *Sharecroppers All* (Chapel Hill: University of North Carolina Press, 1941), pp. vi–vii.

60. Ibid., p. 33.

61. John Hope Franklin, *From Slavery to Freedom: A History of American Negroes* (New York: Alfred A. Knopf, 1947), p. 311.

62. A brief history and considerable bibliography of the literature on black economic development can be found in Bennett Harrison, "Ghetto Economic Development: A Survey," *The Journal of Economic Literature* 12 (1974): 1–37. The double-duty dollar was a notion popular in black communities, especially in Chicago, in the 1930's. The idea was that when "buying black" a dollar both bought goods and "advanced the race."

63. See John H. Bracey, Jr., August Meier, and Elliott Rudwick, eds., *Black Nationalism in America* (Indianapolis: Bobbs-Merrill, 1970) for an especially well selected set of readings on the origins and accomplishments of black nationalism.

64. As noted above, Du Bois especially saw this idea as central. See his "A Negro Nation within the Nation," in *Writings by Du Bois,* ed. Aptheker.

65. Harrison, "Ghetto Economic Development," p. 2.

66. Raper and Reid, *Sharecroppers All,* p. 265.

67. Wilbur Cash, *The Mind of the South* (New York: Alfred A. Knopf, 1941), pp. 163–64.

68. A possible exception to this generalization is Broadus Mitchell, a member of the Johns Hopkins economics department, who began his career as a New South advocate in the early 1920s but turned to socialism as he became disillusioned with southern industry. Perhaps because of his increasing radicalism, Mitchell tended to abstract from regional issues.

69. William H. Nicholls, *Southern Tradition and Regional Progress* (Chapel Hill: University of North Carolina Press, 1960), pp. 2, 20.

70. Ibid., p. 27.

71. Ibid., p. 33.

72. Ibid., p. 162.

73. On this analysis of the convergence of southern and northern incomes, see Joseph Persky, "Regional Competition, Convergence, and Social Welfare—The U. S. Case," in J. Rubery, A. Castro, and Ph. Mehaut, eds., *International Integration and the Organisation of the Labour Market* (Academic Press, forthcoming). For a contrary view that argues that national legislation slowed southern development, see Gavin Wright, *Old South, New South: Revolutions in the Southern Economy since the Civil War* (New York: Basic Books, 1986).

Bibliographic Essay

Given the magnitude of the high-quality southern historical scholarship that exists, I, an interloper from economics, make no claim to a definitive or even a comprehensive reading of this rich literature. I gather here the works I found most exciting, so that other readers may venture in more detail into particular periods.

Historians of economic thought have avoided southern economic writings almost completely. Apart from a bit of Thomas Jefferson, the standard cannon of the history of economic thought includes virtually nothing from the South. At least since Joseph Schumpeter made his distinction between analytical economics and economic scribblings, historians of economic thought have tended to ignore the less-than-rigorous writings that characterize so much of "popular economics." As a result, any study of southern economic thought relies heavily on the work of historians in general and intellectual historians in particular, for whom economics is often a secondary consideration.

Of course there are exceptions, most notably Joseph Dorfman's monumental history, *The Economic Mind in American Civilization* (New York: Viking Press, 1961), where southern writers play a real role. Not surprisingly, Dorfman's work provided my starting point and repeated guide. Full of wise insights, *The Economic Mind* presents an encyclopedic panorama. Dorfman, although aware of the colonial theme in southern thought, pays only passing attention to it. He limits his explicit consideration of "colonial dependency" to the prerevolutionary period. A second exception requires mention: William Grampp's *Economic Liberalism* (New York: Random House, 1967). Grampp does a fine job of analyzing Jeffersonian economics, although I suspect he has little sympathy for relating such writings to modern dependency theory.

Turning back to history, the beginning of southern economic thought was in the mercantilist period. David Bertelson's *The Lazy South* (New York: Oxford University Press, 1967) is an often-overlooked but excellent treatment of early southern thinking on work, leisure, and sin. Bertelson pays serious attention to economics, making clear the tensions between mercantilist and libertarian thought in the colonial South. He emphasizes southern ambivalence over leisure rather than southern preoccupation with dependency. A similar contrast between mercantilist and libertarian thought is drawn in John C. Rainbolt's *From*

175

Prescription to Persuasion: Manipulation of Eighteenth-Century Virginia Economy (Port Washington, N.Y.: Kennikat Press, 1974), which is presented as a straight history but deals extensively with economic thought.

On the revolutionary generation, the sheer volume of historical research becomes truly overwhelming. The work I found most useful was T. H. Breen's *Tobacco Culture: The Mentality of the Great Tidewater Planters on the Eve of Revolution* (Princeton, N.J.: Princeton University Press, 1985). Making use of the concept of mentalité, Breen provides a plausible view of the influence of the experience of southern revolutionaries on their economic thinking. While somewhat controversial and perhaps now a bit passé, this approach strikes me as a sensible midpoint between a mechanistic economic determinism and a naive idealism. In this respect I also found James Henretta's "Families and Farms: Mentalité in Pre-Industrial America" (*William and Mary Quarterly* 35 (1978): 3–32) quite useful. Pauline Maier's work *The Old Revolutionaries: Political Lives in the Age of Samuel Adams* (New York: Alfred A. Knopf, 1980) has a similar bent.

Joseph Davis's *Sectionalism in American Politics, 1774–1787* (Madison: University of Wisconsin Press, 1977) provides a rich source on the important sectional battles in the early Republic, just in case anyone thought all the Founding Fathers were nationalists. Staughton Lynd, in his *Class Conflict, Slavery, and the United States Constitution: Ten Essays* (Indianapolis: Bobbs-Merrill, 1967), makes a similar point, couched in a radical antislavery ideology. While I am sympathetic to his argument, Lynd loses sight of the legitimate concern of southerners over their economic dependency. Charles Beard's fascinating *Economic Origins of Jeffersonian Democracy* (New York: Macmillan, 1949) suffers from the same problem.

Drew McCoy's *The Elusive Republic: Political Economy in Jeffersonian America* (Chapel Hill: University of North Carolina Press, 1980) makes perhaps the finest contribution to the study of republican thought. Far more than most historians of the period, he appreciates the content and quality of the formal economics the revolutionary generation absorbed. He has a solid grasp of the national problems of economic development faced by the revolutionary generation but tends to homogenize northern and southern thought. Someone who thinks I have overemphasized southern distinctiveness might start with this volume.

John Taylor of Caroline, Pastoral Republican (Columbia: University of South Carolina Press, 1980), by Robert Shalhope, provides a first-rate treatment of Taylor's philosophy. Paul Conkin's original *Prophets of Prosperity: America's First Political Economists* (Bloomington: Indiana University Press, 1980) considers Taylor along with several of the classical southern economists and several northerners, including Henry Carey. Allen Kaufman, in his ambitious work *Capitalism, Slavery, and Republican Values: Antebellum Political Economists, 1819–1848* (Austin: University of Texas Press, 1982), recognizes the complex conflict between southern and northern republicans rooted in their quite different economic positions. Kaufman in effect builds on Norman Risjord's *The Old Republicans: Southern Conservatism in the Age of Jefferson* (New York: Columbia University Press, 1965).

Thomas Cooper's economics prove something of a disappointment, but his life makes fascinating reading. Dumas Malone's 1926 biography, *The Public Life of Thomas Cooper* (New Haven, 1926; Columbia: University of South Carolina Press, 1961) is dated but quite exciting. I really think it should be made into a movie. Melvin Leiman's analysis of Cardozo's economics in *Jacob N. Cardozo: Economic Thought in the Antebellum South* (New York: Columbia University Press, 1966) presents perhaps the most serious discussion of any southern economist's work. Cardozo, however, showed considerably more restraint than most of his fellow Carolinians in using the colonial analogy.

Charles Sydnor, in *The Development of Southern Sectionalism: 1819–1848* (Baton Rouge: Louisiana State University Press, 1948), explicitly considers the colonial analogy in a sympathetic fashion. However, I found more useful Robert Russel's *Economic Aspects of Southern Sectionalism, 1840–1861* (Urbana, Ill., 1924; New York: Russell and Russell, 1960), a classic study that seems to have fallen out of favor, although I can't see that it has been superseded by a superior treatment of these matters. Another older book full of the list of southern complaints in the thirty years before the Civil War is John G. Van Deusen's *Economic Bases of Disunion in South Carolina* (New York, 1928; New York: AMS Press, 1970). More recent research works, such as Fred Bateman and Thomas Weiss's *A Deplorable Scarcity: The Failure of Industrialization in the Slave Economy* (Chapel Hill: University of North Carolina Press, 1981), tend to interpret the antebellum economy in terms of smooth market adjustments, leaving little room for colonial dependency. Like the northerners of the antebellum period, Bateman and Weiss tell the southerners that markets clear and all capital earns more or less the same return. Most southerners did not buy that argument, and I tend to agree with them. An interesting biography of this time is *James Henry Hammond of the Old South: A Design for Mastery* (Baton Rouge: Louisiana State University Press, 1982), by Drew Gilpin Faust.

George Fitzhugh's economic sociology has long been recognized as important. Harvey Wish's solid biography, *George Fitzhugh, Propagandist of the Old South* (Baton Rouge: Louisiana State University Press, 1943), does a fine job at introducing Fitzhugh's thought, but there's no reason not to read the originals. The most important commentators on Fitzhugh are Hartz and Genovese, whose contributions are discussed in my text.

The New South has received considerable attention in recent years. Of course, C. Vann Woodward's exquisite *Origins of the New South, 1877–1913* (Baton Rouge: Louisiana State University Press, 1951) laid the foundation for all more-recent treatments. Woodward spends a good deal of effort on judiciously scaling the extent to which the postbellum southern economy suffered from colonial dependency. Paul Gaston's *The New South Creed: A Study in Southern*

Mythmaking (New York: Alfred A. Knopf, 1970) made a breakthrough by seriously analyzing the economic thought of newspapermen and promoters of the region. Laurence Shore's *Southern Capitalists: The Ideological Leadership of an Elite, 1832–1885* (Chapel Hill: University of North Carolina Press, 1986) shows, perhaps a bit too eagerly, the connections between New South and antebellum proponents of diversification. Patrick Hearden's *Independence and Empire: The New South's Cotton Mill Campaign* (DeKalb: Northern Illinois University Press, 1982), while even more enthusiastic, most clearly delineates the sectionalist undertone in the New South program. Through all of these works runs a serious debate over the extent to which proponents of the New South plan broke from the conservative agricultural interests of the region.

The populist revolt has been admirably studied by a host of historians. Again the story starts with C. Vann Woodward, in both his *Origins of the New South* and his early and remarkable biography of Tom Watson, *Tom Watson: Agrarian Rebel* (New York: Rinehart, 1955), dating from 1938. Woodward initiated the notion that the New South advocates and the populists represented the divided mind of the region in responding to industrialism. Lawrence Goodwyn's fine study *Democratic Promise: The Populist Moment in America* (New York: Oxford University Press, 1976) deals thoughtfully with populist economics, as does Bruce Palmer's *Man Over Money: The Southern Populist Critique of American Capitalism* (Chapel Hill: University of North Carolina Press, 1980). While both of these excellent works acknowledge the agrarian roots of populist economic ideas, I think they underestimate the extent to which the southern populists took Jeffersonian economics seriously. There is something yet to be done on this score.

The 1980s produced a flurry of excitement over the Nashville Agrarians. Five solid and classy books paid serious attention to their work: Daniel Singal's *The War Within: From Victorian to Modernist Thought in the South, 1919–1945* (Chapel Hill: University of North Carolina Press, 1982), Michael O'Brien's *The Idea of the American South, 1920-1941* (Baltimore: Johns Hopkins University Press, 1979), William C. Havard and Walter Sullivan, eds., *A Band of Prophets: The Vanderbilt Agrarians after Fifty Years* (Baton Rouge: Louisiana State University Press, 1982), Richard Gray's *Writing the South: Ideas of an American Region* (Cambridge: Cambridge University Press, 1986), and Paul Conkin's *The Southern Agrarians* (Knoxville: University of Tennessee Press, 1988). I particularly like Singal's treatment, which emphasizes the transition from Victorian to modernist thought in the South. He puts the agrarians on the edge—"modernist by the skin of their teeth." In some sense this judgment seems relevant to the entire history of the colonial critiques. Unfortunately, all of these authors pay only modest attention to the actual economics of the agrarians. Both Singal and O'Brien also treat the Chapel Hill sociologists at some length. The question of what African-American writers thought of the southern economy has not yet been fully researched.

Index

Designed by David denBoer

Composed by The EPS Group, Inc.
in Fairfield text and Fenice display

Printed by Thomson-Shore, Inc., on
60-lb. Glatfelter Offset, B-16, and bound in
Holliston Roxite